PSYCHOPATHY

PSYCHOLOGY AND CRIME

General Editors: Brian Bornstein, University of Nebraska, and Monica Miller, University of Nevada, Reno

Psychopathy

An Introduction to Biological Findings and Their Implications

Andrea L. Glenn and Adrian Raine

NEW YORK UNIVERSITY PRESS

New York and London

NEW YORK UNIVERSITY PRESS
New York and London
www.nyupress.org

References to Internet websites (URLs) were accurate at the time of writing.
Neither the author nor New York University Press is responsible for URLs that
may have expired or changed since the manuscript was prepared.

Library of Congress Cataloging-in-Publication Data

Glenn, Andrea L.
Psychopathy : an introduction to biological findings and their implications / Andrea L.
Glenn and Adrian Raine.
pages cm. -- (Psychology and crime)
Includes bibliographical references and index.
ISBN 978-0-8147-7705-3 (cloth : alk. paper) -- ISBN 978-0-8147-4544-1 (pbk.   )
1. Antisocial personality disorders. 2. Antisocial personality disorders--Genetic aspects. 3.
Psychopaths. 4. Mental illness--Genetic aspects. I. Raine, Adrian. II. Title.
RC555.G54 2014
616.85'82--dc23

2013039338

New York University Press books

Manufactured in the United States of America
10 9 8 7 6 5 4 3 2 1

Also available as an ebook

Dedicated to Yu Gao, Robert Schug, and Yaling Yang.

CONTENTS

Introduction

In November 2009, evidence from functional magnetic resonance imaging (fMRI), a technology used to approximate brain functioning, was presented for the first time in a criminal court case. The defendant, Brian Dugan, was already serving two life sentences for murders he committed in the 1980s, and was now on trial for an earlier murder in which he had kidnapped a 10-year-old girl, raped her in the back seat of his car, and beat her to death. Brain imaging evidence was used to argue that Dugan, a highly psychopathic individual, demonstrated deficits in brain functioning that contributed to his extremely violent behavior, and therefore he should not be sentenced to death.

The case incited much debate, not only about what this type of brain imaging evidence can and cannot tell us about an individual, but also regarding the general idea that psychopaths, who are able to distinguish between right and wrong, may be excused for their behavior because of how their brains function. Dugan's trial illustrates the ways in which biological research on psychopathy is gaining traction in the public domain and beginning to have real-world effects. As we learn more from this research, new questions are arising. How much control does a psychopath have over his or her behavior? How much of that behavior is influenced by biology versus the environment? If research shows that the brains of psychopaths are different, what chance do we have of preventing these individuals from causing harm?

The prevalence of psychopathic personality traits takes a major toll on society. In criminal populations, offenders with psychopathic traits are responsible for a disproportionate amount of crime, particularly violent crime. In the rest of society, psychopathic traits are a driving force behind much of the corruption, exploitation, manipulation, and deception that occurs on both large and small scales. Psychopathy causes undue physical, emotional, and financial trauma in the lives of countless individuals. Because of this, in recent years, much attention has been devoted to understanding psychopathy, including identifying the ways in which the biology of these individuals may be different, and how these differences lead to the development of psychopathic traits.

Unlike much of the research in the field of criminology, which has focused primarily on the social causes of crime, early researchers in the scientific study of psychopathy took a particular interest in examining the biological correlates of the disorder, and this biologically based approach has continued among many researchers in the field. Studies using brain imaging, skin conductance recordings, and other biological methods have identified differences between individuals with and without psychopathic traits, and behavioral genetics studies have determined that there is a significant genetic contribution to the disorder.

The purpose of this book is to provide an overview of this biologically based research on psychopathy, which has spurred the interest of scholars in many fields and is beginning to have real-world applicability. To those who are not familiar with biological methods, it may be difficult to sort through descriptions of complex technologies and statistical methods, learn the role of dozens of brain regions, hormones, and neurotransmitters, and gain a clear understanding of what the research can and cannot tell us about psychopathy. A goal of this book is to help scholars navigate this literature and to summarize some of the key findings in biological research. In addition, we also want to clarify many of the misunderstandings that often arise regarding the purpose of biological research and how findings should be interpreted.

Unsurprisingly, biologically based research on crime has led to much debate over issues such as free will, criminal responsibility, and punishment. This book aims to provide a context for understanding this research, to discuss the ethical issues related to it, and to demonstrate the ways in which understanding biological factors, in addition to social and environmental factors, may help us to solve the problem of psychopathy in the future.

What Is Psychopathy?

Although the term "psychopath" is used colloquially in many different contexts, psychopathy is a personality disorder describing individuals with a specific set of traits. Interpersonally, these individuals are described as grandiose and self-centered; they come across as having an exaggerated sense of self-importance and tend to blame others for their failures and shortcomings. They readily take advantage of others using charm, manipulation, and deception. Their emotions tend to be shallow and insincere. They experience little guilt or remorse when they harm others. They have a pronounced lack of empathy and are described as callous and cold. They are also described as being fearless and tend to be more reckless and take risks in several domains. They have diminished concerns about punishment, physical injury, or social repercussions. Psychopaths are impulsive and seek reward and novelty. In life they are often irresponsible and fail to make appropriate life plans. They tend to have a volatile temperament and can easily become irritable and hostile. They show disregard for social norms and frequently engage in behavior that would be considered immoral to most. The observation that this "constellation" of traits could be identified in individuals again and again, albeit in different forms, led to the idea that these traits represent a single disorder.

Psychopathic traits increase the risk for engaging in criminal behavior and alcohol and drug abuse. However, these traits not only are observed in criminal populations, but also can be observed in individuals at many different levels of society, including in some people who have achieved high professional status. The crux of psychopathy is not the display of antisocial behavior, per se, but rather the distinctive personality traits, including emotional deficits, that characterize these individuals.

Original Description of Psychopathy

Throughout modern history the term "psychopath" has been used to describe a variety of different types of individuals. However, current conceptualizations of psychopathy in the scientific literature are based largely on the writing of Hervey Cleckley in his 1941 book *The Mask of Sanity*. Cleckley's book provided the first extensive description and interpretation of psychopathy. He describes psychopathy based on his experiences with inpatients in a psychiatric hospital and details several case histories that he believes exemplify psychopathic personality. He then presents a list of 16 specific criteria for psychopathy:

1. Superficial charm and good intelligence
2. Absence of delusions and other signs of irrational thinking
3. Absence of nervousness or psychoneurotic manifestations
4. Unreliability
5. Untruthfulness and insincerity
6. Lack of remorse and shame
7. Inadequately motivated antisocial behavior
8. Poor judgment and failure to learn by experience
9. Pathologic egocentricity and incapacity for love
10. General poverty in major affective reactions
11. Specific loss of insight
12. Unresponsiveness in general interpersonal relations
13. Fantastic and uninviting behavior with drink and sometimes without
14. Suicide threats rarely carried out
15. Sex life impersonal, trivial, and poorly integrated
16. Failure to follow any life plan

The title of *The Mask of Sanity* represents Cleckley's idea that psychopathy represents severe pathology masked by a façade of robust mental health. In contrast to individuals with other psychiatric conditions who outwardly demonstrate signs of depression, confusion, or agitation, psychopaths give the impression of being confident, personable, and well-adjusted. It is only through continued observation that the clinician begins to notice signs that things are not as they seem.

Modern Conceptualization and Measurement of Psychopathy

From the late 1950s through the 1970s, Cleckley's descriptions of the characteristics of psychopathy served as the basis for research. For example, early work by Dr. Robert Hare and colleagues used a clinical rating of how closely an individual's personality and behavior matched the description provided by Cleckley (Hare, Frazelle, and Cox 1978). However, the idea that psychopathy is a disorder that is "masked," and that repeated interactions may be necessary before signs of psychopathy become evident, presented a significant challenge for early attempts to accurately measure the disorder. The scientific study of psychopathy began to burgeon with the creation of a reliable and valid tool for assessing it. In order to clarify Cleckley's criteria, Hare developed an interview-based inventory, the Psychopathy Checklist (PCL; Hare 1980) to distinguish between psychopathic and nonpsychopathic individuals in forensic settings. The PCL (most recently revised in 2003; PCL-R; Hare 2003) is a 20-item scale that trained clinicians complete based on an extensive interview with a criminal offender and a review of institutional records.

Although Cleckley described psychopathy in a psychiatric unit and the first reliable method for measuring psychopathy was developed for forensic populations, individuals with high levels of psychopathic traits can be found at all levels of society and in many different contexts, including business, politics, and law enforcement. In the past 20 years, several additional measures have been developed to assess psychopathy in nonincarcerated samples. Several of these measures are based on self-reports, making the measures easier to administer to large samples of individuals than the PCL-R, which involves extensive interviews. Some self-report measures are derived from the PCL-R, such as the Self-Report Psychopathy Scale and its revisions (Hare 1985, Williams and Paulhus 2004, Paulhus, Neumann, and Hare in press) and the Levenson Self-Report Psychopathy Scale (Levenson, Kiehl, and Fitzpatrick 1995). Other measures contain items intended to assess the core features of psychopathy, but in different formats from that of the PCL-R, and may include fewer assessments of criminal behavior than measures designed for use in incarcerated populations. These include the Psychopathic Personality Inventory and its revision (Lilienfeld and Andrews

1996, Lilienfeld and Widows 2005), and the Elemental Psychopathy Assessment (Lynam et al. 2011). These scales generally relate to external correlates of psychopathy, such as aggression and other personality measures, in a similar way as PCL-R-based measures. Recently, an additional measure called the Business-Scan (Mathieu et al. 2013) has been developed to assess psychopathic traits in business settings. One of the challenges of self-report measures of psychopathy is that individuals with psychopathic traits are prone to lying and therefore may not be truthful when completing the measures. Self-report measures must be carefully worded with language that does not signal disapproval so that people with psychopathic traits will feel free to endorse them (Levenson, Kiehl, and Fitzpatrick 1995). The PCL-R has also been used to assess psychopathy in community samples. The information gathered from prison files, which is required in the PCL-R, can be replaced by official criminal records and other sources of information gathered about an individual during a laboratory visit (Raine et al. 2003). Overall, the development of precise measures of psychopathy has greatly advanced research in the field and has clarified communication among researchers.

Structure of Psychopathy

Research on psychopathy has determined that psychopathic traits exist on a continuum, meaning that these traits vary in the population and there is no distinct point at which a person is designated a "psychopath" (e.g., Guay et al. 2007); each individual falls at some point on the spectrum of psychopathic traits. For research purposes, cutoff scores are sometimes arbitrarily designated to group together individuals with high levels of psychopathic traits, but these distinctions do not mean that the individuals above and below the cutoff point are qualitatively different.

Researchers have also attempted to uncover the basic structure of the construct. For example, statistical methods called factor analyses have been conducted to examine how the different items on psychopathy scales may reflect underlying groups of variables. This research has led to much debate in the literature about whether psychopathy comprises two, three, or four underlying factors (Benning et al. 2003, Cooke and Michie 2001, Mahmut et al. 2011, Hare 2003).

For example, factor analyses of the PCL-R reveal two overarching factors, each of which can be divided into two additional factors or facets. The overarching Factor 1 subscale assesses the core personality traits of psychopathy, including manipulativeness, callousness, and lack of guilt or remorse. This factor can be subdivided into Interpersonal features (Facet 1) and Affective features (Facet 2). The overarching Factor 2 subscale assesses features of the antisocial lifestyle, including impulsiveness, irresponsibility, and antisocial behavior. This factor can be subdivided into Lifestyle features (Facet 3) and Antisocial behavior (Facet 4). Figure I.1 illustrates the features of each of the four facets.

As mentioned previously, different measures of psychopathy encompass these features differently. For example, some conceptualizations of psychopathy emphasize callous-aggressive tendencies, involving taking advantage of and victimizing other people (Hare 2003, Lynam and Derefinko 2006). Other conceptions emphasize deficits in emotional reactivity, such as fearlessness and a lack of anxiety (Cleckley 1976, Lilienfeld and Widows 2005). Thus, psychopathic traits may be emphasized and grouped differently according to the assessment measure being used. These distinctions may be important in understanding why some biological factors may relate to the subfactors of psychopathy differently depending on the measure used to assess psychopathy. For clarity, throughout this book we primarily refer the structure utilized by the PCL-R, but we attempt to highlight cases in which different measures may reflect different constructs. The two overarching factors of psychopathy are labeled as Interpersonal-Affective Factor 1 and Lifestyle-Antisocial Factor 2. We refer to the four facets as Interpersonal Facet 1, Affective Facet 2, Lifestyle Facet 3, and Antisocial Facet 4.

As mentioned above, Cleckley viewed psychopathy as more of a configuration of disparate tendencies. On one hand, individuals with psychopathic traits come across as personable, lacking anxiety, lacking delusions, and psychologically well-adjusted. On the other hand, they have problems regulating their behavior and maintaining relationships and empathizing with others. However, The PCL-R was designed to measure psychopathy more as a unitary construct than as a condition in which two (or more) separable dispositions co-occur in some individuals. Although the idea that psychopathy is a unitary construct has been dominant in the field, some have suggested that Cleckley's original

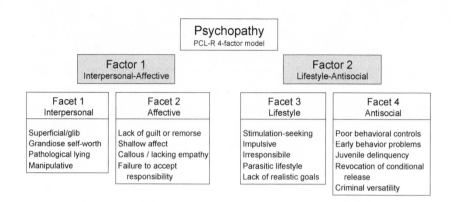

Figure I.1. Factor structure of psychopathy as defined by the Psychopathy Checklist–Revised (Hare 2003).

conception of psychopathy as a grouping of distinct constructs may be more accurate (Patrick and Bernat 2009, Patrick, Fowles, and Krueger 2009). For example, psychopathic individuals demonstrate features that are thought to reflect tendencies common with a general externalizing spectrum, which underlies antisocial behavior, substance use, and impulsive and disinhibited personality traits (Krueger et al. 2007). In addition to this, they also demonstrate trait fearlessness, or under-reactivity to treats. These two dispositions may result from deficits in different biological systems. This is particularly important to consider when unpacking the biological research on psychopathy. Do common or distinct neurobiological factors underlie the different features of psychopathy? Although further research is needed, in the following chapters we highlight research that may speak to this issue. Progress toward understanding the development of psychopathy may be improved by considering the idea that the different features may be the result of separable deficits.

Psychopathy, Aggression, and Criminal Behavior

Psychopathy is often incorrectly equated with criminal behavior and violence. The reality is that in some individuals, psychopathic traits are accompanied by criminal behavior, evidenced by the fact that psychopathic individuals are overrepresented in forensic settings. It is estimated that they compose about 25 percent of the prison population (Hare 2003). Other individuals with psychopathic traits may be better able to achieve success in life, and may thrive in careers in which some degree of psychopathic traits may be advantageous. Overall, whereas some psychopathic individuals engage in crime, sometimes violent crime, others may never come into contact with the legal system. These individuals likely engage in acts that would be considered antisocial or immoral, such as lying or manipulating others, but may never engage in, or at least be caught engaging in, behaviors that are explicitly illegal. Psychopathic individuals with criminal convictions have been referred to as "unsuccessful psychopaths," compared to "successful psychopaths" who have not had encounters with the law, and some of whom may have achieved substantial personal success. In Chapter 9, we review the research that has examined the biological similarities and differences between unsuccessful and successful psychopaths.

Psychopathy is also sometimes incorrectly equated with antisocial personality disorder (APD or ASPD). APD is a listed in the *Diagnostic and Statistical Manual of Mental Disorders* (American Psychiatric Association 1994) as a personality disorder describing individuals with persistent antisocial behavior, such as serious violations of the law, frequent deception, and aggressive behaviors. Many individuals with high levels of psychopathic traits may meet the criteria for APD, as the criteria are similar to the Lifestyle-Antisocial (Factor 2) features of psychopathy. However, what sets psychopaths apart is the presence of the core Interpersonal-Affective (Factor 1) features. Many individuals with APD would not exhibit these features. APD is a much more inclusive and heterogeneous category; approximately 75 percent of individuals in a prison setting would be diagnosed with APD. Much research has been conducted on APD, as well as on criminal offending in general. In most of these studies, it is not clear what proportion of individuals in the sample has psychopathic traits, so it is difficult to generalize the findings to psychopathy. In this book, we attempt to focus the discussion of biological findings on studies that have examined psychopathic traits specifically. However, we also believe it is important to highlight some of the similarities and differences between individuals with psychopathic traits and antisocial individuals more generally.

When psychopathic individuals do demonstrate aggressive behavior, it tends to be more instrumental in nature. Instrumental aggression is planned, predatory, unprovoked aggression that is used to achieve a goal. Individuals with other disorders associated with aggression, such as schizophrenia, intermittent explosive disorder, and posttraumatic stress disorder, and individuals with conduct disorder or APD who do not demonstrate psychopathic traits generally do not demonstrate instrumental aggression. Instead, the aggression of these individuals is primarily reactive in nature. Reactive aggression is triggered by a frustrating or threatening event and involves unplanned attacks on the source of the threat or frustration. Individuals with psychopathy also demonstrate reactive aggression, in addition to instrumental aggression (Cornell et al. 1996).

In sum, psychopathy is set apart from disorders such as APD by the presence of interpersonal and affective personality traits. It can be but is not necessarily accompanied by criminal behavior. In terms of diagnostic categories, psychopathy represents a more specific set of traits, but still may reflect separable underlying dimensions.

Subtypes of Psychopathy

In addition to the distinction between successful and unsuccessful psychopathy, other subtypes have also emerged. Early researchers in the study of psychopathy suggested that there may be etiologically distinct subtypes (Lykken 1957, Karpman 1941). More recent research has supported this idea. Models assessing personality characteristics of individuals with high overall scores on psychopathy measures reveal two subgroups—one group described as being emotionally stable and generally unreactive to stress, and another group characterized by negative emotionality, impulsivity, and hostility (Hicks et al. 2004, Hicks, Vaidyanathan, and Patrick 2010). These two groups have been referred to as primary and secondary psychopaths.

Secondary psychopathy has been found to be associated with higher levels of anxiety (e.g., Newman and Schmitt 1998, Skeem et al. 2007) and poorer interpersonal functioning (i.e., demonstrating greater irritability, greater social withdrawal, lack of assertiveness) than primary psychopaths, yet rates of antisocial behavior are similar (Skeem et al. 2007). Evidence suggests that different factors may influence the development of these two subtypes of psychopathy (Kimonis et al. 2011, Skeem et al. 2003). In addition, each may be characterized by different neurobiological abnormalities.

Psychopathy in Youth

A growing body of research has found that psychopathic personality traits, although traditionally conceptualized in adults, are also observable in children and adolescents. The construct resembles psychopathy in adults and remains relatively stable during the transition from adolescence to adulthood (Frick et al. 2003, Loney et al. 2007). Similar to adults with psychopathic traits, youth with psychopathic traits engage in more severe and versatile antisocial behavior that begins at an earlier age (Edens, Campbell, and Weir 2007, Frick et al. 1994). One of the most defining features of psychopathy in youth appears to be the presence of callous (e.g., manipulative, unempathic) and unemotional traits (e.g., lack of guilt and remorse, shallow affect).

Several measures have been developed for measuring psychopathic traits in youth. These include the Psychopathy Checklist: Youth Version (Forth, Kosson, and Hare 2003), which is a modified variant of the PCL-R designed to be used in adolescent offenders ages 13 to 18, the Youth Psychopathic Traits Inventory (Andershed et al. 2002), the Child Psychopathy Scale (Lynam 1997), and the Antisocial Process Screening Device (Frick and Hare 2001), which is designed to assess psychopathic tendencies in children ages 6 to 13. In addition, the Inventory of Callous-Unemotional Traits (Frick 2004) provides a more extensive assessment of the affective traits of psychopathy in youth. Evidence for distinct primary and secondary subtypes of psychopathy in youth has been limited (Lee, Salekin, and Iselin 2010). In this book, we also review research examining the biological factors associated with psychopathic or callous-unemotional traits in youth.[1]

Biological Research on Psychopathy

As mentioned above, early researchers of psychopathy recognized the importance of understanding the biological mechanisms underlying the disorder. Cleckley wrote in 1941, "[W]e must also consider the possibility that the psychopath may be born with a biologic defect that leaves him without the capacity to feel and appreciate the major issues of life or to react to them in a normal and adequate manner" (p. 286). Since Cleckley's writing, the idea that there may be a biological basis to psychopathy has been an exciting area for exploration. Research findings have drawn the attention of a broad audience of individuals who are interested in understanding what makes psychopaths the way they are, and what the implications are for policy and treatment. To a lesser extent than research investigating other psychological disorders, studies exploring the biological factors associated with psychopathy or criminal behavior can be a sensitive topic, as they have implications for a number of ethical issues that people feel strongly about, including culpability, the punishment of criminals, and the existence of free will. Suggestions that psychopaths may not be responsible for their behavior because of biological deficits or that persistent criminal behavior should be considered a mental disorder are often met with harsh criticisms. This research also raises civil rights concerns, with some suggesting that biological research on crime may open the door to discrimination based on genes or that it may lead to individuals being labeled or punished before they have committed any crime. Some have even alleged that research examining the genetic factors that may contribute to crime is similar to "the kind of racist behavior we saw on the part of Nazi Germany" (Palca 1992).

Although biological research on crime certainly has implications for a number of ethical issues, many of these strong reactions may stem from a misunderstanding of the purpose and conclusions of biologically based research. These misunderstandings are often propagated by the media. For example, we frequently come across headlines such as "Can Your Genes Make You Murder?" (*National Public Radio*, July 1, 2010), "Is the Psychopathic Brain Hardwired to Hurt?" (*Vancouver Sun*, June 9, 2012), "Child Brain Scans to Pick Out Future Criminals" (*Telegraph*, February 22, 2011), or "Criminal Behavior May Be Hard-Wired in the Brain, Researchers Find" (*Los Angeles Times*, November 17,

2009). Articles such as these summarize studies that have found genetic associations or differences in the structure or functioning of the brains of psychopaths, and often draw conclusions that may be somewhat misguided. A few common examples are the following:

1. Aha! Psychopaths behave the way they do because of how their brains function.
Technically, this is true. But in reality, *all* people behave the way they do because of how their brains function. In theory, each thought we have and decision we make can be traced to a pattern of neurons firing. The purpose of research on the brains of psychopaths is really to discover *how* their brains are different, rather than to propose this as an explanation for their behavior. Brain functioning is the most proximate, direct cause of everyone's behavior, not just that of psychopaths.

Take, for example, the case of Charles Whitman, the straight-laced and intelligent 25-year-old man with no prior criminal history who one day in 1966 went on a killing spree at the University of Texas at Austin, killing 13 people and wounding many more. An autopsy determined that he had developed a tumor in this brain that likely led to the radical change in his behavior. These types of cases provide strong evidence that our personalities and behavior are the product of how our brains function. However, there is an important distinction to make: A more *proximate* cause of Whitman's extremely violent behavior was that specific parts of his brain were not functioning properly. The cause of his poor brain functioning was the tumor. But the *ultimate* causes that led to the development of tumor are unknown, and may be genetic or environmental in origin. Thus, when brain imaging research reports that a particular brain region is smaller or functions differently in a particular individual or population, it really says nothing about the *ultimate* cause(s) of an individual's behavior. Brain imaging studies are important for describing what the differences are so that we can work toward determining what some of the ultimate causes (genetic and/or environmental) might be.

2. It's biological.
People often conclude that the identification of brain deficits in psychopaths means that the disorder is biologically based. This is

understandable because we often categorize things as "nature versus nurture" or "biological versus environmental," and information about the *brain* seems to fall into the biological category. But in reality, the brain is just the machine that the biological and environmental factors act upon. The factors that make our brains function the way they do can be either genetic or environmental in origin, or, more likely, a combination of the two. Our genes are determined at conception. The environment is influential from that point forward; it affects how our genes are expressed, how our brains develop, and how our brains function. Thus, the identification of a brain abnormality in psychopathic individuals should not be viewed as evidence that the disorder results more from biological than environmental factors.

This also applies to other types of "biological" research that we review in this book, including psychophysiology, and the study of hormones and neurotransmitters. These are either indicators of brain functioning or the mechanisms that drive it, and therefore should not be viewed any differently. Environmental factors influence these measures as well as genetic factors. For example, abuse or trauma in early childhood may cause lasting changes in hormone levels, which, in turn, affect brain functioning. Exposure to toxins in utero may affect the way the brain develops. Thus, although this book reviews much of the research in these "biologically based" areas, it is important to understand that this describes the biological *mechanisms*, rather than suggesting that biology plays more of a role than the environment.

3. If their brains are broken, nothing can be done.
The headline above, "Criminal Behavior May Be Hard-Wired in the Brain," implies that individuals are predisposed for crime early in life and that there is little we can do—biology is destiny. In our view, it is quite the opposite. As we discuss in this book, the environment plays a significant role in shaping how the brain develops and how it functions, even in adulthood. Environmental factors can even alter the way that genes are expressed, meaning that being a carrier of a particular gene does not necessarily mean that the functions of that gene will be realized. Rather than eliminating any possibility for a solution, understanding the biology of psychopathic individuals puts us one step closer to understanding how psychopathic traits develop. *How* do specific genes

predispose for psychopathic traits? *How* do environmental factors predispose for psychopathic traits? Answering these questions will help us to develop more targeted and sophisticated methods for prevention and intervention, which is the ultimate goal.

Levels of Biology

In this book, we present findings from several different areas of biological research. Each represents a step in the biological pathway that underlies behavior. Genes embody the first step in this pathway, representing the first source of biological variation between individuals. Very early on, genes play a role in the development of the structure and organization of the brain. Genes are unique in this pathway because genes and environmental factors are the only two ultimate causes of behavior. The other steps in the pathway simply represent the mechanisms by which genes and the environment have an effect. When we say that a person behaves a particular way because he or she has a deficit in a specific brain region, we really mean that genetic or environmental factors caused this deficit in the brain, which resulted in the behavior.

Genetic and environmental factors continue to be influential throughout the life span via their effects on neurotransmitter and hormone systems, which in turn influence brain functioning, the most proximate cause of traits and behaviors such as those observed in psychopathy. Figure I.2 depicts the basic levels at which the biology of a disorder can be studied. The intermediate biological mechanisms that form the link between genes and the disorder are called endophenotypes. Endophenotypes include sources of variation at the molecular level (e.g., altered hormone levels) or on a larger systems level that involve the structure and function of brain regions and brain networks. In addition, indirect assessments of brain functioning, such as psychophysiological responding, may also be considered endophenotypes.

Brain structure and brain functioning are unique in the biological pathway because they represent a more direct, proximate cause of behavior. All behavior is caused by brain functioning. Genetic and environmental influences ultimately are associated with behavior because of their effects on brain structure and functioning. Environmental factors can exert an influence at any one of these levels. This means that the

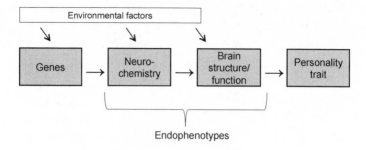

Figure I.2. The biological pathway leading to the development and maintenance of a set of behaviors or personality traits.

relationships between two levels may be modest because additional factors are entering the equation. However, information about each level has the potential to increase our understanding of the many factors along the biological pathway that lead to the development of these traits.

Overview of Book

The goal of this book is to provide an overview of the different areas of biological research on psychopathy, explaining the techniques that are used, reviewing the existing findings, and discussing their implications for our understanding of psychopathy. We begin in Chapter 1 with a discussion of one of the ultimate causes of behavior—genes. We review two types of genetic research on psychopathy: behavioral and molecular genetics. From there, we turn to the various endophenotypes that form the biological pathway. In Chapter 2, we examine research on the potential role of hormones in the development and maintenance of psychopathy. These neurochemicals are important in facilitating brain functioning. Chapters 3, 4, and 5 focus on actual brain functioning, measured with different techniques. In Chapter 3, we review research that estimates brain and peripheral nervous system functioning using psychophysiological techniques, which include skin conductance activity, heart rate, and electroencephalogram. In Chapter 4, we explore research that estimates brain functioning based on performance on standardized neuropsychological tests that have been developed to assess the degree of dysfunction in a particular brain region or set of regions. Neuropsychological techniques have been vigorously used in the study of psychopathy and have provided a wealth of information regarding the specific nature of the psychopath's deficits. In Chapter 5, we discuss the more direct method for assessing the brain—structural and functional brain imaging. These studies have utilized tasks assessing empathy, moral decision making, and emotional responding, among others, to uncover the brain regions that appear to function differently in individuals with psychopathic traits.

After reviewing findings from studies implementing these various biological techniques, in Chapter 6, we turn to the environmental factors that have been linked to psychopathy, or to the impairments that have been observed in psychopathy. We devote particular attention to examining how environmental factors may interact with biological factors in predisposing individuals to psychopathy, as well as how environmental factors may alter biology during development. In Chapter 7, we focus on a particular subtype of psychopath—the successful psychopath—and review studies that have examined biological similarities and differences between successful and unsuccessful psychopaths.

In Chapter 8, we provide an in depth discussion of a number of ethical and legal issues that have arisen based on biological research on psychopathy and criminal behavior. We address issues such as whether psychopathic individuals are truly responsible for their crimes given evidence of biological deficits and whether brain imaging evidence should be allowed in court, and discuss the purpose of punishment.

In Chapter 9, we look toward the future of biological research and discuss how it may enable us to more accurately develop methods for prevention and intervention that ideally can be implemented at an early age. We briefly review existing studies involving treatment for psychopathy and discuss the potential for future studies that may take biological factors into consideration. Finally, in the concluding chapter we focus on the theoretical concept that psychopathy has a neurodevelopmental basis and review the evidence that the neurobiological processes associated with psychopathy likely have their origins early in life, emphasizing the need for future work examining the development of psychopathy and ways in which we may ultimately prevent it.

The idea that there is a significant biological component to the development of psychopathy has attracted great interest from a variety of fields. This book aims to provide a concise, nontechnical overview of the biological findings in psychopathy research. We intend this book to be useful for undergraduates, graduate students, and academics both within psychology and outside the field who are interested in an introduction to biological research on psychopathy and a discussion of the ethical and legal implications associated with these findings.

Note

1. For more information regarding research on psychopathic traits in youth, see the handbook edited by Salekin and Lynam (2010).

1

Genetics

In his book *Without Conscience* (1999), Dr. Robert Hare describes a set of female twins who differ like "night and day," "heaven and hell." One twin grows up to be a lawyer with ambitious career prospects, while the other develops drug addiction, has numerous encounters with the law, and demonstrates many of the traits of psychopathy. Despite years of intensive self-scrutiny, the twins' supportive and attentive mother cannot identify a mistake, event, or way in which the girls might have been treated differently that could have resulted in the troublesome behavior of one of the twins. Despite sharing the same womb and being raised in the same nurturing family environment, the twins are drastically different. Yet one notable factor is that the sisters are not identical twins—they are fraternal.

Children have the physical, cognitive, and emotional means of being physically aggressive toward others by 12 months of age, and individual differences in the frequency and severity of this aggression can be observed shortly thereafter (Tremblay 2008). To what extent are these individual differences due to genes versus the environment of the child? The idea that antisocial or criminal behavior is heritable is one that has been very controversial over the years, but it has gained substantial scientific evidence to support it (Raine 2008, Moffitt 2005). Recently, studies have also begun to specifically examine the genetics of psychopathic personality traits. This chapter outlines evidence from two overarching fields of genetic research: behavioral genetics and molecular genetics. Behavioral genetics studies aim to disentangle how much a disorder is the result of genes versus environmental factors; this approach includes twin and adoption studies. The next step is to identify specific genes that may confer risk for the disorder, which is the task of molecular genetics. The main findings from these studies are that psychopathic traits appear to be moderately to highly heritable and share some common genetic factors with antisocial behavior more generally, but they also are attributable to unique genetic factors. Studies examining specific genes that may confer risk for psychopathic traits are just beginning, but have provided some clues as to the biological pathways that may underlie psychopathy.

As discussed in the introduction, genes represent the first source of biological variation between individuals; they facilitate the development of the structure and organization of the brain, and continue to have an influence throughout the life span through their effects on neurotransmitter and hormone systems, which facilitate brain functioning. The functioning of a particular gene may depend on the presence of other genes, as well as environmental factors, which have the capability of altering the way that genes are expressed (e.g., they may be able to turn genes "on" or "off"). Therefore, the association between a single gene and a behavior or trait is typically very small. This is also due to the fact that the pathway from the activity of a single gene to behavior is complex, and countless additional factors are introduced at each step, introducing additional variance. Thus, large sample sizes are often required in studies attempting to link a single gene to a particular disorder. Identifying the genes that are associated with psychopathy has the potential to further our understanding of the causal chain of events that lead to its development.

Behavioral Genetics

In studying the genetics of psychopathy, the first step is to establish whether psychopathic traits are heritable and the extent of the potential heritability. Behavioral genetics studies have begun to answer these questions and others. Before outlining evidence from these studies, the methodologies used in the field of behavioral genetics are first briefly outlined.

Behavioral Genetics Methodology

Behavioral genetics studies usually involve twin or adoption studies. Since there are currently no adoption studies of psychopathy, we focus on the twin methodology. Twin studies typically compare samples of monozygotic (MZ) or "identical" twins, who share 100 percent of their genes, to dizygotic (DZ) "fraternal" twins, who share approximately 50 percent of their genes. It should be noted that when we say 50 percent, we are actually referring to only the genes that can vary across individuals; all humans share about 99 percent of their genes, but the remaining 1 percent varies, and it is this portion that is of interest in genetics studies. Furthermore, DZ twins share 50 percent of their variable genes *on average*, but this can vary considerably, with some DZ twins being more similar and others less similar.

In behavioral genetics studies, the similarity of MZ twins on a given trait is compared to the similarity of DZ twins on that trait. If MZ twins are more similar than DZ twins, then it can be inferred that the trait being measured is at least partly due to genetic factors. Across large samples, statistical modeling techniques can determine the proportion of the variance in a particular trait or phenotype (in this case, psychopathy or a subcomponent of it) that is accounted for by genetic versus environmental factors.

Genetic factors either can be additive or nonadditive. Additive means that genes summate to contribute to a phenotype. For example, hypothetically, alleles at five different locations may contribute to the determination of an individual's height (the phenotype). An additive effect means that the individual's height is the sum of the effect of each of these alleles on height. Additive effects are passed on in families. The more alleles you have that are similar to your parent or sibling (e.g., alleles coding for height), the more similar you are on a given trait (e.g., height). If a genetic effect is additive, then the correlation between DZ twins will usually be about half of the correlation of MZ twins (because they share half the number of genes).

Nonadditive effects mean that genes are configured in a unique way to form the personality trait, rather than simply being the cumulative effect of several genes. This means that if just one gene is different, the personality trait may not exist. Nonadditive effects come in three types—dominance, epistasis, and emergensis. Dominance means that if one of two alleles is dominant, the phenotype will reflect the dominant allele, rather than a summation of the two alleles. For example, alleles for brown eyes tend to be dominant, whereas alleles for blue eyes are recessive. If an individual has one allele for brown eyes and one allele for blue eyes, the result is that the individual will have brown eyes, rather than a mix between brown and blue. In the case of dominance, DZ twin correlations are expected to be about 25 percent of the MZ correlations. Epistatic and emergenic effects simply mean that multiple genes must interact or be configured in a specific way in order for the phenotype to be present. Because these configurations are so specific, these types of effects do not run in families and can be thought of as random; thus, the correlation between DZ twins is typically close to zero, whereas the effect will be present in MZ twins who share the exact same genes.

Environmental effects can also be divided into two types—shared and nonshared. Shared environmental effects are those that are common to both twins such as socioeconomic status and parental discipline. Nonshared environmental effects are those that are unique to each twin; the most common example of a nonshared environment is a peer group.

Aside from addressing the extent of heritability of psychopathic traits, behavioral genetics studies can help to answer a number of additional questions about psychopathy. For example, are psychopathic traits more heritable than criminal behavior in general? Also, how much genetic variation is shared across the different features of psychopathy (i.e., do the interpersonal, affective, and antisocial traits stem from common genetic factors?), suggesting that this is in fact a unified disorder? Or are these independently derived maladaptive personality traits that combine in some individuals to form what we think of as psychopathy? Answers to these questions may provide useful information regarding the conceptualization of psychopathy.

Evidence from Behavioral Genetics Studies

Although several studies have claimed to study the genetics of psychopathy, most of these studies have focused on the antisocial deviance features of psychopathy and not the core personality traits (Blonigen et al. 2003). However, in the past several years, several studies have assessed the genetics of psychopathic traits specifically (see Table 1.1). These studies include participants from as young as age 7 to as old as age 92. These studies have used a variety of measures for assessing psychopathy (or callous-unemotional traits in youth), but all have relied on either self-report or teacher-report ratings. Despite the variance in methodology, four key findings have emerged from these studies.

1. Psychopathic traits are moderately to highly heritable.
The general consensus from these studies suggests that genetic factors account for approximately 40 to 60 percent of the variance in psychopathic traits, an estimate that is consistent with the results of behavioral genetics studies that have examined the heritability of other personality dimensions (Bouchard and Loehlin 2001). This means that, on average, genetic and environmental factors contribute approximately equally to the disorder. It will be important to keep this estimate in mind in the following chapters as we discuss differences in brain functioning and hormone levels—it is important to remember that these biological differences result from *both* genetic *and* environmental factors. It is also important to keep in mind that this figure represents an average across a large number of people, and that in some individuals, genes may have a stronger influence on the development of psychopathic traits than the environment, and in other individuals, the opposite may be true.

The majority of behavioral genetics studies of psychopathy report that genetic effects are additive. This means that the genes summate to contribute to the disorder; the more risk genes an individual has, the more likely he or she will be to develop psychopathic traits (for an exception, see Blonigen et al. 2003). We can tell that the genetic effects are additive because studies show that the correlation for DZ twins, who share about half of their genes, is approximately half of the correlation for MZ twins. Genetic factors have also been found to contribute to the stability of psychopathic traits over time. Several studies have established that psychopathic personality is stable (Loney et al. 2007, Lynam et al. 2007). A study by Forsman et al. (2008) found that genetic factors contribute to this stability. In contrast, changes in psychopathic traits over time were found to result primarily from environmental factors,

Table 1.1. Behavioral Genetics Studies of Psychopathy

Study	Measure	Age	Sex	Number of twin pairs		Correlation between twin pairs		Additive genetic effects	Dominant genetic effects	Epistasis or emergensis	Shared environmental effects	Non-shared environmental effects
				MZ	DZ	rMZ	rDZ	a^2	d^2	i^2	c^2	e^2
Blonigen et al. 2003	Psychopathic Personality Inventory	~39–42	M	165	106	.46	−.26			.47		.53
	• Machiavellian Egocentricity					.28	−.09			.29		.71
	• Social Potency					.54	.21	.54				.46
	• Fearlessness					.54	.03			.51		.49
	• Coldheartedness					.34	−.16			.38		.62
	• Impulsive Nonconformity					.51	−.05			.50		.50
	• Blame Externalization					.57	.16	.56				.44
	• Carefree Nonplanfulness					.31	−.16			.38		.62
	• Stress Immunity					.43	−.08			.42		.58
Blonigen et al. 2005	Multidimensional Personality Questionnaire (MPQ)	26–33	M/F	411	215							

Table 1.1 (continued)

Study	Measure	Age	Sex	Number of twin pairs		Correlation between twin pairs		Additive genetic effects	Dominant genetic effects	Epistasis or emer-gensis	Shared environ-mental effects	Non-shared environ-mental effects
				MZ	DZ	rMZ	rDZ	a^2	d^2	i^2	c^2	e^2
	• Fearless Dominance (MPQ estimated)					.44	.20	.45				.55
	• Impulsive Antisociality (MPQ estimated)					.50	.24	.49				.51
Johansson et al. 2008	Self-Report Psychopathy Scale (SRP-III)	33–43	M	91	110	.55	.29	.54				.46
	• Interpersonal					.49	.21					
	• Affective					.37	.16					
	• Lifestyle					.44	.24					
	• Antisocial					.45	.21					
Larsson et al. 2006[a]	Youth Psychopathic Traits Inventory	16–17	M/F	419	347							
	• Latent Psychopathy Factor							.63				.37
	• Grandiose/Manipulative							.51			.03	.46
	Boys					.48	.30					

Table 1.1 (continued)

Study	Measure	Age	Sex	Number of twin pairs		Correlation between twin pairs		Additive genetic effects a^2	Dominant genetic effects d^2	Epistasis or emergensis i^2	Shared environmental effects c^2	Non-shared environmental effects e^2
				MZ	DZ	rMZ	rDZ					
	Girls					.61	.26					
	• Callous/Unemotional											
	Boys					.47	.26	.43				.57
	Girls					.44	.17					
	• Impulsive/Irresponsible											
	Boys					.57	.20	.56				.44
	Girls					.57	.31					
Taylor et al. 2003	Minnesota Temperament Inventory	10–12 16–18	M	128 58	142 70							
	• Detachment (similar to callous)							.42				.58
	Younger					.41	.15					
	Older					.43	.25					
	• Antisocial							.39				.61
	Younger					.42	.17					
	Older					.36	.09					

Table 1.1 (continued)

Study	Measure	Age	Sex	Number of twin pairs		Correlation between twin pairs		Additive genetic effects	Dominant genetic effects	Epistasis or emergensis	Shared environmental effects	Non-shared environmental effects
				MZ	DZ	rMZ	rDZ	a^2	d^2	i^2	c^2	e^2
Vernon et al. 2008	SRP-III	17–92	M/F	75	64	.54	.44	.64			.04	.32
Viding et al. 2005	Teacher Ratings	7	M/F									
	• Extreme Callous/ Unemotional			459 (MZ + DZ)		.73	.39	.67[b]			.06	.27
	• Extreme Callous/Unemotional + Antisocial Behavior			187 (MZ + DZ)		.76	.36	.81[b]			.05	.14

Note:

[a] Additional studies from this sample include Larsson et al. (2007) and Forsman et al. (2008, 2010).

[b] Measured as heritability (h²) but likely additive genetic effects since the correlations for DZ twins are approximately half the correlations of MZ twins

meaning that any changes in the level of psychopathic traits over time appear to be due to environmental influences.

2. Nonshared rather than shared environment accounts for the rest of the variance.

This is a key finding that distinguishes behavioral genetics studies of psychopathy from those of antisocial behavior more generally. Studies of antisocial behavior have most often found that the environment that is shared between twins has an effect on antisocial behavior (Rhee and Waldman 2002, Larsson et al. 2007). However, across all the studies reviewed here on psychopathic personality traits, the influence of shared environmental factors was negligible. This means that although environmental factors are important in the development of psychopathic traits, it is not the environment that is shared between the twins, such as socioeconomic status, school, or neighborhood, that is important. It is the environmental factors that are unique to each twin that are involved. Some researchers hypothesize that peer relationships may account for some of the nonshared environmental influences on psychopathy (Larsson, Andershed, and Lichtenstein 2006), as peer relationships are thought to substantially contribute to differentiation between siblings during adolescence (Pike and Plomin 1997).

This finding represents a divergence in etiology between psychopathic traits and general antisocial behavior. It has been suggested that this finding may reflect the distinction between core personality traits (i.e., psychopathic traits) and "characteristic adaptations," which are behaviors that result from a combination of core personality traits and environmental influences (i.e., antisocial behavior could be viewed as a characteristic adaptation) (Larsson et al. 2007). The finding of the influence of the nonshared environment but not the shared environment is more consistent with other studies of personality dimensions, which find that almost none of the environmental variance in personality is due to sharing a common environment (Bouchard and Loehlin 2001).

3. Different facets of psychopathy have both common and unique genetic factors.

The idea that the different features of psychopathy are unified and stem from common factors has long been hypothesized (Hare 1970), but has been difficult to confirm. Behavioral genetics studies have a unique ability to provide information about whether the different features of psychopathy actually represent a unified disorder. The finding that there are common genetic factors influencing the distinct aspects of psychopathy would suggest that it is indeed a unified construct. Thus far, two studies have found that some of the same genetic factors contribute to the different facets of psychopathy (Taylor et al. 2003, Larsson, Andershed, and Lichtenstein 2006). Both of these studies found sizable genetic correlations between the different factors of psychopathy, including callous-unemotional features and impulsive-antisocial features. These studies suggest that there is a strong relationship among the genetic factors that are associated with the different aspects of psychopathy. Furthermore, Larsson, Andershed, and Lichtenstein (2006) found that the different facets of psychopathy covary with a latent overall psychopathy factor, which is also substantially influenced by genetic factors.

One exception to these findings is the study by Blonigen at al. (2005), which found no genetic correlation between the Fearless Dominance and Impulsive Antisocial factors of psychopathy, suggesting that the two factors may derive from independent etiological processes. Although this finding stands in contrast to the strong genetic correlation between psychopathy factors observed by Taylor et al. (2003) and Larsson, Andershed, and Lichtenstein (2006), both of the latter studies also found that there are some unique genetic effects that are important for the different psychopathy factors (i.e., there are unique genetic effects that influence the different psychopathy factors over and above the genetic influence from the latent psychopathy factor). This suggests that despite the fact that the factors of psychopathy tend to co-occur, there may be some etiological factors that differentiate them. Additional studies will be necessary to clarify the degree of shared versus unique genetic contributions to the psychopathy factors, but overall research suggests that there are both common and unique genetic factors underlying the different aspects of psychopathy.

A final interesting point to note regarding the heritability of the psychopathy factors is that each of these studies has shown that the degree of heritability of the different factors of psychopathy (e.g., emotional, interpersonal, lifestyle) tends to be approximately the same, meaning that there are not features of psychopathy that are more heritable than others (Blonigen et al. 2005, Larsson, Andershed, and Lichtenstein 2006, Taylor et al. 2003).

4. Psychopathy shares common genetic factors with antisocial/externalizing behavior.
The genetic correlations between psychopathy factors in the studies discussed above refer only to the "personality" features of psychopathy, and do not include assessments of criminal behavior that are measured on the PCL-R (i.e., items included in the "antisocial" subfactors from these studies reflect traits such as deceitfulness or irresponsibility rather than crime). However, Blonigen et al. (2005) assessed whether the psychopathic personality features shared common genetic factors with externalizing behavior and found that there was significant genetic overlap between externalizing behavior and both the Impulsive Antisociality factor and the Fearless Dominance factor of psychopathy (the latter only in males). Furthermore, Larsson et al. (2007) measured psychopathic personality and deviant behavior in adolescent twins and found that a common genetic factor substantially contributed to psychopathic personality traits and to deviant behavior. Finally, Viding et al. (2005) showed that extreme antisocial behavior was much more heritable in youth with callous-unemotional traits than in youth without those traits (in whom antisocial behavior resulted primarily from shared environmental factors), suggesting that there are potentially shared genetic factors underlying callous-unemotional traits and antisocial behavior. Importantly, these studies suggest that genetic factors largely account for the co-occurrence of psychopathic personality traits and antisocial behavior. However, it is still unclear whether this set of genes is common to psychopathy and antisocial behavior because they predispose to externalizing psychopathology more generally, or whether they may primarily predispose for psychopathic personality traits and have an indirect effect on antisocial behavior as a result of increased psychopathic traits.

One study attempted to partially clarify this question by examining the direction of effects between psychopathic personality traits and antisocial behavior and assessing the degree of genetic involvement.

Forsman et al. (2010) found that genetic factors played a role in the association between psychopathic traits at age 16 to 17 and antisocial behavior (primarily rule breaking rather than aggression) at age 19 to 20, suggesting that genetically driven personality features may predispose to antisocial behavior. However, they also found a genetically driven effect from persistent antisocial behavior to psychopathic personality. Thus, although behavioral genetics studies have potential for furthering our understanding of the developmental relationship between psychopathic traits and antisocial behavior, to date the evidence seems inconclusive.

Mechanisms of Genetic Effects

Establishing that psychopathic traits are heritable does not provide information about *how* a group of genes may confer risk for the disorder (i.e., how genes influence brain structure or functioning). It is likely that these genes influence brain structure or functioning in some way. One recent study of psychopathic traits attempted to determine which regions of the brain may show variable gray matter concentrations as a result of genes associated with psychopathy (Rijsdijsk et al. 2010). The first step was to examine the heritability of gray matter concentrations in regions of the brain that have previously been associated with psychopathic traits. Rijsdijsk et al. (2010) found that gray matter concentrations in two areas of a part of the brain called the cingulate gyrus—the posterior cingulate (the part of the cingulate closer to the back of the brain) and the right dorsal anterior cingulate (the part of the cingulate closer to the front and top of the brain)—demonstrated moderate heritability. The gray matter concentration in these regions had previously been found to be reduced in individuals with psychopathic traits. The second step was to establish whether common genetic factors were associated with reduced gray matter concentrations in these regions and with psychopathic traits. Using twin study methodology, the authors found that in the posterior cingulate, nearly half of the genetic influences between gray matter concentration and psychopathic traits overlapped, suggesting that a subset of genes may confer risk for psychopathic traits via their effects on gray matter concentrations in this region. Common genetic factors were also observed for the right dorsal anterior cingulate. This is the first study to directly explore the mechanisms by which genetic factors may operate in psychopathy.

Behavioral Genetics: Conclusions and Future Directions

Taken together, the results from behavioral genetics studies indicate that genetic and nonshared environmental factors account for individual differences in psychopathic traits from childhood through adulthood. Future behavioral genetics studies will likely be beneficial in helping to fine-tune our understanding of the different aspects of psychopathy and how they are etiologically related to each other and to antisocial behavior. Future studies may also benefit from examining primary and secondary subtypes of psychopathy to examine the hypothesis that primary psychopathy is more genetically based, whereas secondary psychopathy results more from environmental influences (Poythress and Skeem 2006).

It will also be important to use findings from behavioral genetics studies to aid our understanding of the mechanisms by which genetic factors have an effect. For example, the finding that there are both common and unique genetic influences for the different factors of psychopathy raises questions about how the general and specific variance within psychopathy is related to emotional and cognitive processes. In addition, the finding that there is a latent psychopathic personality factor that is highly influenced by genetic factors makes this factor a novel target for future research examining the biological pathway that may stem from these genetic factors. Studies exploring the brain mechanisms by which genes may operate have great potential for furthering our understanding of the relationships among genes, the brain, and behavior. Future studies may examine variation in other types of structural brain factors, as well as in brain functioning to determine how genes may influence the brain and thus predispose to psychopathic traits.

Overall, behavioral genetics studies do not identify specific genes or specific environmental factors that contribute to the development of psychopathy, but they do shed light on the broader etiological framework for psychopathy by improving our understanding of the etiology of the different components of psychopathy, how psychopathy is related to antisocial behavior, and how genes may act on the brain to predispose to psychopathic traits. The next section focuses on initial attempts to identify specific genes that may confer risk for psychopathy.

Molecular Genetics

Given the substantial evidence that genetic factors do in fact contribute to the development of psychopathic traits, the field is now also tackling the important questions of *which* genes predispose to psychopathy, and under what circumstances and in what combinations they have an effect. Molecular genetics research on psychopathy is still in its infancy, but initial answers to these questions are beginning to emerge. Determining which genes are involved may aid in the development of treatment methods that can be tailored to an individual's biology. It also may improve our understanding of the biological pathways that lead to the disorder (e.g., from genes, to brain, to behavior).

Molecular Genetics Methodology

To date, two types of molecular genetics studies have been conducted in psychopathy—candidate gene studies and genome-wide association studies. The most common molecular genetics approach in research on psychological disorders is the study of candidate genes.

What are candidate genes?
A candidate gene is a gene that has been hypothesized to be associated with a disorder for one reason or another. The function of the gene is usually known to some extent (e.g., it codes for a protein such as a neurotransmitter receptor). Research on candidate genes involves genotyping individuals to determine which alleles (variations) of the gene the individual possesses. Many commonly studied candidate genes have two alleles (e.g., a long version and a short version). Since an individual inherits one allele from each parent, there would be three possible genotypes for a gene with two alleles (e.g., long/long, long/short, or short/short). Studies then examine whether there are differences between individuals with the different genotypes; these differences can be on indicators of biological or neuropsychological functioning, or in the prevalence of a trait or disorder.

As mentioned previously, linking a single gene variant (called a polymorphism) to a complex psychological disorder such as psychopathy can be difficult because the contribution of an individual gene is typically very small (Canli and Lesch 2007). Psychological disorders are influenced by many genetic polymorphisms, as well as by environmental factors. Therefore, studies attempting to link a candidate gene to a disorder often require very large sample sizes to detect an effect, and observed effects may account for only a small proportion of the variance in the disorder (Lesch et al. 1996).

How do you decide which gene to study?
One way to identify candidate genes is to select a gene that is related to a biological system that is believed to be associated with the disorder—in other words, a gene that could plausibly be related to the disorder. For example, studies of alcohol and drug dependence have examined genes associated with the neurotransmitter dopamine, which is the primary neurotransmitter associated with the reward system of the brain. Researchers can look at genes associated with various aspects of this system, including genes that code for dopamine receptors, genes that code for dopamine transporters (proteins that remove dopamine from the synapse and transport it back to the cell), or genes that code for enzymes that break down dopamine. In addition, genes associated with other neurotransmitter systems that may modify dopamine function could be considered potential candidate genes.

Another approach to identifying candidate genes for a disorder is to build upon previous candidate gene research on a disorder that commonly co-occurs with the disorder of interest (i.e., a comorbid disorder) and to examine genes that have been associated with comorbid disorders in previous studies. The idea is that disorders that frequently co-occur likely have common genetic factors that contribute to both. For example, genes that contribute to a more general externalizing factor may be related to both alcohol dependence and antisocial personality; therefore, it may be beneficial to examine the genes that have been previously associated with alcohol dependence when studying antisocial personality. This is the approach that has primarily been implemented in newly emerging studies of psychopathy. Several studies of psychopathy have examined genes that have previously been associated with alcohol or substance dependence because there is high comorbidity between substance dependence and psychopathy, and it is likely that some genes confer risk for both.

A final approach is to identify candidate genes that have been associated with endophenotypes that have previously been associated with the disorder. Endophenotypes are essentially the intermediate biological mechanisms that represent the pathway between the ultimate causes of a disorder (genes and the environment) and the behavioral symptoms of the disorder. When attempting to identify candidate genes, if a particular gene has been linked to an endophenotype, it could be hypothesized that the gene may be associated with disorders in which the endophenotype has been observed. For example, reduced functioning of a particular brain region may be an endophenotype associated with psychopathy. Genes that have been linked to reduced functioning in that region would therefore be good candidates to explore in relation to psychopathy. Although this approach has rarely been used in psychopathy research to date, it has great potential in helping to identify candidate genes that are worthy of testing, particularly as more and more research establishes links between gene variants and endophenotypes.

Genome-wide association studies.

Genome-wide association (GWA) studies provide a more systematic approach than candidate gene studies. These studies scan the genome for polymorphisms that may be more common in one group (e.g., individuals with psychopathic traits) versus another (e.g., individuals low in psychopathic traits). These studies can be very expensive if genotyping is conducted separately for each individual. An alternative method is for the DNA for each group to be pooled so that the average allele frequency can be calculated, although a disadvantage of this method is that some statistical power is lost. Similar to candidate gene studies, GWA studies require large sample sizes, as the association between a single polymorphism and a complex trait is typically very small. Well-powered GWA studies rarely identify polymorphisms that account for more than 1 percent of the variance on a complex trait (Viding et al. 2010). These studies also generate large amounts of data from many sites in the genome without regard to biological plausibility and thus may be prone to false associations (Pearson and Manolio 2008). However, these studies have the potential to be very valuable in identifying genetic polymorphisms that can be the focus of further study.

Evidence from Molecular Genetics Studies

Candidate gene studies.

Several studies have begun to specifically examine the relationship between candidate genes and psychopathic traits. To date, polymorphisms of approximately eight genes have been studied, and most findings have yet to be replicated. Thus, the field is very open for new research.

Table 1.2 lists the genes that have been examined in relation to psychopathy and summarizes their function and the reason they have been hypothesized to be associated with it. Several of these polymorphisms have been associated with reward systems of the brain (e.g., dopamine or endocannabinoid systems) and have been found to be associated with disorders that commonly co-occur such as substance and alcohol dependence. The hypothesis is that there may be common genes associated with the reward systems of the brain that may predispose one to the reward-seeking tendencies observed in psychopathy and also increase vulnerability to developing addictive behaviors (Hoenicka et al. 2007). Specific polymorphisms may affect the functioning of brain regions involved in reward, such as the nucleus accumbens, resulting in heightened reward-seeking tendencies or impulsivity resulting from a diminished ability to delay rewards. Similarly, brain regions involved in stimulus-reinforcement learning (i.e., the ability to learn from reward and punishment), such as the amygdala, may be affected by altered transmission of dopamine and endocannabinoids resulting from genetic polymorphisms.

Additional genetic polymorphisms that have been studied relate to other neurotransmitter systems, such as the serotonin system, as well as to molecules that break down neurotransmitters. There are various reasons that these polymorphisms have been hypothesized to be associated with psychopathy. Some of these hypotheses are based on endophenotypes such as brain functioning. For example, the gene coding for fatty acid amide hydrolase (FAAH), which breaks down endocannabinoids, has been associated with reduced threat-related activity in

Table 1.2. *Candidate Genes Explored in Psychopathy*

Polymorphism	Gene Function	Reason for Hypothesis
Reward systems		
TaqIA SNP	ANKK1	• Affects the dopamine system, which is associated with reward and learning • Associated with alcoholism (Blum et al. 1991) and antisocial traits (Lu et al. 2001) and may relate to a general vulnerability to impulsive and reward-seeking behavior Located near the D2 dopamine receptor gene and is associated with increased D2 receptors in the striatum, resulting in increased dopamine synthesis (Laakso et al. 2005)
C957T	DRD2	• Affects the dopamine system, which is associated with reward and learning Codes for the D2 dopamine receptor and is associated with D2 receptor availability in the striatum (Hirvonen et al. 2004)
10-repeat allele	SLC6A3	• Affects the dopamine system, which is associated with reward and learning • Associated with alcoholism (Ueno et al. 1999) and ADHD (Cook et al. 1995) Codes for the dopamine transporter, which clears dopamine from the synapse
At least one allele with 10 or fewer repeats	CNR1	• Located on the same neurons as dopamine receptors in the striatum and therefore may affect the dopamine system • Associated with drug dependency (Comings et al. 1997) and ADHD in alcoholics (Ponce et al. 2003) Codes for cannabinoid receptor type 1 (CB1), which may modulate dopamine release in the striatum

Table 1.2 (continued)

Polymorphism	Gene Function	Reason for Hypothesis
Neurotransmitter systems		
5-HTTLPR	SLC6A4	Codes for the serotonin transporter	• Biological and behavioral findings in individuals with the long allele parallel findings from studies of psychopathy (Glenn 2011)
Five-locus haplotype	OXT and OXTR genes	Codes for oxytocin and the oxytocin receptor	• Oxytocin is associated with social bonding and the ability to recognize social cues
Degradation/metabolic systems		
C385A	FAAH	Codes for fatty acid amide hydrolase (FAAH), an endocannabinoid metabolizing enzyme	• Associated with reduced threat-related amygdala activity and increased reward-related ventral striatal activity (Hariri et al. 2009) • Associated with drug use (Sipe et al. 2002)
Val158Met	COMT	Codes for catechol-O-methyl-transferase (COMT), an enzyme that degrades neurotransmitters such as dopamine, epinephrine, and norepinephrine	• Associated with impaired prefrontal cortex functioning (Tunbridge, Harrison, and Weinberger 2006) • Associated with antisocial behavior (Thapar et al. 2005)
30-bp variable number of tandem repeats	MAO-A	Codes for monoamine oxidase A (MAO-A), an enzyme that breaks down neurotransmitters such as serotonin, norepinephrine, and dopamine	• Associated with amygdala functioning (Meyer-Lindenberg et al. 2006) • Associated with antisocial and violent behavior (Craig 2007)

the amygdala, a region that generates the body's response to threat and stress. It has also been associated with increased reward-related activity in the ventral striatum, a region important in reward processing (Hariri et al. 2009). Previous brain imaging studies of psychopathy have found similar results—reduced activity in the amygdala to threat-related stimuli (e.g., Birbaumer et al. 2005) and increased volume of the striatum (Glenn, Raine, et al. 2010). Thus, there is good reason to hypothesize that *FAAH* may confer risk for psychopathy.

Another genetic polymorphism that has been hypothesized to be associated with psychopathy based on research from endophenotypes is the serotonin transporter gene (*SLC6A4*) (Glenn 2011). There are a number of parallels between findings from the serotonin transporter gene polymorphism and findings from psychopathy. Individuals homozygous for the long allele of the serotonin transporter polymorphism have been found to show several effects that are similar to those shown in psychopathic individuals, including reduced amygdala responding, reduced stress-induced reactivity of the hormone cortisol, and deficits in fear conditioning. The parallels between findings in individuals homozygous for the long allele and psychopathic individuals are listed in Table 1.3. The number of similarities between these studies suggests that the long allele of the serotonin transporter may confer risk for psychopathic traits.

A summary of the findings from studies of candidate genes associated with psychopathy is provided in Table 1.4. Although a few studies have explored the direct associations between psychopathic traits and variants in the serotonin transporter, results remain unclear. Herman et al. (in press) examined the relationship between the serotonin transporter genotypes and psychopathy in a sample of individuals with alcohol dependence and found that males homozygous for the long allele scored higher in psychopathy than did carriers of the short allele, as would be hypothesized; however, the opposite effect was observed in females, suggesting that gender may moderate the effects. Similarly, Sadeh et al. (2010) found that adolescents homozygous for the long allele demonstrated increased callous-unemotional and narcissistic traits, although this was observed only in individuals of low socioeconomic status (SES). In contrast, Fowler, Langley, Rice, van de Bree, et al. (2009) found higher

Table 1.3. Parallels between Findings in Psychopathic Individuals and L-Homozygotes

	Psychopathic individuals relative to controls	Study	L-homozygotes relative to s-carriers	Study
Brain level				
Amygdala responsivity to negative stimuli	Reduced	Kiehl et al. (2001) Glenn, Raine, and Schug (2009) Birbaumer et al. (2005)	Reduced	Hariri et al. (2002) Heinz et al. (2005)
Connectivity between amygdala and VMPFC	Reduced	Marsh et al. (2008) Craig et al. (2009)	Reduced	Heinz et al. (2005) Pezawas et al. (2005)
Error processing in the prefrontal cortex	Reduced error-related negativity Reduced positive ERP amplitude (Pe)	von Borries et al. (2010) Brazil et al. (2009)	Reduced error-related negativity Trend toward reduced positive ERP amplitude (Pe)	Fallgatter et al. (2004) Fallgatter et al. (2004)
Psychophysiology				
Heart rate (resting)	Reduced	Hansen et al. (2007)	Reduced	Crisan et al. (2009)
Heart rate variability	Increased	Hansen et al. (2007)	Increased	Crisan et al. (2009)
Fear potentiated startle	Reduced	Flor et al. (2002) Others reviewed in Patrick (1994)	Reduced	Brocke et al. (2006) Lonsdorf et al. (2009)
Reduced skin conductance responding during fear conditioning	Reduced	Flor et al. (2002)	Reduced	Garpenstrand et al. (2001)

Table 1.3 (continued)

	Psychopathic individuals relative to controls	Study	L-homozygotes relative to s-carriers	Study
Hormones and Neurotransmitters				
Cortisol response to the Trier Social Stress Test	Reduced	O'Leary, Loney, and Eckel (2007) O'Leary, Taylor, and Eckel (2010)	Reduced	Gotlib et al. (2008) Alexander et al. (2009) Way and Taylor (2010)
Central serotonin functioning (fenfluramine challenge)	Elevated	Dolan and Anderson (2003)	Elevated	Reist et al. (2001)
Neuropsychology				
Attention to negative stimuli in the periphery	Reduced	Glass and Newman (2009) Newman et al. (2010)	Reduced	Beevers et al. (2007) Osinsky et al. (2008) Fox, Ridgewell, and Ashwin (2009)
Passive avoidance learning	Poor	Newman and Kosson (1986) Blair et al. (2004)	Poor	Finger et al. (2007)
Risk taking (Balloon Analog Risk Task)	Increased risk taking	Hunt, Hopko, and Bare (2005)	Increased risk taking	Crisan et al. (2009)
Decisions based on reward and punishment	Poor	Blair et al. (2006)	Poor	Roiser et al. (2006)

Source: Reprinted from Glenn (2011).

total psychopathy scores in carriers of the short allele in adolescents with attention-deficit/hyperactivity disorder (ADHD).

Interestingly, many of the polymorphisms that have been studied tend to be associated with the core personality features of psychopathy (Interpersonal-Affective Factor 1) more so than with the lifestyle and antisocial features (Lifestyle-Antisocial Factor 2). Although replication of these studies is needed, this suggests that these polymorphisms may be examples of genetic factors that are unique to the core features of psychopathy rather than being genes that confer risk for antisocial behavior more generally. Another pattern worth noting is that several of the findings are limited to particular circumstances (e.g., the finding applies only to males, or only to individuals of low SES). This emphasizes the idea that many factors other than genes are involved in the steps along the pathway from genes to behavior, and therefore it is important to consider the context in which the genes may operate.

A few studies have examined multiple candidate genes within a single sample. One study that examined three polymorphisms simultaneously found that each polymorphism appeared to independently contribute to the variance in the Interpersonal-Affective Factor 1—that is, the more "risk" genotypes that the individual possessed, the higher the Interpersonal-Affective Factor 1 scores (Figure 1.1; Hoenicka et al. 2007). This is in line with the evidence from behavioral genetics studies, which suggest an additive genetic effect—the more risk genes an individual has, the greater the probability of developing psychopathic traits. At some point in the future it may be possible to test for a large number of candidate genes simultaneously to determine which genetic polymorphisms contribute independently to the variance in psychopathy, such as the polymorphisms in the Hoenicka et al. (2007) study, and which polymorphisms may interact with one another to confer risk. It may also be possible to develop intervention or treatment programs that target individuals with specific combinations of risk genotypes.

The discrepancies within and between these studies emphasize the difficulties in establishing a direct link between gene variants and complex disorders. However, candidate gene studies can be extremely valuable in helping to uncover the ways in which particular genetic polymorphisms may interact with other genes or environmental factors such as SES in conferring risk for a disorder.

Table 1.4. Key Findings from Candidate Genes Studies in Psychopathy

Polymorphism/Gene	Reference	Sample	Scale	Main finding
TaqIA & B SNP	Smith et al. (1993)	58 male inmates with substance abuse	PCL-R	No association with total psychopathy scores
	Hoenicka et al. (2007)	137 alcohol dependent males	PCL-R	A+ genotype associated with Factor 1, but not total scores
	Ponce et al. (2008)	176 alcohol dependent males; 150 controls	PCL-R	A+ genotype associated with Factor 1, but not total scores
C957T (DRD2)	Ponce et al. (2008)	176 alcohol dependent males; 150 controls	PCL-R	CC genotype associated with total, Factor 1, and Factor 2 scores
SLC6A3 (dopamine transporter gene)	Hoenicka et al. (2007)	137 alcohol dependent males	PCL-R	No association with total or factor scores
CNR1 (cannabinoid receptor gene)	Hoenicka et al. (2007)	137 alcohol dependent males	PCL-R	Associated with Factor 1, but not total scores
5-HTTLPR (serotonin transporter gene)	Fowler, Langley, Rice, van de Bree, et al. (2009)	89 adolescents previously diagnosed with ADHD	PCL-YV	Higher psychopathy scores in carriers of the short allele, driven by the affective factor
	Sadeh et al. (2010)	Youth from treatment/legal agencies and controls; male and female	APSD	Higher scores on the impulsivity dimension of psychopathy in short allele carriers; higher scores on the callous-unemotional dimension in individuals homozygous for the long allele of lower socioeconomic status

Table 1.4 (continued)

Polymorphism/Gene	Reference	Sample	Scale	Main finding
	Herman et al. (in press)	862 alcohol dependent males and females	CPI	Higher psychopathy scores in males homozygous for the long allele; higher psychopathy scores in females homozygous for the short allele
OXTR	Beitchman et al. (2012)	Psychopathy screening device	Callous-unemotional traits associated with the A allele of the OXTR_rs237885 gene	
FAAH	Hoenicka et al. (2007)	137 alcohol dependent males	PCL-R	Associated with Factor 1, but not total scores
COMT	Fowler, Langley, Rice, van de Bree, et al. (2009)	99 adolescents previously diagnosed with ADHD	PCL-YV	Val/Val genotype associated with higher Factor 1 scores
MAO-A	Fowler, Langley, Rice, van de Bree, et al. (2009)	88 adolescent males previously diagnosed with ADHD	PCL-YV	Low activity allele associated with higher total and affective factor scores

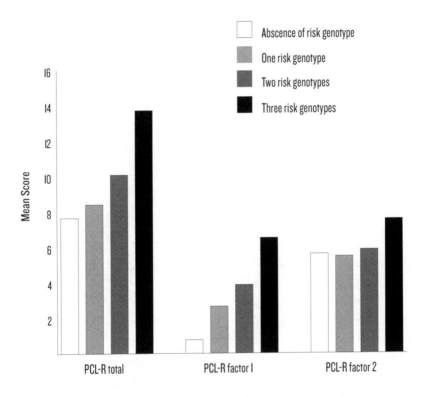

Figure 1.1. Psychopathy Interpersonal-Affective Factor 1 scores increase linearly with each additional risk genotype. Source: Reprinted from Hoenicka et al. (2007).

Genome-wide association studies.

Viding et al. (2010) undertook the first GWA study of psychopathic traits in a sample of children scoring high on both callous-unemotional traits and antisocial behavior. This study did not find any genetic associations that reached genome-wide statistical significance (i.e., accounting for more than 1 percent of the variance). However, they identified 273 polymorphisms that showed marginally significant associations and focused on the top 30 of these. One polymorphism in this group that has biological plausibility is the ROBO2 polymorphism, which is a gene involved in neural development. Several previous studies have shown

differences in brain structure and function in children with psychopathic traits (De Brito et al. 2009, Jones et al. 2009, Marsh et al. 2008),
suggesting that genetic factors may underlie the neurodevelopmental
abnormalities observed in psychopathy. Indeed, the study by Rijsdijsk
et al. (2010) reviewed above showed that some of the structural brain
differences in children with psychopathic traits were driven by the same
genetic factors that increase risk for psychopathic traits. The ROBO2
polymorphism may be one such example of a gene that confers risk for
psychopathic traits via its effects on the structural development of the
brain.

Molecular Genetics: Conclusions and Future Directions

The molecular genetics studies reviewed in this chapter provide initial evidence for links between psychopathic traits and specific genes.
Future studies replicating these findings in larger samples, as well as
testing new genetic polymorphisms, will be beneficial in furthering
our understanding of the biological pathways that lead to psychopathy.
GWA studies have the potential to identify important leads regarding
which genes may be associated with psychopathic traits. These leads
can then be followed up in candidate gene studies. When considering
the real-world applications of identifying gene candidates, it is important to remember that the impact of any particular gene variant is prob-
abilistic, as its effects are influenced by other gene variants and by environmental factors. Thus, it will be important to also examine the role
of these genes within a larger context to identify the factors that may
moderate gene expression.

To date, most candidate gene studies have examined psychopathic
traits within populations of individuals with substance use disorders
or ADHD. Although these samples are good sources for high rates of
psychopathic traits, it is possible that co-occurring disorders may mask
some of the unique biological contributors to each disorder (Gunter,
Vaughn, and Philibert 2010). Therefore, it will also be important to
examine relationships between psychopathy and candidate genes in
unselected samples.

Another important challenge for molecular genetics research on
psychopathy will be to identify not just which genes are associated with

psychopathic traits, but also which among these genes code for the brain impairments found in psychopathic individuals. While these initial molecular genetics findings require replication, it appears that several of the genes identified have also been associated with structural or functional brain impairments, suggesting that they may predispose for psychopathic traits via their influence on the brain.

Interpretations of Genetic Research

Research on the genetics of criminal behavior has been the source of much controversy. Thus, it is important to clarify what conclusions can and cannot be drawn from this work.

1. There is no "crime gene."

By no means is there a single gene, or even a small group of genes, that will enable us to predict which individuals will commit crime in the future. Genes confer risk for traits such as those observed in psychopathy, which may heighten the risk for criminal behavior, but we will never be able to use genes to predict which individuals will become psychopathic or persistent criminals. In reality, hundreds and maybe thousands of genes are involved, each of which makes a small contribution by coding for proteins and enzymes that in turn affect brain functioning, psychological processes, and ultimately behavior. Criminal behavior and the traits associated with it are like the countless other human traits and behaviors that are influenced by genes. The general consensus is that "many genes of small effect" underlie the majority of these complex behaviors and traits (Plomin, Haworth, and Davis 2009).

To further emphasize this point, consider the fact that many genetic polymorphisms that are examined in candidate gene studies are very common in the population. For example, in the U.S. population, approximately 25 to 35 percent of individuals carry two long alleles of the serotonin transporter gene, which we discussed as potentially conferring risk for psychopathy. Clearly such a large percentage of the population is not considered highly psychopathic. This gene likely contributes to only a very small fraction of the variance in psychopathic traits. The overwhelming majority of individuals who have this genotype will not be psychopathic, and a significant portion of individuals who are

considered psychopathic will likely not have this genotype. In addition
to the small effect that the gene may have, whether the gene confers *any*
risk within a given individual may be dependent on environmental factors, as well as the presence of other genes with which it may interact.

2. Environmental factors play a substantial role.
As reviewed in this chapter, behavioral genetic studies suggest that
genetic and environmental factors contribute approximately equally to
the development of psychopathic traits. However, these factors may be
much less distinct than we may realize. Research has begun to explore
the ways in which the environment is able to influence the way that
genes are expressed, or turned on and off. For example, evidence has
shown that separating rat pups from the mother in the first three weeks
of life results in increased expression of a gene associated with stress
hormones in the hippocampus and prefrontal cortex of the brain, two
regions that are critically involved in regulation of the stress response.
In addition, the rats who were separated from their mother also demonstrated fearlessness and a reduced stress response in adulthood
(Weaver, Meaney, and Szyf 2006). This suggests that environmental factors early in life, such as maternal behavior, can directly change gene
expression and thus alter the way in which the brain develops. These
structural modifications to DNA may have profound influences on
neuronal functioning and, hence, the development of traits such as
those observed in psychopathy. In sum, many genes may be controlled
by the environment, functioning differently depending on environmental conditions. The interaction of genes and environmental factors is
discussed in depth in Chapter 6.

3. Genes are not destiny.
The influence of the environment on gene expression leads to the exciting idea that, although approximately half of the variance in psychopathic traits is thought to be genetic in origin, genes are not fixed, static,
and immutable. Individuals with genetic risk factors are not destined
to develop along a fixed track. Environmental conditions may have the
ability to diminish or exacerbate the negative effects that risk genes may
have. By attempting to prevent adverse environmental conditions that
alter gene expression, we may be able to block some of the negative

effects that are associated with risk genes. Similarly, environmental enrichment may help to diminish negative effects and thus alter the course of individuals with genetic risk factors.

In the future, genetic information may help us to identify which individuals are at somewhat greater risk for traits associated with criminal behavior, and may help us to provide environmental enrichment or implement preventative measures in order to reduce the likelihood that psychopathic traits develop. If we can learn more about how genes interact with the environment, we can begin to design treatment and prevention programs that are tailored to individuals with specific risk factors.

Conclusions

Despite the relative recency of research on the genetics of psychopathy, there are emerging clues regarding the possible genetic underpinnings of psychopathic traits. Behavioral genetics studies are beginning to uncover how genetic factors contribute to the various aspects of psychopathy, as well as how it is genetically related to antisocial behavior. Molecular genetics studies are beginning to identify specific genes that may be involved, providing a basis for future intervention and treatment programs that may be genetically informed.

2

Hormones

Throughout our evolutionary history, hormones have been important in facilitating key functions that are necessary for survival. They help to mobilize our bodies when we are confronted with threats in the environment and to seek out rewards such as food and sexual partners. They also help us to navigate social hierarchies, influencing whether we respond in a particular situation in a dominant or submissive way. They influence how we respond to cues that another individual is angry or in distress. Hormones also influence our ability to learn from punishment and reward and our willingness to take risks. Hormone systems are also known to become dysregulated. For example, in posttraumatic stress disorder, the body develops an overgeneralized and exaggerated response to threat, resulting in excessive fear and anxiety. In this chapter, we discuss the ways in which dysregulated hormones may contribute to the symptoms observed in psychopathy.

Hormones are chemical messengers that travel through the bloodstream and bind to receptors in the brain and body. When hormones bind to receptors in the brain, they can affect the functioning of brain regions. Hormones can be thought of as an intermediate step between genetic or environmental factors and brain functioning. Genes code for these molecules, as well as the proteins that transport, receive, and metabolize them. In addition, hormone systems are highly sensitive to environmental and psychological factors such as stress. Thus, hormones represent one mechanism by which genetic and environmental factors have an effect on the brain.

In psychological research, hormones may be assessed as an endophenotype, or biological marker for a particular disorder. By measuring hormones, we can gain an index of how a hormone system of interest is functioning and also make inferences about how particular brain regions may be functioning, because signals from the brain are required to trigger the release of hormones. In essence altered hormone levels may reflect altered brain functioning. In addition, because hormones, in turn, have an *effect* on the brain, they also may be considered a potential target for treatment. By altering hormone levels either through biological (e.g., psychopharmacological, nutritional) manipulations or by changing the environment in a way that affects hormone levels (e.g., through behavioral therapy), we may be able to produce changes in how the brain functions.

Hormones are typically measured through either saliva or blood samples. Most hormones can be measured from saliva reliably and in a manner that is less stressful than collecting blood samples, as the process is noninvasive. Hormones can be measured either at rest or in response to some type of stressor or event to gain information about the reactivity of the system.

The two primary hormones that have been associated with psychopathy are cortisol and testosterone. Cortisol and testosterone have been associated with several features that are observed in psychopathy, including blunted stress reactivity, fearlessness, aggression, and stimulation seeking. In this chapter, the research on hormones in psychopathy is discussed, including how hormones such as cortisol and testosterone might affect the development and maintenance of psychopathic features and how hormones contribute to current neurobiological theories of psychopathy. Finally, the implications of future hormone research in psychopathy for intervention and treatment are discussed.

Importance of Hormone Research in Psychopathy

There are several reasons why studying the role of hormones in psychopathy is important. First, understanding the functioning of hormone systems in individuals with psychopathy helps us to gain a more complete picture of the biology of the disorder, which may provide clues regarding how psychopathy develops. Brain imaging studies have found reduced structural and functional differences in regions such as the amygdala and orbitofrontal cortex in psychopathic individuals. Impaired functioning in these brain regions is thought to underlie a wide range of findings in psychopathy, including deficits in stress reactivity, sensitivity to punishment, autonomic functioning, fear conditioning, and decision making (Blair 2007). To date, the underlying causes of the impairments in brain structure and functioning in psychopathy remain unknown (Kiehl 2006). Abnormalities in hormone systems may contribute to these disruptions in brain structure and functioning.

If hormones do contribute, we may be able to gain more information about how the deficits develop. For example, if psychopathy is found to be associated with abnormalities in hormones associated with the stress response system, then factors that are known to cause disruptions in this system could be identified as potential causes of the development of the disorder. Environmental factors such as chronic stress or prenatal substance use have a strong influence on hormone systems and are therefore potential sources of disruptions. Maternal smoking, for example, has been found to disrupt prenatal testosterone levels (Rizwan, Manning, and Brabin 2007). Insights into the environmental factors that may contribute to psychopathy can aid in the development of prevention measures.

Understanding how hormones may be disrupted in psychopathic individuals may also help us to identify some of the genes that may confer risk for the disorder. For example, genetic polymorphisms associated with reduced cortisol reactivity in stressful situations may be worth examining in molecular genetics studies of psychopathy.

Finally, because hormones are relatively easy to measure relative to brain imaging, hormones may be useful as an assessment tool for measuring an individual's biological functioning so that treatments could be designed that are tailored specifically to the individual. For example, individuals with high testosterone levels may respond best to reward- rather than punishment-based forms of learning. By assessing hormone levels, we may be able to group individuals into treatment programs that are most likely to be effective. Such biological assessments could also be used to identify individuals who may be at risk for psychopathy so that attempts at early intervention such as environmental enrichment could be implemented. Overall, understanding the functioning of hormone systems in psychopathy is important for several lines of future research.

Hormone Systems

Cortisol and testosterone are hormones that are released by two different systems. These systems in particular are theoretically relevant to psychopathy because they are involved in several functions that are impaired in psychopathy. Cortisol is the hormone that is released by the hypothalamic-pituitary-adrenal (HPA) axis, which is part of the body's system for responding to stress. It is involved in potentiating the state of fear, generating sensitivity to punishment, and promoting withdrawal behavior (Schulkin, Gold, and McEwen 1998); psychopathic individuals have deficits in these areas. They are described as having a fearless temperament, as less responsive to situations that most would find stressful, and as less sensitive to punishment. This leads to the hypothesis that the HPA axis may be underactive. Testosterone is released by the hypothalamic-pituitary-gonadal (HPG) axis. Testosterone is hypothesized to be associated with psychopathy because its levels are much higher in males than in females and may correspond to the increased prevalence of psychopathic personality and antisocial behavior in males compared to females. It has also been associated with several features that are observed in psychopathy including reward seeking (Daitzman and Zuckerman 1980), dominance (Archer 2006), and aggression (Dabbs, Jurkovic, and Frady 1991). Research has found that there is a large degree of interaction between the HPG and HPA axes.

Cortisol: Product of the HPA Axis

As part of the HPA axis, cortisol is a hormone that is released in response to a stressor. When a stressor occurs signals from the limbic

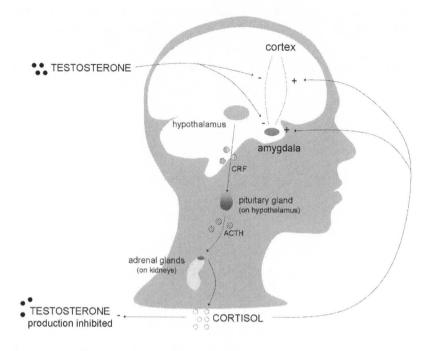

Figure 2.1. Hormone effects in the brain. In the event of a stressor, signals from limbic (e.g., amygdala) and cortical regions trigger the HPA axis, resulting in the production of cortisol. Cortisol circulates in the body, where it inhibits the production of testosterone, and the brain, where it increases the excitability of the amygdala and strengthens the connections between limbic regions such as the amygdala, and regions of the cortex. Testosterone has the opposite effect in the brain, inhibiting amygdala activity and weakening the connections between limbic and cortical regions.

and cortical brain regions, which receive the information about the stressor, trigger a brain region called the hypothalamus to release corticotrophin releasing factor (CRF) into the blood. CRF stimulates the secretion of adrenocorticotrophic hormone (ACTH) from the anterior pituitary gland. ACTH then triggers the adrenal gland to release cortisol (Figure 2.1). Unlike adrenaline, which is released very quickly in response to stress, this process takes some time and represents a slower-acting stress response; cortisol typically peaks in saliva about 20 minutes after a stressor occurs.

The role of cortisol is to mobilize the body's resources and to provide energy in times of stress (Kudielka and Kirschbaum 2005). Cortisol in the blood travels to the brain, where it binds to receptors on neurons in brain regions such as the amygdala, hippocampus, and prefrontal cortex. The amygdala is a small brain region in the limbic system that is associated with the processes of inducing fearfulness, responding to punishment and reward, and generating the fight-or-flight response. Levels of circulating cortisol may be an index of the functioning of structures such as the amygdala that are involved in generating the responses to fear and stress. In addition, if cortisol is reduced, it may affect the functioning of the amygdala during stress (Rosen and Schulkin 1998). Psychopathy has been associated with reduced stress responsivity (Patrick 1994), fearlessness (Benning, Patrick, and Iacono 2005a), and reduced amygdala functioning (Birbaumer et al. 2005). Therefore it has been hypothesized that cortisol levels may be reduced in psychopathic individuals.

Low resting cortisol levels have been associated with impaired fear reactivity in young children (Kagan, Reznick, and Snidman 1988), increased sensation seeking in men (Rosenblitt et al. 2002), and increased monetary risk taking (van Honk et al. 2003). In the latter study, van Honk and colleagues suggested that low cortisol levels may decrease punishment sensitivity and increase reward dependency.

A few recent studies have found relationships between cortisol and psychopathy. Holi et al. (2006) measured blood serum cortisol levels in young adult male psychopathic offenders with a history of violence and found a negative correlation with psychopathy scores. Cima, Smeets, and Jelicic (2008) found that psychopathic offenders showed lower cortisol levels than did nonpsychopathic offenders. One study also observed low salivary cortisol levels in adolescents with callous-unemotional traits (Loney et al. 2006). However, others have failed to replicate this finding (van Honk et al. 2003; Glenn, Raine, Schug, et al. 2011).

O'Leary, Loney, and Eckel (2007) measured cortisol reactivity, or changes in cortisol in response to an environmental stressor. The stressor involved a public speaking task, performed in front of two to three confederates and a video camera, followed by five minutes of mental arithmetic (e.g., counting backward from 2,083 in increments of 13).

Results showed that undergraduate males scoring higher on a self-report psychopathy measure lacked cortisol responsivity to a social stress test when compared to low-scoring males; no differences were observed in prestressor levels of cortisol. This finding was replicated in another sample of males, and also in females when controlling for phase of the menstrual cycle (O'Leary, Taylor, and Eckel 2010). In another study, no association was observed between cortisol reactivity to a stressor and psychopathy in an adult sample recruited from temporary employment agencies (Glenn, Raine, Schug, et al. 2011); however, interactions with testosterone were observed, which will be discussed below.

Studies examining cortisol reactivity may be especially important in understanding the patterns of stress responsivity in psychopathic individuals. Together, studies of cortisol in psychopathy provide some initial evidence for an association, but results are not consistent, and more studies with larger sample sizes are needed to clarify the relationship. Furthermore, it is unclear whether low cortisol levels are a factor that *leads* to the development of psychopathy or simply an *indicator* of reduced functioning in certain brain regions.

Testosterone: Product of the HPG Axis

As part of the HPG axis, testosterone is a sex hormone that is primarily released by the testes in males and the ovaries in females. Males have several times the amount of testosterone as females. Because there are large sex differences in antisocial behavior, with the male-to-female ratio being about 4:1 for antisocial personality disorder and as large as 10:1 for violent crimes (van Honk and Schutter 2007), it has been hypothesized that testosterone is a potential contributing factor to aggressive behavior.

Studies of testosterone have produced observations that are strikingly similar to those found in psychopathy (Table 2.1). Many studies have found that individuals with high testosterone levels have characteristics that have been observed in psychopathy. For example, individuals with elevated testosterone levels have been described as impulsive (Bjork et al. 2001), sensation seeking (Daitzman and Zuckerman 1980), and more forward than individuals with low testosterone (Dabbs et al. 2001). They have more sexual partners (Daitzman and Zuckerman 1980), have more

Table 2.1. *Parallels between Testosterone and Psychopathy Findings*

High testosterone levels associated with:	Reference	Psychopathy associated with:	Reference
Impulsivity	Baucom, Besch, and Callahan (1985), Bjork et al. (2001)	Impulsivity	Hare (2003, PCL-R item)
Sensation seeking	Daitzman and Zuckerman (1980)	Stimulation seeking	Blackburn (1979)
Sociability	Daitzman and Zuckerman (1980)	Sociability	Benning, Patrick, Blonigen, et al. (2005)
Disinhibition	Daitzman and Zuckerman (1980)	Poor behavioral controls	Hare (2003, PCL-R item)
Showing off	Udry and Talbert (1988)	Grandiose sense of self-worth	Hare (2003, PCL-R item)
Forwardness	Dabbs et al. (2001)	Promiscuous sexual behavior; increased number of sexual partners	Hare (2003), Lalumiere and Quinsey (1996)
More criminal violence	Dabbs, Jurkovic, and Frady (1991)	More criminal violence	Hare (1991)
Not marrying; marital instability; poor marital quality	Booth and Dabbs (1993)	Many short-term marital relationships	Hare (2003, PCL-R item)
Law breaking	Mazur and Booth (1998)	Law breaking	Hare (2003)
Reckless driving	Aromaki, Lindman, and Eriksson (1999)	Poor behavioral controls, risk-taking behavior	Hare (2003, PCL-R item)
Failure to plan ahead	Aromaki, Lindman, and Eriksson (1999)	Impulsivity/failure to plan ahead	Hare (2003, PCL-R item)
Judged more harshly by parole board; violate prison rules more often	Maras et al. (2003)	Revocation of conditional release	Hare (2003, PCL-R item)
Juvenile delinquency	Maras et al. (2003)	Juvenile delinquency	Hare (2003, PCL-R item)

Table 2.1 (continued)

Injections of testosterone associated with:	Reference	Psychopathy associated with:	Reference
Reduced emotional response to fearful faces	van Honk, Peper, and Schutter (2005)	Reduced brain activity to fearful faces	Deeley et al. (2006)
Reduced empathetic behavior (facial mimicry)	Hermans, Putman, and van Honk (2006)	Callous/lack of empathy	Hare (2003, PCL-R item)
Reduced fear-potentiated startle	Hermans, Putman, Bass, et al. (2006)	Deficient fear-potentiated startle	Benning, Patrick, Blonigen, et al. (2005), Justus and Finn (2007), Vaidyanathan et al. (2011)
Reduced skin conductance responding to affective stimuli	Hermans et al. (2007)	Reduced skin conductance responding to affective stimuli	Hare (1978), Lorber (2004)
Poor decision making on the Iowa Gambling Task	van Honk et al. (2004)	Poor performance on the Iowa Gambling Task	Mitchell et al. (2002), Mahmut, Homewood, and Stevenson (2008)

marital instability (Booth and Dabbs 1993), and are more likely to engage in violent crime (Dabbs, Jurkovic, and Frady 1991).

Other parallels come from studies that have examined behavioral changes following injections of testosterone. For example, injections of testosterone have been shown to reduce fear-potentiated startle (Hermans, Putman, Baas, et al. 2006), reduce skin conductance responding to affective stimuli (Hermans et al. 2007), and impair performance on the Iowa Gambling Task (van Honk et al. 2004), which likely occurs due to reduced sensitivity to punishment and increased sensitivity to reward. Psychopaths demonstrate reduced fear-potentiated startle (Patrick 1994) and reduced skin conductance responses (Hare 1978) and exhibit poor performance on the Iowa Gambling Task (Mitchell et al. 2002). The parallels between these studies lead to the hypothesis that psychopathy is associated with high testosterone levels.

Despite the strong theoretical evidence that psychopathy may be associated with high levels of testosterone, only a few studies have tested the hypothesis and results are inconsistent. One study found testosterone levels to be associated with scores on the Lifestyle-Antisocial Factor 2 of the PCL-R in forensic psychiatric patients, although results may be confounded by comorbid substance abuse and other psychiatric disorders (Stalenheim et al. 1998). A more recent study in a large sample of individuals recruited from temporary employment agencies found no relationship between psychopathy (or its factors) and testosterone (Glenn, Raine, Schug, et al. 2011). Similarly, another study found that testosterone levels were not different in boys with callous-unemotional traits compared to healthy controls (Loney et al. 2006).

In other antisocial and aggressive groups, higher testosterone levels have been observed in girls with conduct disorder (Pajer et al. 2006), adolescent boys with externalizing behaviors (Maras et al. 2003), young criminals (Kreuz and Rose 1972; Dabbs, Frady, and Carr 1987; Dabbs, Jurkovic, and Frady 1991), and criminal women (Banks and Dabbs 1996). Furthermore, testosterone has been associated with a variety of antisocial behaviors including difficulties on the job, nonobservance of the law, marriage failures, drug use, alcohol abuse, and violent behaviors (Mazur and Booth 1998). Although a direct link between testosterone and psychopathic traits has not been established, some evidence suggests that testosterone may interact with other hormones to predispose to psychopathy.

Combined Effects

Some researchers have suggested that the emotional and behavioral deficits observed in psychopaths may result from an imbalance in *both* cortisol and testosterone (van Honk and Schutter 2006), specifically through a ratio involving increased testosterone and decreased cortisol (Terburg, Morgan, and Van Honk 2009). This model highlights the fact that the HPA and HPG axes interact (i.e., they mutually inhibit one another) and that the relative activity of the two axes can significantly influence brain regions and pathways that have been implicated in psychopathy. One brain region that is affected by this imbalance is the amygdala, which, as noted above, has been widely implicated in psychopathy (Blair 2006b, 2007). The amygdala is a major binding site for both cortisol and testosterone (Figure 2.1), and thus the ratio of the two hormones can alter amygdala responsivity to fearful or threatening stimuli (Schulkin 2003). As described above, cortisol is involved in potentiating the state of fear and increasing sensitivity to punishment, whereas testosterone is associated with reward sensitivity, fear reduction, and increased approach behavior. Therefore, an imbalance involving decreased cortisol (low fear) and increased testosterone levels (high approach/reward seeking behavior) can change the responsivity of the amygdala to reduce sensitivity to punishment cues or fearful stimuli, and increase sensitivity to reward. This imbalance may contribute to the fearlessness, insensitivity to punishment, impairment in fear conditioning, and reward-seeking behavior observed in psychopaths. Thus, decreased cortisol and increased testosterone may be an underlying cause for the reduced amygdala functioning and related behavioral deficits observed in psychopathy.

In addition to effects on the amygdala, the hormonal imbalance involving decreased cortisol and increased testosterone may also disrupt the connectivity between subcortical (e.g., limbic) regions such as the amygdala and cortical structures. Studies have used electroencephalography (EEG) to demonstrate relative increases or decreases in subcortico-cortical "cross-talk." Injections of testosterone have been shown to reduce the communication between these regions (Schutter and van Honk 2004), whereas cortisol has been shown to strengthen it (Schutter and van Honk 2005; van Wingen et al. 2010; van Peer, Roelofs, and

Spinhoven 2008). Neuroimaging data in psychopathic adults and youth suggest that connectivity between the amygdala and prefrontal regions is indeed compromised (Craig et al. 2009; Marsh et al. 2008). The decoupling between subcortical and cortical regions that may result from increased testosterone relative to cortisol may have effects in two ways. First, during decision making, emotion-related information from the amygdala that signals cues of threat, risk, or harm to others may not be able to reach cortical areas in order to inform the decision. This may result in the callousness, lack of empathy, risk taking, and goal-directed aggression observed in psychopathy. Second, cortical regions may be less able to send inhibitory signals to subcortical regions, resulting in deficits in emotion regulation and inhibition (van Honk and Schutter 2006), which contribute to reactive aggression and emotional instability observed in psychopathy. Thus, through these processes, a high ratio between testosterone and cortisol reactivity may contribute to a variety of psychopathic traits, including both instrumental and reactive forms of aggression.

One study tested the hypothesis that the ratio of testosterone to cortisol is associated with psychopathy. In a large sample of individuals recruited from temporary employment agencies, Glenn, Raine, Schug, et al. (2011) found that psychopathy was associated with the ratio of baseline testosterone to cortisol reactivity to a stressor; this accounted for 5 percent of the variance in psychopathic traits. No significant relationships were observed between psychopathy and individual hormone measures, which included baseline testosterone and cortisol, and cortisol reactivity to a stressor; it appeared that only when both hormones were taken into consideration did a significant relationship emerge. These findings highlight the importance of examining multiple hormone systems in order to gain a complete understanding of how systems may interact to predispose to psychopathy.

Other Hormones

Two other hormones are also potentially important in the study of psychopathy. Dehydroepiandrosterone (DHEA) is a precursor to testosterone; it is an androgen that originates from both the adrenal glands and the gonads. From around age 6, children exhibit an increase in DHEA in a period called the *adrenarche* (Parker 1999). Some evidence suggests that DHEA, rather than testosterone, may be more important in studies of prepubertal youth, and that the testosterone-aggression relationship may not emerge until during or after puberty. Although the precise mechanisms by which DHEA is related to aggression are unknown, it has been hypothesized that because DHEA is eventually converted to testosterone, it may add to a larger pool of endogenous testosterone (Brown et al. 2007).

No studies to date have examined DHEA in youth with callous-unemotional traits. However, two studies have found increased DHEA levels in children and adolescents with conduct disorder (Dmitrieva et al. 2001; van Goozen et al. 1998), while one study of aggressive children found no relationship (Constantino et al. 1993). One study (Buydens-Branchey and Branchey 2004) of adults with cocaine addiction found that DHEA levels were increased in adult males with a retrospective diagnosis of conduct disorder in childhood. This suggests that mechanisms underlying adrenal androgen alterations in childhood could still be at play in adulthood. No studies have examined DHEA in adults with psychopathic traits, however.

Another chemical that may be important in psychopathy is alpha-amylase, which actually is not a hormone but a salivary enzyme that can be assessed in a similar manner to hormones. Alpha-amylase release is thought to reflect the functioning of the sympathetic nervous system (SNS) of the brain; more specifically, it is an indicator of the release of the neurotransmitter norepinephrine (NE) into the blood (Chrousous and Gold 1992). Along with the HPA axis, the SNS is part of the body's stress response system. Technological advances have allowed researchers to begin to implement alpha-amylase measures in biobehavioral studies, allowing for the simultaneous assessment of the HPA axis (cortisol) and SNS (alpha-amylase) functioning via noninvasive saliva samples. The novel advantage of measuring alpha-amylase is that it allows for a parallel investigation of two stress response systems (endocrine and neurotransmitter) through saliva samples.

However, a recent review suggests that alpha-amylase may not be a very reliable indicator of SNS functioning. Bosch et al. (2011) argue that although initial evidence seemed compelling, there is currently no strong evidence for the use of salivary alpha-amylase as a reliable indicator of SNS functioning; it may respond to a large number of contributing factors, including activity in the parasympathetic nervous system. Future studies will be necessary to determine the accuracy in using alpha-amylase as a proxy for SNS functioning.

Conclusion and Future Directions

In sum, hormones reflect an intermediate step in the biological pathway; hormone systems can be influenced by genes and by environmental factors, and in turn influence the functioning of the brain. The involvement of hormones in the development and maintenance of psychopathy is significant because it may help to explain numerous findings in the field. Decreased cortisol levels and increased testosterone levels may help to explain poor decision making, blunted stress reactivity, fearlessness, poor conditioning, and increased instrumental aggression, all of which have been observed in psychopathy. In addition, examining the role of hormones may also lead to a deeper understanding of neurobiological findings in psychopathy. Brain imaging studies have highlighted several key brain regions that appear to be hypofunctioning in psychopathy, but have thus far not been able to explain the source of this hypofunctioning. The consistent findings of reduced amygdala and orbitofrontal cortex activity may be a result of an imbalance in cortisol and testosterone levels.

Future studies are needed to clarify the role of hormones in psychopathy. It is not clear whether hormones may be altered by environmental factors at some point, or if altered levels exist early in life. Longitudinal studies involving periodic hormone assessments beginning at a very early age and following through to adulthood may help to determine how hormones may contribute to the development of psychopathy. One hypothesis is that there may be some type of "burnout" effect, where chronic stress or other environmental factors overwork the stress response system to the point that it no longer responds properly.

Most important, hormone studies may have significant implications for treatment. If future research begins to clarify the role of hormones in psychopathy, it may be possible to use hormone therapies to increase the functioning of key brain regions such as the amygdala that have been found to be impaired in psychopathy. If studies were to establish a definitive relationship between cortisol levels and psychopathy, additional studies could seek to determine which factors might be able to change cortisol levels, how much cortisol levels can be changed, and whether changing cortisol levels can change the functioning of brain regions such as the amygdala. The same could be true for testosterone levels. With respect to the interaction between the two hormones, pharmacological therapies could restore the homeostatic balance between cortisol and testosterone. This could be a key neurobiological first step in sensitizing a psychopath's emotional system so that previously failed attempts at behavioral therapies may begin to have efficacy. In addition, identifying the factors that lead to altered hormone levels will also be important in informing prevention efforts. Future research to explore the potential of hormones as a biomarker for psychopathy is an important step in furthering our ability to identify, prevent, and treat the disorder.

3

Psychophysiology

Psychophysiological research has significantly contributed to our empirical understanding of the biological factors associated with psychopathy. In 1957, David Lykken published seminal work involving psychophysiological processes in psychopaths—work that largely marks the beginnings of the modern neurobiological investigation of antisocial behavior in general (Lykken 1957). Lykken's studies sought to empirically test Cleckley's assertion that the main clinical characteristic of psychopaths was a lack of normal emotional responses. He tested this by examining small changes in sweat generated on an individual's hand in response to different stimuli. Lykken hypothesized that the emotional deficit of psychopaths was specific to emotions such as fear or anxiety. Indeed, he found that psychopathic individuals were not as physiologically responsive when anticipating aversive events such as an electric shock or loud noise. In other words, they did not seem to be fearful or anxious about the idea of an impending aversive experience. He developed the hypothesis that low fearfulness is one of the primary deficits in psychopathy.

By recording physiological activity through the skin and scalp, psychophysiological measures provide estimates of brain functioning, which is a more proximal cause of behavior. The purpose of this chapter is to review the body of psychophysiological research that has been conducted in psychopathy and to discuss how this research has improved our understanding of the neurobiological correlates. Psychophysiological research involves the study of two overarching systems: the autonomic nervous system, which controls mostly visceral functions and is measured by skin conductance and heart rate, and the central nervous system, which consists of the brain and spinal cord and is measured by electroencephalogram (EEG). One primary strength of psychophysiological research is its excellent temporal resolution; detectable electrical changes can be recorded just milliseconds after an event, meaning that an individual's reactivity to specific and transient events can be measured. After a brief introduction to the measurement techniques used in psychophysiological research, we review the key findings in research on psychopathy. We also refer the interested reader to a review by Patrick (2008) for a summary of research findings on the psychophysiological correlates of antisocial and aggressive behavior.

Autonomic Nervous System

The autonomic nervous system (ANS) serves as a link between the central nervous system (i.e., brain and spinal cord) and internal organs (e.g., heart, lungs, salivary glands, sweat glands). There are two components of the ANS—the sympathetic nervous system and the parasympathetic nervous system. The sympathetic nervous system is critically involved in mobilizing the body for action when threatened, stressed, or emotionally aroused. The parasympathetic nervous system facilitates activities that occur when the body is at rest, such as digestion. The most frequently used measures of the ANS include skin conductance (SC) and heart rate.

Heart Rate

Heart rate reflects both sympathetic and parasympathetic nervous system activity, making it a somewhat complex measure to interpret. Heart rate can be measured both at rest (number of beats per minute) and in response to a stimulus (heart rate reactivity). There are two basic measures of phasic heart rate activity. In response to the onset of a stimulus, the heart normally slows down for a brief period. This slowing is followed by a speeding of heart rate, termed an acceleratory response. Such responses are particularly common to aversive stimuli. Heart rate acceleration is thought to be a marker of affective arousal.

In a meta-analysis of 17 studies, Lorber (2004) found no evidence of a relationship between psychopathy and resting heart rate or heart rate reactivity in adults, although lower resting heart rate was related to aggression more generally. However, in a later study of psychopathy, Serafim et al. (2009) found that, unlike controls and nonpsychopathic murderers, psychopathic murderers failed to show an increase in heart rate when viewing unpleasant, pleasant, or neutral pictures. Furthermore, interpersonal and affective features (Interpersonal-Affective Factor 1) of psychopathy were correlated with lower variation in heart rate over the course of picture viewing. Similarly, in another study, youth with callous-unemotional traits were found to display lower magnitude of heart rate change than conduct disordered youth without callous-unemotional traits and controls while watching an emotionally evocative film (Anastassiou-Hadjicharalambous and Warden 2008). Thus, more recent evidence suggests that individuals with psychopathic traits may have lower heart rate reactivity in response to affective stimuli. This may reflect reduced emotional responsiveness to these stimuli.

Skin Conductance

Skin conductance, or electrodermal activity, is a relatively simple but powerful measure of ANS processing. It reflects very small changes in the electrical activity of the skin, with increased sweating leading to an increase in skin conductance. Skin conductance is controlled exclusively by the sympathetic nervous system and can reflect baseline levels of arousal (skin conductance levels) and also how well the system responds (skin conductance responses). Because the sympathetic nervous system is sensitive to stress and emotional arousal, skin conductance reactivity can be used to assess stress reactivity to aversive or arousing events.

Skin conductance is recorded by attaching electrodes onto the palmer surface of the hands (usually the nondominant hand) or fingers (distal phalanges of the index and middle fingers), where the concentration of sweat glands is highest. Electrode jelly is used as the conductive medium between the electrodes and the skin, and adhesive collars are used to control the area of contact between the electrode and the skin. Variables such as age, sex, race, and stage of menstrual cycle, as well as environmental factors including temperature, humidity, time of day, day of week, and season, are found to affect skin conductance (Boucsein 1992) and therefore need to be considered as potential covariates in skin conductance data analyses. Skin conductance recordings have excellent temporal resolution.

Resting

The most basic skin conductance measure is resting levels of electrodermal activity. In a meta-analysis of studies, Lorber (2004) found that psychopathy was significantly associated with lower resting electrodermal activity across 18 studies, although the effect was small. Psychopathic adults have also been found to demonstrate fewer skin conductance fluctuations (Raine, Venables, and Williams 1996), or spontaneous changes in skin conductance, which are also thought to reflect arousal.

Orienting

Skin conductance orienting is a paradigm that is commonly used in psychophysiology studies to measure the orientation of attention toward potentially significant events. Skin conductance orienting measures the individual's response to a novel stimulus. In most people, skin conductance increases in response to the presentation of novel stimuli; this increase is called an orienting response (Dawson, Schell, and Filion 2000), or the "what is it?" response. In a typical orienting paradigm, three or more identical stimuli (usually a neutral tone, but may include speech-like sounds, baby cries, etc. [Isen et al. 2010]) are presented sequentially. A skin conductance response is expected to occur within 1 to 3 seconds after the onset of each stimulus. After repeated presentations of the neutral stimulus, individuals tend to give smaller and smaller responses until the skin conductance response ultimately extinguishes; this is called habituation, a process that can also be explored. After habituation, a new set of neutral stimuli may be presented and an orienting response occurs again. The initial responses after the stimulus changes are typically of most interest when examining the orienting response.

Individual differences in the size of an individual's response to an orienting stimulus are thought to reflect the degree to which the individual allocates attentional resources to the processing of that stimulus (Dawson, Filion, and Schell 1989, Dawson, Schell, and Filion 1990); reduced orienting responses may indicate attentional deficits that may interfere with the normal processing of stimuli in the environment. Thus, although skin conductance is a peripheral measure that more directly assesses the ANS, it can also be viewed as an indicator of central nervous system processing.

Reduced orienting responses have been linked to antisocial behavior in both youth and adults (e.g., Herpertz, Wenning, et al. 2001). Several studies have also examined the orienting response in individuals with psychopathic traits. Early studies of psychopathy found reduced responding to orienting stimuli in psychopathic individuals (Hare 1968). One study found that psychopathy-prone adolescents had larger skin conductance responses to an initial tone (Borkovec 1970). In psychopathic adults, Raine and Venables (1988b) found differences in the rise time (i.e., time to reach peak amplitude) of the initial response to verbal sounds. A prospective longitudinal study measuring skin conductance orienting at age 3 found that individuals who scored higher on a self-report psychopathy scale at age 28 demonstrated *higher* orienting responses at age 3 (Glenn et al. 2007). Finally, in 9- to 10-year-old twins, Isen et al. (2010) found lower skin conductance reactivity to orienting stimuli in boys, but not girls, scoring higher in psychopathic traits. Overall, these results suggest that psychopathy may be associated with reduced orienting responses, though this may be dependent on gender and stage of development.

Aversive Stimuli

In addition to orienting paradigms, skin conductance responses have also been examined during a number of different tasks. Psychopathic individuals have been found to demonstrate reduced skin conductance responses to facial expressions of sadness and fear (Blair 1999, Blair et al. 1997), imagined threat scenes (Patrick, Cuthbert, and Lang 1994), anticipated threat (Hare 1965, 1982, Hare, Frazelle, and Cox 1978, Ogloff and Wong 1990), and emotionally evocative sounds (Verona et al. 2004). Overall, in a meta-analysis of 28 studies, Lorber (2004) found psychopathy to be associated with reduced skin conductance activity during tasks. Age was a significant moderator, with studies of adults yielding larger effects than studies of children and adolescents. The effect for negative stimuli was also larger than the effect for nonnegative stimuli. Across 14 studies, skin conductance reactivity was also found to be significantly reduced in psychopathy (Lorber 2004). Skin conductance hyporesponsivity during anticipation of aversive stimuli has since been reported in psychopathy-prone adolescents (Fung et al. 2005), similar to that observed in adult psychopaths.

Aversive Conditioning

Aversive conditioning paradigms are also often used in skin conductance studies. Aversive conditioning involves learning that an unpleasant event, such as an electric shock, loud noise, or foul odor, is associated with a particular cue. In a typical conditioning paradigm, a neutral, nonaversive tone or image (conditioned stimulus, CS) is presented to the participant, followed a few seconds later by an unpleasant stimulus (unconditioned stimulus, UCS). When participants receive the unpleasant stimulus, they generate a skin conductance response. After a number of pairings of the conditioned and unconditioned stimuli, they also begin to generate a skin conductance response to the CS, which signals that the aversive stimulus will follow. One key measure is the size of the skin conductance response elicited by the CS after a number of CS-UCS pairings. The larger the response to the CS after repeated pairings with the UCS, the better the conditioning is. Another important measure is the differentiation between the CS+ (CS paired with UCS) and CS- (CS that is not followed by anything).

Several studies have found that psychopathic individuals have altered skin conductance responses during aversive conditioning (Hare 1978, Raine 1993, Lykken 1957). For example, Hare and Quinn (1971) showed that skin conductance responding to the CS preceding shocks was reduced in psychopaths. Flor et al. (2002) found reduced differentiation between CS+ and CS- in individuals with psychopathic traits compared to controls. Aversive conditioning is thought to be important in the development of appropriate moral behavior and in the development of conscience. Empirical studies have generally supported this hypothesis. For example, a longitudinal study conducted by our laboratory has shown that poor skin conductance conditioning at age 3 years predisposes to criminal offending at age 23 years (Gao, Raine, Venables, et al. 2010).

It has been hypothesized that impairments in aversive conditioning reflect dysfunction in the amygdala (Blair 2006b) because the amygdala is involved in the formation of conditioned associations (Cardinal et al. 2002). Patients with lesions to the amygdala have been found to have deficits in aversive conditioning (Bechara et al. 1995). One brain imaging study of psychopathy has provided support for this hypothesis, demonstrating reduced activity in the amygdala during aversive conditioning in psychopathic individuals (Birbaumer et al. 2005).

Startle Blink Reflex

Another common psychophysiological measure is to assess the modulation of the startle reflex. The startle reflex is the automatic jump reaction people show when they suddenly hear a loud noise or feel an unexpected touch. This response is enhanced by exposure to threatening or anxiety-provoking stimuli. For example, being in darkness and hearing suspenseful music during a movie enhance the startle reflex. When individuals view negative emotional stimuli, such as images that elicit fear or disgust, the subsequent startle reflex is also enhanced. This is sometimes referred to as fear-potentiated startle (FPS). In contrast, when individuals view positive emotional stimuli, the startle reflex is reduced (Lang, Bradley, and Cuthbert 1990). The startle reflex is measured by placing electrodes under the eye to record the blink response. Potentiation of the startle reflex to negative stimuli is thought to be an index of defensive reactivity, and may be considered a physiological indicator of trait fearlessness/fearfulness (Vaidyanathan, Patrick, and Bernat 2009).

Extensive evidence shows that individuals with psychopathic traits do not show enhancement of the startle reflex in response to negative

visual stimuli (Levenston et al. 2000, Pastor et al. 2003, Patrick, Bradley, and Lang 1993, Justus and Finn 2007, Benning, Patrick, and Iacono
2005a, Vanman et al. 2003, Vaidyanathan et al. 2011). Flor et al. (2002)
also found reduced startle potentiation in noncriminal psychopaths
when primed with foul odorants rather than unpleasant images, suggesting that the deficit may not be specific to stimuli that induce fearfulness, but to aversive stimuli more generally. Reduced startle blink
modulation has also been replicated in samples of females with psychopathic traits (Anderson et al. 2011, Sutton, Vitale, and Newman 2002).
In the majority of studies, reduced startle modulation was primarily
associated with Factor 1, the interpersonal and affective features of psychopathy (Vaidyanathan et al. 2011, Justus and Finn 2007), suggesting
that this neurobiological correlate may be distinctly associated with
that factor.

Like aversive conditioning, startle reflex modulation is thought to
be dependent on the functioning of the amygdala (Angrilli et al. 1996).
Evidence from animal research suggests that FPS occurs when signals
from the amygdala are projected to the nucleus reticularis pontis cau-
dalis, a region of the startle circuit that lies between the sensory input
component and the motor output component (Davis 1989). Thus,
reductions in startle reflex potentiation in individuals high on the interpersonal and affective features of psychopathy may be an indicator of
deficits in the amygdala (Blair, Mitchell, and Blair 2005, p. 116).

When examining the startle reflex, aversive conditioning, or the
response to aversive stimuli, one interesting finding is that psychopaths
do not appear to have reduced physiological responses to the *actual*
aversive stimulus such as the shock or loud noise blast (exceptions
include Hare and Quinn 1971, Lykken 1957, Fung et al. 2005). Instead,
the deficits appear to be primarily in the ability to respond to *cues that
signal* that an aversive event will occur. For example, in the startle probe
experiments, psychopathic individuals do not respond differently than
nonpsychopaths to the white noise blast when it is preceded by neutral images, suggesting that they do not have a deficient response to the
noise blast itself. Rather, when unpleasant images are presented, they
fail to use these cues to increase arousal in anticipation of an aversive
event occurring. Similarly, in aversive conditioning paradigms, psychopathic participants typically demonstrate a normal skin conductance

response to the UCS (loud noise blast, shock, or foul odor), but show reduced responding to the cues that signal that the aversive event will occur (Flor et al. 2002). In the studies we reviewed that examine responsiveness to aversive stimuli, most of them assess responsiveness not to direct physical threat, but to cues that signal a threat—cues that may have to be learned. For example, facial or vocal expressions are not stimuli that pose a direct threat to the individual; they are stimuli that may *signal* threat. It has been suggested that the basic startle response is facilitated primarily by the hypothalamus and the periaqueductal gray, two brain regions that are also involved in the basic threat system. In contrast, the augmentation of the startle response following cues is thought to be reliant on the amygdala (Davis 2000, Blair 2010a). Although data will be required to test this hypothesis, it demonstrates how findings from psychophysiological research may help us to better understand the specific nature of the neurobiological impairments in psychopathy.

In sum, studies generally suggest that psychopathic individuals demonstrate reduced cardiovascular and electrodermal responding. Reduced responding to orienting stimuli suggests deficits in the allocation of attentional resources to novel stimuli. Reduced responding to conditioned stimuli as well as reduced FPS suggest that deficits in the amygdala may impair the acquisition of associations between stimuli.

Central Nervous System
Electroencephalogram and Event-Related Potentials

Electroencephalography (EEG) is a noninvasive way of recording electrical activity in the brain through the skull and scalp. To measure EEG, electrodes are placed in specified locations on the head with reference to certain points on the scalp. Standardized placement of electrodes has been made easier by the use of EEG caps, which are spandex caps in which electrodes have been embedded. Electrical activity picked up by the electrodes is then fed through a series of amplifiers and filters and finally to a computer for offline analysis.

EEG is thought to measure activity in the cortex of the brain (the part nearest to the surface), although structures below the cortex are also involved in cortical activity. The spatial resolution of EEG recordings, or the ability to distinguish different physical regions, is not nearly as precise as brain imaging techniques such as magnetic resonance imaging (MRI), discussed in Chapter 5, but the temporal resolution, the ability to distinguish events in time, is much better—on the order of milliseconds rather than the several seconds it takes for changes in blood oxygenation to be detected by MRI. EEG is also relatively inexpensive to conduct and is portable, allowing more flexibility in research.

EEG data are divided into different bands based on the frequency components of the EEG wave pattern, ranging from slow-wave frequencies (delta [generally below 3 Hz] and theta [4–7 Hz]), to more moderate (alpha [8–12 Hz]) and high-frequency activity (beta [above 15 Hz]). Increasing frequency is associated with increased arousal: delta and theta waves are predominant during sleep, alpha waves are common during wakeful relaxation, and beta waves are indicative of increased activation and arousal (Hugdahl 2001). Numerous studies have identified altered EEG abnormalities in violent offenders. Commonly reported are slow-wave (i.e., theta and delta) abnormalities, reflecting underarousal within frontal and temporal regions (Gatzke-Kopp et al. 2001), although other regional cortical abnormalities have also been noted (Lindberg et al. 2005). Only one published study to date has examined EEG abnormalities in individuals with psychopathic traits. Blackburn (1979) found no differences in EEG wave patterns between psychopathic and nonpsychopathic offenders, but found that individuals with the interpersonal and affective features of psychopathy were more aroused than those with the impulsive and antisocial features.

Event-Related Potentials

EEG reflects thousands of simultaneously ongoing brain processes, making it difficult to decipher a response related to a single stimulus. However, if a stimulus is repeated many times, the brain activity to each trial can be averaged together so that changes in the electrical activity of the brain in response to a specific type of stimuli become visible; these averaged measurements are called event-related potentials (ERPs). ERPs are recorded using the same equipment as EEG, with the addition of computer software to average the signal of multiple ERP trials. An

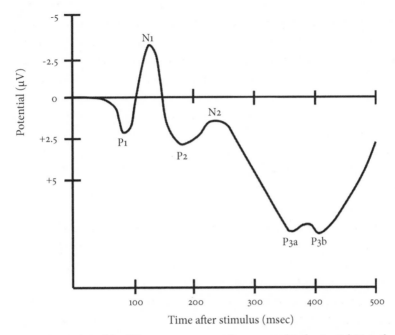

Figure 3.1. Depiction of the different components of an event-related potential. Note that positive deflections are depicted in a downward direction, whereas negative deflections are depicted in an upward direction.

example of an ERP is depicted in Figure 3.1. The ERP can be divided into several components. Most ERP components are referred to by a letter indicating whether there is a positive or negative deflection in the electrical signal, and a number indicating the approximate time after the stimulus that the deflection occurs, or the order in which it occurs. As mentioned, a deflection in brain electrical activity may be positive (P) or negative (N). Traditionally, positive deflections are depicted as downward deflections and negative deflections are depicted as upward. Three commonly studied ERP components are N1, P2, and P3. These occur at about 100, 200, and 300 milliseconds (ms) after the stimulus, respectively, and therefore are also called N100, P200, and P300.

ERPs that follow specific types of events, such as when an individual makes an error, may have components that are referred to by acronyms, such as error-related negativity (ERN), referring to a change in electrical signal measured shortly after the error has been committed. Overall, ERP components are thought to be correlates of specific psychological processes (Hugdahl 2001) such as orienting or error processing. Many researchers have examined differences in ERP components between psychopathic and nonpsychopathic individuals in order to explore how the brain may process information differently in psychopathic individuals.

P100

The P100 is thought to reflect attentional processes such as alerting, which involves achieving and maintaining an alert state and preparing to react to stimuli, and orienting, which involves allocating attention to potentially significant events. The P100 that is measured in the occipital lobe, the region of the brain that processes visual information, can be used to assess these alerting and orienting responses to visual stimuli. It provides a relatively direct and sensitive index of where attention is directed in space; the more a participant's attention is directed toward an upcoming target, the larger the amplitude of the P100. Racer et al. (2011) found that adolescents high in psychopathic traits demonstrated reduced P100 amplitude to a visual alerting cue compared to adolescents scoring lower in psychopathic traits. The reduced P100 may reflect deficits in neurobiological systems involved in attentional alerting, such as the locus coeruleus and right frontal and parietal regions (Racer et al. 2011). These regions may be important in the ability to properly redirect attention and change responding in response to cues in the environment. One of the deficits observed in psychopathy is that individuals have difficulty shifting attention from a current goal to take in peripheral information that may be important. For example, the individual may continue to engage in behaviors despite the fact that the behavior is no longer rewarding, or it elicits punishment (Newman and Kosson 1986, Newman, Patterson, and Kosson 1987).

P300

The P300 is one of the ERP components that is the most robust and that has received the most attention in cognitive research. The P3 is thought to reflect processes involved in the orienting ("what is it?") response. The oddball paradigm is a common test for measuring the P3 ERP component. In this paradigm, two stimuli (e.g., a low- and a high-pitched tone) are presented repeatedly, with the low-pitched tones presented more frequently than the high-pitched tones. The participant is asked to respond selectively to the high-pitched tones, which are less frequent. When a high-pitched tone is presented, the amplitude of the P3 tends to be enhanced. ERP components are measured at different sites in the brain. The P300 has been found to have two components—an earlier component (P3a), which is strongest at frontal sites and is thought to be elicited by detecting the novelty of the stimulus, and a later component (P3b), which is strongest at parietal sites and is thought to be associated with the process of generating a response to the stimulus.

The P3 is thought to reflect a few cognitive processes associated with orienting. When a stimulus is presented frequently (e.g., the low-pitched tone), it is maintained in working memory with minimal attention. If a change in stimulus is detected (e.g., the high-pitched tone), additional attentional resources are allocated and the memory representation is updated, eliciting the P3 (Donchin and Coles 1988). Thus, the amplitude of the P3 has been considered an index of the allocation of neural resources and cognitive processing capability. The P3 can occur between 300 and 600 ms after the stimulus. Peaks at the shorter end of this range are thought to reflect superior cognitive performance in allocating attentional resources for memory processing (Houlihan, Stelmack, and Campbell 1988).

Studies examining the P300 in psychopathic individuals have yielded inconsistent and often contradictory results. In a meta-analysis, Gao and Raine (2009) examined 11 studies assessing the P300 in psychopathic individuals. Findings were mixed, revealing no overall effect. For example, Jutai, Hare, and Connolly (1987) used an oddball task with speech stimuli but found no differences in P3 amplitude or latency, though the study did not measure activity at parietal lobe sites. Using emotional faces as visual stimuli in an oddball task, Campanella, Vanhoolandt, and Philippot (2005) found no differences in amplitude of the P300, but found that the P3a occurred earlier and the P3b occurred later in psychopathic individuals. Raine and Venables (1988a) used visual stimuli in an oddball task and found *increased* amplitude of the P300 in psychopaths. Two studies by Kiehl et al. (1999, 2000) found *reduced* P300 amplitudes in psychopaths, but one found only slight reductions using an auditory oddball task (Kiehl et al. 2006). Differences in task methodologies and sample populations may contribute to these inconsistencies.

Stronger associations have been observed between the P3 and antisocial behavior more generally. Across all studies of antisocial individuals, Gao and Raine (2009) found that P3 amplitudes were smaller and the latency was somewhat longer. Thus, reduced P3 may be associated with antisocial behavior more generally, but not the core interpersonal and affective features of psychopathy.

Indeed, a later study by Carlson, Thai, and McLarnon (2009) found that different features of psychopathy were associated with divergent patterns of P3 amplitude. Reduced P3 amplitudes were associated with Self-Centered Impulsivity (similar to Lifestyle-Antisocial features), whereas increased P3 amplitudes were associated with Fearless Dominance (similar to Interpersonal-Affective features). Similarly, Gao, Raine, and Schug (2011) examined the P3 in successful (unconvicted) and unsuccessful (convicted) psychopaths. Although it was not specified in the report, successful psychopaths may score higher on the interpersonal and affective features of psychopathy, whereas unsuccessful psychopaths may score higher on the impulsive and antisocial features. In line with the findings by Carlson, Thai, and McLarnon (2009), they found that compared to normal controls, unsuccessful psychopaths showed reduced P3 amplitudes to target stimuli. In contrast, successful psychopaths exhibited larger P3 amplitudes to irrelevant nontarget stimuli than unsuccessful psychopaths. However, it should be noted that these P3 amplitudes were not recorded at the same sites in the two studies. In addition, Anderson et al. (2011) found increased P3 amplitude in relation to *both* factors of psychopathy in undergraduate females scoring higher in psychopathic traits.

Thus, inconsistencies remain. The studies that have examined the P300 in individuals with psychopathic traits use different tasks for ERP generation, different participant populations, and different methods for assessing psychopathy, making it difficult to draw firm conclusions from these studies. Additional research will be necessary to clarify how the P300 may be altered in individuals with psychopathic traits. However, despite inconsistencies, the identification of abnormalities in the P300 in relation to psychopathic traits supports the idea that psychopathy is related to differences in the allocation of attentional resources.

Late Negativities

Psychopathy has also been associated with differences in later negative ERP components. Adults with psychopathic traits have demonstrated reduced frontal N275 amplitudes during a go/no-go task (Kiehl et al. 2000). In a go/no-go task, two types of stimuli are presented (e.g., red and green shapes). Participants are told to press a button in response to one type of stimulus (e.g., green), but refrain from pressing the button when the other stimulus type is presented. The task requires sustained attention and the ability to inhibit responses. Amplitudes of the N275 are thought to reflect the process of response inhibition. However, Munro et al. (2007b) failed to replicate this finding; they found no relationships between psychopathy and amplitude of the N2 or P3 during a go/no-go task.

Reduced N300 amplitudes have also been observed in psychopathic individuals while processing positively and negatively valenced emotional faces (Campanella, Vanhoolandt, and Philippot 2005); in this study, the N300 was thought to index a reaction to the affective features of the stimuli. These results suggest that psychopathic individuals may be less efficient in the processing of emotional faces. Studies have found that adults and children with psychopathic traits have impairments in identifying the emotions of facial expressions of others (Blair, Colledge, Murray, et al. 2001) and also have reduced autonomic responses to images depicting distress in others (Blair et al. 1997, Blair 1999).

Error-Related Negativity

ERP studies have also examined how psychopathic individuals may process error differently. One of the features of psychopathic individuals is that they have difficulty adjusting their behavior in response to punishment and reward. They may be less able to monitor the results of their actions, leading to a failure to learn from experience, impulsivity, and poor decision making. This may be due to deficits in regions of the brain that detect a mismatch between the actual and expected results of one's actions. It has been suggested that when an error occurs, a signal is sent from the basal ganglia to the anterior cingulate cortex (ACC) region of the brain (Holroyd and Coles 2002). This results in the generation of an ERP with a negative deflection, which has been termed error-related negativity (ERN). This negative deflection in electrical signal occurs 80 to 100 ms after the error, and is thought to reflect signaling in the ACC.

One task that is commonly used for measuring error processing is the flanker task. In a basic version of the task, strings of five letters are presented, and participants are instructed to identify the middle character via a button press. The letter strings are either congruent ("SSSSS" or "HHHHH") or incongruent ("SSHSS" or "HHSHH"). Three studies using this task have found that the ERN is not affected in psychopathy (Munro et al. 2007a, Brazil et al. 2009, Brazil et al. 2011). However, variants of this task do result in differences.

Dikman and Allen (2000) gave feedback after participants gave responses. In one session, participants received punishment (i.e., loud noise blasts) after incorrect responses. In another session, participants received a reward (i.e., a small amount of money) for correct responses. They found that participants scoring lower in socialization (a measure of some features of psychopathy) demonstrated reduced ERN amplitudes during the sessions involving punishment. The authors suggested that participants scoring higher in psychopathy may (1) find errors to be less salient, (2) monitor their errant responses less closely, and/or (3) be less concerned about the consequences of having made an error. In another variant of the task, Munro et al. (2007a) used pictures of fearful and angry faces in place of letters. They found that, unlike in the letter version of the task, the ERN during the emotional flanker task was reduced in individuals scoring higher in psychopathy. These studies suggest that abnormalities in error processing in psychopathic individuals may be specific to contexts involving negatively valenced stimuli or feedback.

In addition to the ERN, which occurs very quickly after error commission, a second ERP component is also generated approximately 200 to 400 ms after the error, referred to as error positivity (Pe). Pe is thought to be associated with conscious error recognition. Brazil et al. (2009) found that during the (neutral) letter flanker task, psychopathic individuals showed unimpaired ERN, but reduced Pe amplitudes, suggesting that these individuals have deficits in a later stage of error processing. One possibility is that this may reflect reduced emotional appraisal following errors. The Pe is also thought to reflect the functioning of the anterior cingulate.

In addition to examining the ERN that occurs after one's own errors, one recent study also examined what is called the "observed ERN," which is generated when people observe an error committed by another individual. The observed ERN has been localized to the same area in the middle frontal cortex that is responsible for the traditional ERN. Similar to previous findings, Brazil et al. (2011) found no reductions in the ERN in psychopathic offenders when monitoring their own errors, but they did observe reduced ERNs when these individuals processed the consequences of others' actions. The authors suggest that this disturbance in monitoring the performance of others may play an important role in the abnormal acquisition of social behavior, since psychopathic individuals may be less able to process observed cues in social settings, leading to reduced availability of usable information about outcomes (Brazil et al. 2011).

Feedback-Related Negativity

The studies discussed thus far have used paradigms such as the flanker task in which no learning is involved. Participants are instructed how to respond, rather than having to learn how to respond based on feedback cues, such as the receipt of punishment or reward. When participants receive feedback, the ERP that follows is referred to as feedback-related negativity (FRN), or sometimes feedback ERN. This ERP occurs 200 to 300 ms after the feedback stimulus and is thought to be generated in the same region of the brain as the ERN (Ridderinkhof et al. 2004). Whereas the ERN can be thought of as an internal error signal (i.e., individuals realize they have made a mistake), the FRN can be thought of as an external error signal (i.e., individuals receive a cue indicating they have made a mistake).

The processing of this feedback is important in the process of learning. When individuals first attempt to learn how to respond to stimuli, they rely on feedback, and an FRN is generated. However, as they gradually learn the associations, they begin to be able to detect errors at the time of response. Thus, the FRN is "propagated back in time" and becomes an ERN. Thus, over the course of learning, ERN amplitudes increase (Holroyd and Coles 2002).

Von Borries et al. (2010) examined this process in a group of individuals with psychopathic traits. They found that individuals with psychopathic traits showed appropriate FRNs to external negative feedback. However, they did not demonstrate the appropriate increase in ERN amplitude as learning progressed (i.e., the propagation from FRN to ERN was diminished). This suggests that individuals with psychopathic traits have intact processing of external negative feedback but reduced ability to use this feedback to form an internal template of the rules (stimulus-response mappings). This was confirmed in the behavioral data, which showed that psychopathic individuals were less accurate in responding during the task, and that they had a smaller increase in accuracy of responding as learning progressed. This study suggests that although ERN amplitudes do not appear to be reduced in psychopathy in the context of simple error detection in a neutral task (Munro et al. 2007a, Brazil et al. 2009), they are decreased during learning processes involving punishment (von Borries et al. 2010).

In another study examining responding to feedback, Varlamov et al. (2010) examined the FRN during a go/no-go task, described earlier, in which positive feedback was given for correct responses, and negative feedback was given for incorrect or slow responses. No differences were observed in the FRN between psychopathic and control groups. However, psychopathic individuals showed significantly reduced amplitude of the N100 in the lateral frontal regions after receiving negative feedback. The authors suggest that the N100 reflects the ability to automatically detect and attend to a mismatch between expected and obtained outcomes. In contrast, the FRN may reflect more controlled processing. These results suggest that psychopathic individuals may fail to register the response conflict that would *initiate* self-regulation or cognitive control (Varlamov et al. 2010). This finding is similar to the findings by Racer et al. (2011), discussed above, in which the initial P100 is reduced in response to an alerting cue. Detection of error messages may be essential for modifying one's own behavior.

Collectively, results from ERP studies may be difficult to interpret. Although more studies are needed to clarify which ERP components may appear different in psychopathy, ERP studies are making progress in furthering our knowledge about the specific deficits that psychopathic individuals may have in information processing. In order to fully understand the disorder, we need to have this information about how processes required for learning and monitoring one's own behavior are impaired. Not only will this help us to better understand how the brain functions differently in psychopathic individuals, but it may also help us to develop more effective interventions. We may be able to develop interventions that target these particular deficits, or we may be able to develop methods for teaching social and emotional skills in alternate ways that rely on processes that *are* intact in youth with psychopathic traits.

Conclusions

Psychophysiological measures can be viewed as a proxy for directly measuring brain activity that may be able to give us a better look at the discrete steps that are involved in processing information of various types. Much of the psychophysiological research on psychopathy is mixed, such as research on the P3. However, some stronger findings have emerged. Studies using various paradigms suggest that psychopathic individuals demonstrate significantly reduced physiological responses to cues that signal threat or aversive events. Unpleasant pictures or odors do not augment the startle response in psychopathic individuals. These types of studies help us to clarify the precise nature of the deficits in psychopathy. Many discrepancies in psychophysiological research may result from the use of different tasks and populations, but future research has the potential to clarify these discrepancies. In addition, combining EEG and/or skin conductance measures with brain imaging methods (e.g., Birbaumer et al. 2005) may also help scholars gain a more complete picture of the deficits that are present in psychopathic individuals.

4

Neuropsychology

Consider the following case studies: A 60-year-old male begins attempting to molest children for the first time in his life, and is arrested. Over the prior four years, the man's personality had changed remarkably. He had become very disinhibited, causing disturbances at work such as intruding into others' conversations and walking into others' offices uninvited. He also had begun compulsive hoarding and constantly pilfering money and other items from his workplace and restaurants. When questioned about the wrongfulness of his actions, he failed to acknowledge that his actions were harmful, and lacked empathy for those who were negatively affected.

In another case, over the course of 18 months, a woman in her 50s demonstrates progressive changes in her personality. Her family describes her as becoming increasingly disinhibited, frequently talking to strangers and making excessively personal comments. She had begun stealing merchandise from stores, including stores whose owners she knew. She showed reduced concern for others, and insincere emotions. For example, when asked about the death of a close relative, she verbally expressed sadness and then quickly lapsed into laughter. She became compulsive with regard to money and developed food addictions.

These two cases, reported by Mendez (2010), describe individuals with frontotemporal dementia, a progressive, neurodegenerative disorder previously known as Pick's disease, which affects the frontal and temporal regions of the brain (Figure 4.1). Interestingly, these neurological patients demonstrate many of the characteristics of psychopathic individuals, including pervasive immoral behavior and reduced concern for the harm that this behavior may have on others. This suggests that some of the brain regions that are compromised in frontotemporal dementia may also be compromised in psychopathic individuals.

By examining individuals who have incurred damage to specific brain regions, due to disease or physical trauma, we can learn more about the role of these brain regions in psychological and behavioral processes and make inferences about whether these regions may be compromised in specific psychological disorders. Neuropsychology is the study of the behavioral expression of brain dysfunction. In addition to observing the traits and behaviors that neurological patients exhibit, neuropsychologists have designed a number of tests to examine the specific deficits that may result from brain injury. For example, tasks have been developed to measure cognitive processes such as working memory, inhibition, and learning. If a patient with damage to a specific region demonstrates deficits on one of these tasks, we can infer that that region is important for (at least one aspect of) the process being measured.

Neuropsychology has been able to provide information about the brain regions that likely function differently in psychopathy in two ways. First of all, like the case studies described above, we can compare the behaviors and personality features of patients with damage to specific brain regions to the behaviors and personality features of people with psychopathic traits. When similarities emerge, we can infer that the damaged regions may also be compromised (to some degree) in individuals with psychopathic traits. Second, we can administer neuropsychological tests to individuals with psychopathic traits. In some cases, these tasks are thought to reflect functioning in a particular brain region, so performance on these tasks provides information about how that part of the brain may function differently in psychopathy. In other words, just as the psychophysiological methods discussed in the previous chapter

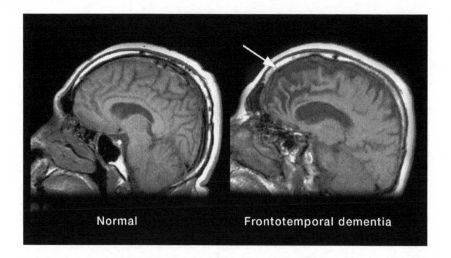

Normal   Frontotemporal dementia

Figure 4.1. The image on the right, particularly in the area near the white arrow, shows the brain shrinkage common in frontotemporal dementia. © Mayo Foundation for Medical Education and Research. All rights reserved.

approximate brain functioning using electrophysiological recordings, neuropsychological techniques approximate brain functioning by examining performance on tasks that are designed to reflect the functioning of those regions. In other cases, the specific brain regions that are necessary to perform a task may be less clear, or the task may require the functioning of a number of regions. However, these tasks can still provide valuable information about the precise nature of the psychopath's impairments. For example, we may be able to determine whether a deficit occurs in the early or later stage of information processing.

Comparisons with Neurological Patients

Neurological conditions include brain damage that has occurred as a result of trauma by an external force or an internal disease such as a tumor or neurodegenerative disease such as frontotemporal dementia. The study of patients who have developed impairments in specific brain regions and have subsequently demonstrated psychopathic-like traits or behaviors has helped to identify the regions that may be impaired in psychopathy. We should emphasize that most psychopathic individuals do not demonstrate significant brain damage that would be visible to the naked eye on a brain scan; rather, the impairments are much more subtle. The purpose of comparing psychopathic individuals with those with brain damage is to gain information about which regions may be compromised, not to imply that the deficits are comparable in scale.

Patients with damage to the ventromedial region of the prefrontal cortex demonstrate symptoms that most closely resemble psychopathic traits. The ventromedial prefrontal cortex is a region located in the front part of the brain, on the lower (ventral) side and toward the middle (medial). The region overlaps with the orbitofrontal cortex, which is the area just behind the eyes (orbito), and the terms are sometimes used interchangeably (Figure 4.2). Damage to this general region has been found to result in characteristics such as impulsivity, a disregard for social conventions, irresponsibility, and reactive aggression. Because these symptoms resemble psychopathic traits, this neurological condition has been referred to as "acquired sociopathy" (Eslinger and Damasio 1985). One of the earliest reported cases of this condition occurred in 1848, when a railway construction worker, Phineas Gage, suffered severe damage to the prefrontal cortex (PFC) after an accidental explosion in which an iron bar was blown through his head. Before the injury, Gage was described as a responsible, intelligent, and courteous man. After the injury, his personality radically changed, and he was described as irreverent and capricious. He became irresponsible and untrustworthy, demonstrating poor decision making and inappropriate social behavior (Harlow 1848, Damasio et al. 1994). Despite these radical changes, he did not appear to have impairments in intelligence, movement, speech, memory, or learning. A modern-day reconstruction demonstrated that damage likely occurred largely in the ventromedial region of the PFC (Figure 4.3; Damasio et al. 1994).

The ventromedial PFC has been found to serve a number of functions that are important for decision making, guiding social behavior, and processing emotional information. For example, the ventromedial PFC is involved in encoding the relative value of different stimuli, and in weighing the relative value of options based on contextual factors.

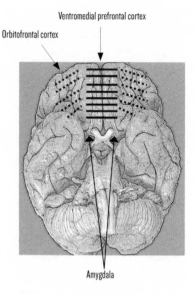

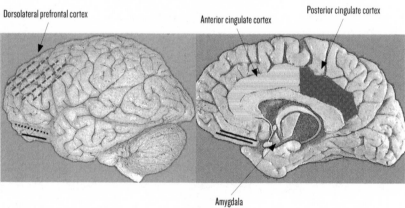

Figure 4.2. The upper image is a view of the underside of the brain. The front of the brain is at the top. Orbitofrontal and ventromedial regions are somewhat overlapping, and the two terms are often used interchangeably. The lower left image depicts the dorsolateral prefrontal cortex. The front of the brain is toward the left. The lower right image is a view of the middle of the brain (divided right to left) and depicts the anterior and posterior cingulate cortices, and the amygdala.

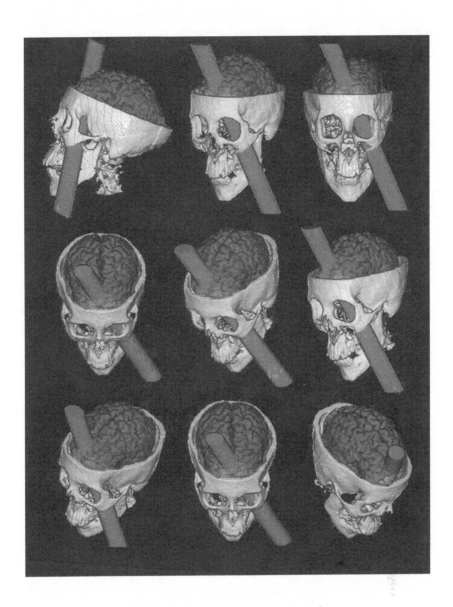

Figure 4.3. Skull measurements were used to reconstruct a three-dimensional image of the trajectory of the rod that passed through the brain of Phineas Gage (Damasio et al. 1994). Reprinted from the cover of *Science* magazine, volume 264, issue 5162.

It is therefore important in decision making, learning associations between stimuli, and processing reward and punishment feedback. It is also involved in anticipating reward or punishment, and is sensitive to situations in which a reward is expected but does not occur. Thus, it is not surprising that damage to this region would result in a variety of impairments.

Phineas Gage did not have deficits in intelligence and reasoning likely because the dorsolateral region of the PFC remained intact. The dorsolateral PFC is a region of the frontal lobe that is toward the top (dorsal) and side (lateral) of the brain. The dorsolateral PFC is a region involved in solving abstract problems, performing calculations, and calling upon appropriate knowledge.

Similar cases to that of Phineas Gage, in which damage occurs primarily to the ventromedial PFC, have also been reported (e.g., Damasio, Tranel, and Damasio 1990). Common features following damage to the ventromedial PFC in these cases include lack of empathy, difficulties with emotion regulation, impulsivity, disinhibited behavior, poor planning, and blunted emotions. When brain damage in the ventromedial PFC occurs early in life, psychopathic-like effects appear to be even more pronounced. Anderson et al. (1999) found that patients who incurred damage to the ventromedial PFC before the age of 16 months developed irresponsible and criminal behavior as adults. They were abusive toward others and demonstrated a lack of empathy or remorse. They were also found to demonstrate more immature levels of moral reasoning, and their antisocial behavior was more severe than those observed in patients who suffered damage to the ventromedial PFC in adulthood. The more severe impairments likely occur because the processes of learning associations are disrupted early in life, thus preventing proper moral socialization.

Patients with damage to the amygdala, a brain region discussed in the previous chapters, also demonstrate some of the same characteristics that are observed in psychopaths. They have been found to have less of a sense of "danger" and come across as dispassionate when recounting highly emotional or traumatic life experiences (Tranel et al. 2006). They also appear to be less fearful. However, their cognition and IQ are normal. Similar to psychopathic individuals, they also show several of the deficits discussed in the last chapter, including a lack of fear-potentiated startle (Angrilli et al. 1996) and impaired aversive conditioning (Bechara et al. 1995). They also exhibit deficits in recognizing fearful facial expressions (Adolphs et al. 1999), which is a feature of psychopathy. The fact that individuals with damage to the amygdala demonstrate these impairments reinforces the idea that amygdala functioning is necessary for these processes, and further supports the idea that these deficits in psychopathic individuals are likely partly a result of differential functioning of the amygdala.

Despite the similarities, patients with damage to either the ventromedial PFC or amygdala do not exhibit all of the features of psychopathy. Patients with ventromedial PFC lesions show primarily reactive aggression, or aggression that is a consequence of frustration or perceived threat (Anderson et al. 1999). Although psychopathic individuals demonstrate reactive aggression too, they also engage in instrumental forms of aggression, which is aggression that is directed toward a goal. Patients with damage to either the amygdala or ventromedial PFC typically do not demonstrate instrumental aggression. Patients with lesions to the amygdala have also been found to express a normal range of affect and emotion (Tranel et al. 2006), although as noted earlier, they may be less troubled by highly emotional or traumatic experiences. Patients with lesions to the amygdala also demonstrate deficits beyond those observed in individuals with psychopathic traits, such as deficits in memory and more pronounced deficits in processing social information. For example, patients with damage to the amygdala have been found to have deficits in their ability to judge traits such as trustworthiness (Adolphs, Tranel, and Damasio 1998). However, psychopathic individuals do not appear to have this deficit (Richell et al. 2005). It is important to keep in mind that the neurobiological deficits observed in psychopathic individuals are much less severe and less widespread than those that occur as a result of disease or physical trauma. However, examining the deficits and behaviors that emerge in people with neurological impairments is useful in helping to understand the result of impaired functioning of certain brain regions that may be implicated in psychopathy. In particular, the study of patients who have incurred brain damage very early in life may be especially useful, as it demonstrates how deficits in brain functioning at an early age may impair social and moral development in the individual. Future research particularly in younger patients with brain damage may be helpful in gaining a more precise understanding of the psychological and behavioral consequences of abnormal functioning in specific regions.

Neuropsychological Testing in Psychopathy

Neuropsychological testing has been widely implemented in the study of psychopathy and has provided a wealth of information regarding the specific nature of the psychopath's deficits. Neuropsychological tests are commonly administered as paper-and-pencil tests or by computer. This makes them portable, inexpensive, and desirable for research settings where brain imaging equipment is not readily available, such as facilities housing incarcerated or institutionalized populations (Schug et al. 2010). Findings from this research have helped to identify the brain structures that are likely to be impaired in psychopathy and also to understand how psychopathic individuals may process information differently.

The similarities between individuals with psychopathic traits and individuals with damage to specific brain regions can be further clarified by comparing the performance of the two groups on neuropsychological tests. Regions include the amygdala, orbitofrontal/ventromedial PFC, and dorsolateral PFC.

Amygdala

On several tasks, individuals with psychopathic traits demonstrate deficits that are similar to those observed in patients with damage to the amygdala. For example, tasks have been designed to examine how well people are able to recognize the facial expressions of others. Patients with damage to the amygdala have been found to have deficits specifically in the recognition of fearful facial expressions (Adolphs et al. 1999). Psychopathic individuals appear to demonstrate similar deficits. In one study, participants were presented with visual displays of facial expressions that were altered so that the facial expression changed from neutral to a specific emotion (e.g., fear, disgust) over the course of 20 successive frames of increasing intensity. The study found that children with psychopathic traits required significantly more stages before they could successfully recognize sad facial expressions, and often misclassified fearful expressions even at full intensity (Blair, Colledge, Murray, et al. 2001). Similarly, in a sample of incarcerated adults, psychopathic individuals showed impairment in the recognition of fearful expressions (Blair, Mitchell, Peschardt, et al. 2004). No deficits were observed for the emotions of happiness, surprise, disgust, or anger.

Psychopathic individuals also show deficits in the ability to recognize fear in auditory cues. For example, in another study, boys with psychopathic traits were presented with neutral words spoken with intonations conveying various emotions; compared to controls, they demonstrated a selective impairment in the recognition of fearful vocal affect (Blair, Budhani, et al. 2005). This finding is similar to the results from two studies of patients with lesions to the amygdala. One study found that damage to the amygdala on both sides impaired the recognition of fear and anger in nonverbal vocalizations (Scott et al. 1997). Another study found that patients with lesions of the temporal lobe (as a treatment for epilepsy), which includes the amygdala, have impaired recognition of vocal expressions of fear and surprise (Dellacherie et al. 2011). Thus, we can infer from these studies that the amygdala may be a region that is compromised in psychopathy. The specific deficits in recognition of fearful facial expressions and vocalizations may be because the amygdala is important in detecting potentially harmful or threatening stimuli.

Disruptions in the ability to recognize fear in other people may disrupt socialization. They may limit the ability to learn from social punishment provided by parents and other individuals. In addition, youth with fear-processing deficits may not find the fearful expressions of others to be aversive, and therefore may engage in harmful acts despite this nonverbal feedback from peers (Blair, Colledge, Murray, et al. 2001). The result may be the development of callous and unemotional traits, including a disregard for the needs of other people, shallow affect, and lack of remorse and empathy.

In animal studies, lesions to the amygdala have also been linked to impairments in the process of stimulus-reinforcement learning (i.e., the ability to learn from reward and punishment) (Schoenbaum, Chiba, and Gallagher 1999). Similarly, psychopathic individuals perform worse on neuropsychological tasks designed to measure this ability. One example is the passive avoidance paradigm. In this task, participants must learn to approach stimuli that become associated with reward (e.g., money) and avoid those that become associated with punishment (e.g., loss of money). Psychopathic individuals perform worse on this task (Newman and Kosson 1986). The amygdala may be important in enabling the individual to learn the goodness and badness of objects and actions (Blair 2007). Dysfunction in the ability to form stimulus-reinforcement associations may mean that during development, individuals will not be able to learn that some behaviors are bad, and thus may be more likely to use antisocial strategies to achieve their goals (Blair 2008). They also may not be able to learn to associate their harmful actions with the pain and distress of others, which may result in a lack of empathy for victims (Blair 2006a).

Ventromedial PFC

In addition to the similar personality features, individuals with psychopathy have been found to perform similarly to patients with damage to the ventromedial PFC on several neuropsychological tasks. One example is performance on the Iowa Gambling Task. As mentioned above, the ventromedial PFC is thought to be involved in tracking reinforcement information and signaling whether reinforcement should be expected. The Iowa Gambling Task is a task that is thought to rely on these functions. In this task, participants attempt to win money by selecting cards from four decks, labeled A, B, C, and D. Two decks are "advantageous," generating modest winnings and mild penalties, whereas the remaining decks are "disadvantageous," yielding larger winnings but more severe penalties. Over time, participants use punishment and reward information to (ideally) learn to select cards primarily from the advantageous decks. Patients with damage to the ventromedial PFC demonstrate deficits on the task (Damasio 1994, Fellows and Farah 2005). Some studies show that individuals with psychopathic traits also show impairments on this task (Blair, Colledge, and Mitchell 2001, Mitchell et al. 2002), although deficits may be specific to the Lifestyle-Antisocial Factor 2 features of psychopathy (Mahmut, Homewood, and Stevenson 2008, Mitchell et al. 2002).

Performance on the Iowa Gambling Task requires a number of different cognitive processes. Evidence suggests that the key process that may be compromised in patients with damage to the ventromedial PFC is reversal learning. Reversal learning is a form of stimulus-reinforcement learning that requires for associations to be updated as reinforcement contingencies change. For example, an individual may initially learn to make a response in order to gain a reward, but then contingencies change so that the correct response no longer results in reward and a new response must be learned to achieve the reward. In the Iowa Gambling Task, cards are ordered so that participants initially receive large rewards from the riskier decks, and thus establish a preference for these decks. Ultimately they must overcome this preference when the large losses begin to accumulate. When cards are rearranged so that reversal learning is not required in the Iowa Gambling Task, patients with lesions to the ventromedial PFC no longer demonstrate impaired performance (Fellows and Farah 2005). Psychopathic individuals also exhibit deficits on other tasks that require reversal learning (Newman, Patterson, and Kosson 1987, Budhani and Blair 2005). Evidence from both human and animal lesion studies suggests that the ventromedial PFC is important for the process of reversal learning (Rolls et al. 1994, Dias, Robbins, and Roberts 1996). Thus, these studies provide further evidence that the ventromedial PFC may be impaired.

Although the poor performance on other reversal learning tasks suggests that psychopathic individuals likely have deficits in the ventromedial PFC, poor performance on the Iowa Gambling Task may also result from deficits in other brain regions. Patients with damage to the dorsolateral PFC also demonstrate worse performance on this task. Patients with lesions to the amygdala may also have impaired performance, as they have been found to have less of an aversion to losing money. One study used a gambling-type task to show that two patients with damage to the amygdala demonstrated a pronounced absence of aversion to monetary loss. However, they retained a normal response to reward magnitude (De Martino, Camerer, and Adolphs 2010). This suggests that amygdala functioning may also contribute to individual differences in performance on gambling tasks. Rather than being involved in comparing reward and punishment information, which is associated with the ventromedial PFC, the amygdala may be important in detecting uncertainty and threatening information in the environment, and triggering arousal or vigilance (De Martino, Camerer, and Adolphs 2010).

In sum, it is important to keep in mind that many of these tasks may rely on the functioning of multiple brain regions.

Finally, studies have also found that damage to the ventromedial PFC alters moral judgment. One popular way for examining moral judgment has been to present individuals with a series of hypothetical moral dilemmas and ask them to make judgments (Greene et al. 2001). One of the most famous of these dilemmas is the trolley problem:

> A runaway trolley is heading down the tracks toward five workmen who will be killed if the trolley proceeds on its present course. You are on a footbridge over the tracks, in between the approaching trolley and the five workmen. Next to you on this footbridge is a stranger who happens to be very large.
>
> If you do nothing the trolley will proceed, causing the deaths of the five workmen. The only way to save the lives of these workmen is to push this stranger off the bridge and onto the tracks below, where his large body will stop the trolley, causing his death.
>
> Is it morally appropriate for you to push the stranger onto the tracks in order to save the five workmen?

When considering this dilemma, most people have a negative reaction to the thought of pushing the man off of the bridge and indicate that this action would not be appropriate. However, people with damage to the ventromedial PFC and individuals with frontotemporal dementia are more likely to say that these types of actions are appropriate (Koenigs et al. 2007, Ciaramelli et al. 2007, Mendez, Anderson, and Shapira 2005). Individuals with psychopathic traits provide similar responses on this task (Bartels and Pizarro 2011). This suggests that the ventromedial PFC (and likely other regions) is important in the process of moral judgment. It may be particularly important in the processing of emotion-related information, including the ability to evaluate options and weigh information about the positive and negative outcomes associated with these judgments. The more severe deficits in moral behavior that occur when an individual incurs damage to the ventromedial PFC early in life may be because these processes are essential for proper moral socialization. In psychopathy, genetic or environmental factors early in life may similarly compromise the functioning of the ventromedial

PFC very early on, resulting in problems in moral socialization that affect behavior throughout the life span. Overall, evidence from neuropsychological testing supports the idea that psychopathy is associated with deficits in the ventromedial PFC. Impairment in this region may contribute to the impaired decision making (and associated risk taking, impulsivity, and antisocial behavior) observed in psychopathy.

Dorsolateral PFC

Psychopathic individuals have also been examined for a variety of deficits in cognitive functioning, which is thought to rely largely on the dorsolateral PFC. Processes such as planning ability, concept formation, cognitive flexibility, and working memory are often collectively referred to as executive functions (Lezak et al. 2004). Tasks designed to measure executive functioning include the Wisconsin Card Sorting Test, the Tower of London, the Porteus Maze Test, and the Stroop Color-Word Inference task (for a review, see Gao, Glenn, et al. 2011). Many of these tasks tap into a number of different processes, which may be difficult to isolate on their own. For example, the Wisconsin Card Sorting Test (WCST) relies on several cognitive functions, including attention, working memory, and inhibition (Psychological Assessment Resources 2003). In the task, cards are presented that depict shapes differing in color, shape, and number. Participants must sort each card into the appropriate stack, but are not told according to which property, only whether their selection is right or wrong. Participants must learn the rules (e.g., sort by shape) based on the feedback they are given. During the course of the test, the rules are changed and the participant must relearn the rules (e.g., now sort by number instead) (Figure 4.4).

A number of studies have been conducted using tasks such as the WCST to explore whether psychopathic individuals have deficits in executive functioning. Results are often mixed in these studies. For example, despite some evidence that psychopathy is associated with deficits on the WCST (Yang et al. 2011), other studies have found that performance on the WCST is not related to total psychopathy scores or to scores on either Factor 1 or Factor 2 (Mol et al. 2009, Roussy and Toupin 2000), or that there is a nonsignificant trend toward worse performance (LaPierre, Braun, and Hodgins 1995).

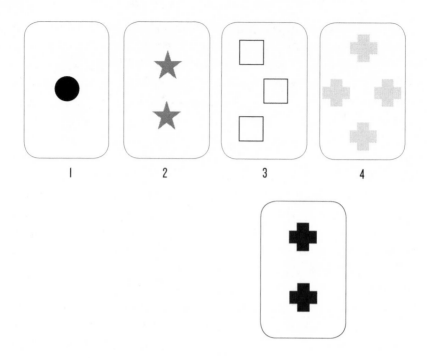

Figure 4.4. Example of Wisconsin Card Sorting Test, which is designed to measure set shifting, or the ability to demonstrate flexibility when reinforcement contingencies change. Participants must initially use trial and error and rely on feedback to determine how to sort the lower card into the appropriate stack (e.g., sort by color, number, or shape). During the test the rules are changed so that participants must switch to sorting by another property (Psychological Assessment Resources 2003).

Two comprehensive meta-analyses have been conducted examining the relationships between executive functioning deficits and psychopathy. Morgan and Lilienfeld (2000) found that there was a small to medium-sized relationship between executive functioning deficits and studies of psychopathy. In a follow-up meta-analysis examining studies published from 1997 to 2008, Ogilvie et al. (2011) found a medium-sized relationship.

Some studies suggest that deficits in executive functioning may primarily be associated with the Lifestyle-Antisocial (Factor 2) features, which are common in externalizing psychopathology more generally. For example, Molto et al. (2007) found that Factor 2 uniquely predicted worse performance on a card playing task requiring flexible responding based on reward and punishment feedback. Individuals scoring high on Factor 2 have also been found to be more prone to interference from distracters in tasks that involve high working memory load (Sadeh and Verona 2008). Impaired executive functions such as poor cognitive control and inhibition may contribute to the chronic irresponsibility, emotional dysregulation, impulsivity, and aggression associated with Factor 2 of psychopathy.

Some researchers have suggested that Factor 1 may actually be associated with *enhanced* executive functioning. For example, Sellbom and Verona (2007) found that individuals scoring higher in psychopathy had fewer perseverative errors than controls on the WCST. Interpersonal features such as being manipulative and deceitful may require the ability to inhibit responding and plan one's actions.

Overall, comparing the performance of individuals with psychopathic traits on neuropsychological tests to that of patients with brain damage in specific regions has enabled us to form hypotheses about the brain regions that are likely compromised in psychopathy. Findings from tasks that are likely dependent on the functioning of the dorsolateral PFC are not as strong as findings from studies designed to measure the functioning of the ventromedial PFC or amygdala. The amygdala and ventromedial PFC are two key regions that are important in the processing of affective information and in learning associations. Deficits in these regions may account for many of the features of psychopathy, including callousness, reduced empathy and guilt, instrumental aggression, poor decision making, and impulsivity.

Neuropsychological Models: Attention-Based Model

In addition to making inferences about which brain regions may function differently in psychopathy, neuropsychological testing has also helped us to understand how psychopathic individuals may process information differently. For example, based on the results of neuropsychological testing, some investigators have suggested that, in addition to deficits in emotion, the development and maintenance of psychopathy may be partly due to abnormalities in attentional processing. Newman and colleagues suggest that some of the reduced responsiveness to aversive stimuli that is observed in psychopathic individuals may actually be due to attentional deficits rather than to reduced emotional responsivity. For example, Newman et al. (2010) found that the widely documented deficits in fear-potentiated startle (FPS; discussed in Chapter 3) observed in psychopathic individuals, which are commonly interpreted as reflecting reduced emotional responsivity, is dependent on the focus of their attention. In the study, FPS was measured as participants categorized red and green letter stimuli under different conditions. In one condition, participants directly responded to the color of the stimuli (red or green), which was the quality that signified whether electric shock would occur or not. In another condition, participants attended to an alternative quality of the stimulus—whether the letter was upper- or lowercase (threat-irrelevant condition). When psychopathic participants *directly* attended to the threat-relevant information (the color of the stimuli), they did not show deficits in FPS. However, when they attended to an irrelevant quality of the stimuli, they demonstrated significant deficits in FPS.

Similarly, psychopathic individuals display normal abilities to avoid monetary punishment when this is their only goal. However, they exhibit deficits in the ability to avoid monetary punishment when the task also involves a goal of earning monetary rewards. It is suggested that when their primary goal is earning reward, they are unable to reallocate attention to cues of potential punishment (Newman and Kosson 1986).

Neuropsychological studies have tried to further clarify the nature of the attentional deficits. Research suggests that there are two mechanisms of attention that regulate the processing of irrelevant, distracting information in the environment. One process occurs early and is involved in perceiving and recognizing external information (perceptual selection), and the other occurs later and is involved in suppressing the effects of irrelevant distractors once they have been recognized (cognitive control). The suggestion is that psychopaths have deficits particularly in this early phase—they do not perceive and recognize appropriate signals in the environment and therefore do not attend to cues that should guide their behavior. As a result, psychopathic individuals may have difficulty shifting their attention from their current goal or task in order to attend to peripheral information that may signal that they should change their behavior (Baskin-Sommers, Curtin, and Newman 2011). This model is based on evidence that psychopathic individuals perform abnormally on tasks that involve the processing of neutral (i.e., nonemotional) stimuli (Hiatt, Schmitt, and Newman 2004), in addition to deficits in processing emotional information.

Like emotion-based models of psychopathy, the attention-based model may also be able to account for the core features of psychopathy. Studies suggest that abnormal attentional processing is specific to the Interpersonal-Affective Factor 1 of psychopathy, rather than the Life-style-Antisocial Factor 2 features (Hiatt, Schmitt, and Newman 2004, Newman 1998). In particular, the core features of psychopathy (Factor 1) appear to be associated with deficits in the early stage of perceiving and recognizing external information (Sadeh and Verona 2008). This may lead to reduced processing of information such as distress cues that promote empathy or cues of threat or punishment that serve as important guides for behavior. In contrast, the Lifestyle-Antisocial (Factor 2) features of psychopathy appear to be associated more with impairments in the later-occurring process of cognitive control, which is facilitated by executive functions (discussed above), and which may be associated with externalizing psychopathology more generally.

The attention-based model suggests that regions important in attention may be compromised in psychopathic individuals. For example, it has been suggested that the septohippocampal area of the brain, which includes regions such as the septum, hippocampus, and posterior cingulate, facilitates the coordination of behavior by detecting whether there is a conflict between sensory information from the environment and the individual's current focus of attention. Impairments in these areas would result in a failure to notice new information that emerges in the environment, such as subtle changes in threat or reward cues, which would typically cause individuals to modify their behavior (Sadeh and Verona 2008). Importantly, the septohippocampal area is highly inter-connected with brain regions implicated in the emotion-based model of psychopathy, including the amygdala, orbitofrontal cortex, and cingulate cortex. The attention-based model suggests that there may be abnormalities in the integration of these brain regions. Future research specifying the attentional deficits in psychopathy and the contexts in which they occur will be necessary to better understand the origin of these impairments and the brain regions that may be implicated.

The field will also benefit from studies designed to directly compare emotion-based and attention-based models. For example, one study was designed to test whether the fear-processing deficits observed in psychopathic individuals may result from attentional impairments. Sylvers, Brennan, and Lilienfeld (2011) used a continuous-flash-suppression paradigm, which is a task designed to assess preattentive processing, or the automatic processing of visual information that occurs before it reaches conscious awareness. This paradigm allows for the investigation of emotional processing that is independent of awareness and attention. Previous studies have found that fearful facial expressions tend to come into awareness more quickly than other types of expressions, suggesting that preattentive processes bring social indicators of threat to people's overt attention faster than nonthreatening indicators. They found that youth with callous-unemotional traits exhibited deficits in preattentive fear recognition. This suggests that threat-processing deficits observed in psychopathy are not merely a product of overt attentional factors. However, this does not rule out the possibility that overt attentional factors may also contribute to the deficits observed in psychopathy. The authors suggest that theoretical explanations for psychopathy may benefit by accounting for both preconscious and conscious processes.

Left Hemisphere Activation and Interhemispheric Integration

Other hypotheses that have stemmed from results of neuropsychological testing in psychopathy are that psychopathic individuals have deficits in the functioning of one hemisphere of the brain (Kosson 1996) or in the transfer of information from one hemisphere of the brain to the other (Hiatt and Newman 2007). When we receive information from the world, it is always processed by the opposite hemisphere of the brain from where the input was received. For example, a tone played in the right ear will be processed by the left hemisphere. Likewise, a visual stimulus presented in the left visual field will be processed by the right hemisphere. Voluntary movements are also controlled by the opposite hemisphere. The act of moving the right hand is controlled by the left hemisphere and vice versa. Some studies have suggested that the antisocial and dysregulated behavior of psychopathic individuals is due in part to deficient information processing under conditions that place substantial demands on the left hemisphere (Kosson 1996, 1998). This hypothesis is called the left hemisphere activation (LHA) hypothesis. It suggests that psychopaths' deficits in cognitive processing are state-specific, occurring primarily when the left hemisphere is activated. For example, compared to nonpsychopathic offenders, psychopathic offenders performed worse on a task in which letters and numbers were presented primarily in the right visual field and a right-handed response was required (i.e., requiring activation of the left hemisphere for both stimulus processing and response generation; Kosson 1998, Llanes and Kosson 2006); they demonstrated no deficits when information was presented to the left visual field and required a left-handed response. Similar findings have been observed in other visual and auditory tasks (Kosson 1996, Suchy and Kosson 2005).

Another way of examining left versus right hemisphere functioning is by examining processes that may be facilitated more by one hemisphere than the other. For example, the left hemisphere is more involved in processing local (detailed) information about visual stimuli, whereas the right hemisphere processes global (holistic) aspects of stimuli. Kosson et al. (2007) found that psychopaths responded more slowly than nonpsychopaths to local (i.e., left hemisphere) but not global targets. The left hemisphere is also involved more in verbal processing, whereas the right hemisphere is involved in nonverbal processing. Suchy and Kosson (2006) found that offenders with psychopathic traits made more errors on a verbal task than did offenders without psychopathic traits, but performed equally well on a nonverbal visuospatial task, suggesting that when processing relies on the left hemisphere, psychopathic individuals demonstrate deficits.

The LHA hypothesis does not imply a specific deficit in cognitive abilities, but predicts that information processing in general (i.e., all cognitive abilities, such as attention, memory, inhibition, etc.) will be disrupted when the left hemisphere is activated (Llanes and Kosson 2006). When the left hemisphere is activated less than, or as much as, the right hemisphere, no deficits should occur. These state-dependent cognitive deficits may account for the fluctuations in behavior across situations that are often observed in psychopathic individuals.

In addition to the LHA hypothesis, it has also been proposed that psychopathic individuals may have deficits in the transfer of information from one hemisphere of the brain to the other. In the brain, signals are transmitted from one hemisphere to the other via the corpus callosum, a bundle of white matter fibers connecting the two hemispheres.

Poffenberger (1912) hypothesized that during laboratory tasks, if information is presented to one side of the body and participants are asked to respond with the hand on the opposite side of the body, responses will be slower than if participants are asked to respond with the hand on the same side of the body as the stimuli were presented. This is because in the former case, information must be communicated across hemispheres. For example, information presented in the left visual field will be processed by the right hemisphere. This information must then be communicated to the left hemisphere in order to initiate a motor response in the right hand. In contrast, information presented in the left visual field that requires a response with the left hand will elicit faster reaction times because no interhemispheric transfer of information is required (i.e., all processing takes place in the right hemisphere).

One study found that psychopathic criminals demonstrate a substantially longer interhemispheric transfer time—the time required to transfer information from one hemisphere to the other (Hiatt and Newman 2007). This effect was most pronounced when participants made responses with the right hand, suggesting that there is slower transfer of information from the right hemisphere to the left hemisphere than vice versa. The authors suggest that reduced connectivity between hemispheres may cause functions primarily facilitated by the left hemisphere, such as approach behavior and language processing, to be relatively unmodulated by functions facilitated predominantly by the right hemisphere, such as behavioral inhibition and emotion processing, and vice versa. Inefficient sharing of information between hemispheres may also interfere with flexible and adaptive responding.

Importantly, in this study, psychopathic individuals did not show deficits in trials that did not involve a crossover (i.e., trials in which information was presented on the right side and a response was required by the right hand). This contradicts previous findings that have demonstrated deficits in psychopathic individuals when processing information on the right side that requires a right-handed response (Kosson 1998). Additional research is needed to clarify this discrepancy.

Finally, it has also been suggested that there may be an interaction between LHA and attention theories, meaning that deficits under LHA conditions may be found only when tasks tax attentional systems. For example, Suchy and Kosson (2006) found that psychopathic offenders made more errors on the verbal task only during trials that placed high demands on executive processing (in this case, forming and switching mental sets).

Disadvantages of Neuropsychological Testing

It is important to keep in mind that performance on neuropsychological tests is a relatively indirect approximation of brain functioning, particularly in comparison to brain imaging and EEG techniques (Rogers 2006). The specificity and sensitivity of many neuropsychological tasks for dysfunction in frontal brain regions are questionable. For example, the WCST is commonly thought to index functioning of the dorsolateral PFC. However, Yang et al. (2011) found that performance on this task was correlated with the thickness of the cortex in the orbitofrontal cortex and the anterior temporal cortex in psychopathic individuals. It has been suggested that the WCST likely relies on multiple cognitive and affective processes and may recruit the orbitofrontal cortex in addition to the dorsolateral PFC (Rogers 2006). Similarly, the performance on the Iowa Gambling Task has been found to be impaired in individuals with damage to either the ventromedial PFC or the dorsolateral PFC (Fellows and Farah 2005). In order to gain a complete picture of the deficits that are present in psychopathic individuals, we advocate a multimethod approach that draws on the strengths of each type of assessment.

Conclusions

Neurocognitive techniques focus on uncovering disruptions in the neural systems that guide behavior. Both neurological case studies and neuropsychological testing suggest that psychopathy likely involves deficits in the ventromedial PFC and amygdala. However, many discrepancies remain in the literature. Future studies will benefit from examining the different factors of psychopathy, as evidence suggests that there may be differential relationships. In addition, it will be important to understand how different tasks tap into different psychological processes, and recruit specific brain regions in order to make accurate inferences regarding the nature of neurobiological deficits.

5

Brain Imaging

In Chapters 3 and 4 we discussed research that is designed to indirectly estimate how the brain may function differently in psychopathy. In this chapter we review the research that examines the brain more directly via brain imaging. Brain imaging is perhaps the fastest moving area of research in psychopathy. Advances in technology are allowing for much better visualization of structural and functional properties of the brain. The clinical implications of this research are significant. Understanding how the brain functions differently in psychopathic individuals will likely be useful in the development of treatment, and in determining the most appropriate type of treatment for a given individual. It may also be able to improve our understanding of how specific genetic and environmental influences lead to the development of psychopathy, which may aid in prevention and intervention.

Brain functioning is a unique type of biological factor because it represents the most direct, proximate cause of behavior. The functioning of the brain reflects the culmination of a variety of genetic and environmental influences and their interactions. The reason that genetic and environmental influences can affect behavior is because they alter brain structure and function.

Before summarizing the key findings from brain imaging studies of psychopathy, a brief overview of brain imaging techniques is given to familiarize the reader with the basic technical aspects of this research. Neuroimaging studies of psychopathy have implemented a variety of brain imaging techniques and paradigms to uncover the brain regions in which the structure or functioning is different in psychopathy. These studies primarily implicate the amygdala and orbitofrontal cortex as the brain structures that function differently in psychopathy, though several additional regions involved in important processes such as moral judgment have been identified. Studies conducted in children with psychopathic traits suggest that alterations in the brain may originate early in life.

Brain Imaging Techniques

The speculations that antisocial or criminal behavior may be linked to the brain can be traced back as early as the 18th century. The study of phrenology, developed by the German physician Franz Joseph Gall, involved examining the topography of the cranial bones with the assumption that this was an indicator of underlying regional brain sizes, which were thought to be abnormal in violent individuals. However, phrenology was largely discarded in the early 20th century when numerous cases of violent individuals were observed to have well-developed skulls. In the early 20th century, a new technique called "pneumoencephalography" allowed for the first time the visualization of the ventricular system of living human beings using an X-ray after injecting air into the subarachnoid space through a lumber puncture and draining the cerebrospinal fluid. This technique was not only very invasive, but often painful and dangerous, and therefore was largely abandoned after the rise of computed tomography (CT) in the early 1970s.

In CT, a sequence of X-ray images is taken across the head. These images are then processed to create a three-dimensional representation of the brain. CT images allow differentiation of soft-tissue with different densities. CT soon became a gold standard in medical diagnosis and was employed in early brain imaging studies of criminal offenders.

For example, using CT, Langevin and colleagues (1988) found that about 50 percent of violent sadists have brain structural abnormalities, especially in temporal lobe regions. Similarly, Blake, Pincus, and Buckner (1995) found brain atrophy in 9 of 19 individuals charged with murder. However, CT presents several limitations, including limited spatial resolution (difficulty in differentiating gray and white matter) and the fact that participants must be exposed to radioactivity. In the late 1980s, positron emission tomography (PET) gained popularity as a method for understanding functional differences in the brain. This technique involves injecting the participant with a short-lived radioactive tracer prior to the brain scan to detect metabolic abnormalities in the brain. A similar technique, single photon emission computed tomography (SPECT), involves injecting the subject with a gamma-emitting tracer to determine the amount of regional cerebral blood flow in any particular brain area.

In 1973, the first image using magnetic resonance imaging (MRI) was published, and this new technology quickly became the most commonly used imaging technique in many research fields. This technique is much safer and less invasive than previous imaging methods. MRI is based on the principle that atoms in the human brain are like small bar magnets that possess magnetic charges in random orientations. When immersed in a strong magnetic field, the nuclei of these atoms tend to align and reach an equilibrium state. A radiofrequency electromagnetic field is then briefly introduced to excite the atoms and induce a transient phase coherence among the nuclei that creates a signal, which can be detected by the MRI scanner receiver. Typically, MRI detects the resonance of hydrogen atoms in water, and because this element is abundant in the brain, images with excellent anatomical details can be produced without the use of radiation.

Several different types of scans can be conducted using MRI to examine different aspects of brain structure and function. In addition, advances in computational imaging analysis methods have permitted researchers to gain more precision in interpreting the images than ever before. Most brain imaging studies of psychopathy have been conducted in recent years, and therefore most have implemented techniques involving MRI. In the following sections, we review the basics of the MRI-based techniques that have been used to study the brain mechanisms

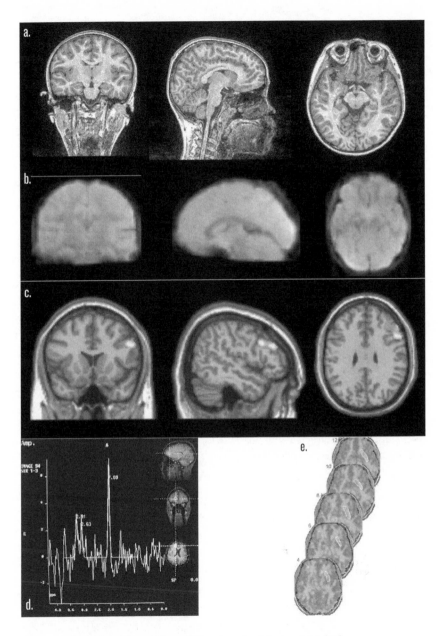

Figure 5.1. Examples of images from different methodologies. (a) A high resolution structural MRI image. (b) A raw functional MRI image. (c) Regions of statistical significance from averaged functional MRI images overlaid on structural MRI images. (d) MRS spectra obtained from one region of the brain. (e) DTI image depicting white matter tracts.

underlying psychopathic personality; each technique can be implemented in an MRI scanner but is designed to assess different aspects of the brain. Figure 5.1 depicts some of the different types of scans.

Structural Magnetic Resonance Imaging

Structural brain imaging scans, sometimes referred to as aMRI (anatomical MRI), are designed to gain a very clear, overall picture of brain structure. These scans last approximately four to eight minutes and collect a highly detailed image of the anatomy of the brain. The images can be used to assess the volume and shape (morphometry) of different brain regions. They are also used in the analysis of functional MRI images, which have poorer resolution; by overlaying functional images on a high-resolution structural image from the same individual, it is possible to more clearly identify the regions in the functional images.

Volume

The volume of brain regions can be assessed using either manual or automated methods. Manual assessment of volume is performed by tracing the brain region (three-dimensional) on a series of two-dimensional cross-sections of the brain. Trained researchers or technicians follow a previously validated protocol that describes in detail the anatomical markers that should be used as boundaries for the region. Although somewhat subjective due to individual anatomical variations and errors introduced by the scorers, this approach has generated several important findings in psychopathy research and remains especially useful in examining the volume of relatively small subcortical structures.

Recently, alternative approaches using fully automated or semiautomated algorithms to identify morphological changes in the brain have been used to examine brain structure in psychopathic individuals. Voxel-based morphometry (VBM), tensor-based morphometry (TBM), and FreeSurfer allow researchers to examine brain structural changes throughout the whole brain (rather than one region at a time) by morphing each individual brain into a standardized space so that comparisons can be made between individuals using an automated method. These methods are much less labor-intensive. However, despite several algorithms currently under development, fully automated methods are not yet accurate enough to trace anatomical structures without human intervention.

One benefit of automated methods is that they can also be used to identify differences in aspects of brain structure other than volume, such as gray matter concentration (using VBM) or the shape of a brain region (using TBM). Other methods, such as cortical thickness pattern matching and surface-based mesh modeling, allow for fine reconstructions of the 3D shape of the brain structure in order to detect morphological differences. Several scholars have begun to employ these methods in studies of psychopathic individuals.

Functional Magnetic Resonance Imaging

Functional MRI (fMRI) is a type of MRI scan that can measure changes in brain activity during a task. This scan acquires images of changing blood flow in the brain by measuring changes in the blood-oxygen-level-dependent (BOLD) signal, which is well correlated with neural activity. Images are acquired very quickly so that researchers can view the changes in brain activity across time as participants view pictures or respond to stimuli.

One disadvantage of fMRI is that in order to obtain sufficient power to detect a signal, the task must involve events of a similar type that are repeated many times (e.g., looking at a series of familiar objects vs. looking at a series of unfamiliar objects). Thus, it may be challenging to create tasks that closely resemble real-world events. Generally, there need to be two or more types of events that can be contrasted. For example, if the research question is "What areas of the brain are active when looking at emotional pictures?" then one would need an "emotional pictures" condition as well as a "neutral pictures" condition in order to "subtract out" the areas that are activated simply by looking at pictures in general.

A number of fMRI tasks have been used to study psychopathy, including tasks involving social and/or emotional processes, such as moral decision making, social interactions, viewing pictures of emotional facial expressions, fear conditioning, and viewing emotionally salient scenes.

Diffusion Tensor Imaging

Diffusion tensor imaging (DTI) is a technique used to map the white matter connections that transmit signals between brain regions. This type of scan can be conducted in an MRI scanner in approximately 10 minutes. DTI provides information about the volume and microstructural integrity of these white matter fiber tracts. Only one study to date has used this method to examine psychopathic individuals (Craig et al. 2009).

Magnetic Resonance Spectroscopy

Magnetic resonance spectroscopy (MRS) is another technique that can be implemented in an MRI scanner. It is used to determine the concentration of a variety of metabolites in the brain. These metabolites are generally seen as a reflection of the viability of neurons. MRS is a technique that is more often used in studies of neurodegenerative diseases, tumors, stroke, or epilepsy, when damage to or loss of neurons is significant. However, it has also proven to be useful in studying psychological disorders, in which abnormalities in the brain are less pronounced (Abbott and Bustillo 2006).

The main metabolites of interest in many MRS studies are N-acetyl aspartate (NAA), creatine (Cr), and choline (Cho). NAA is an amino acid found in high concentrations in neurons and is a marker of neuronal integrity, so reductions in this chemical can indicate neuronal loss or damage (Bertolino and Weinberger 1999). Creatine is found in many tissues and is important in the storage and transfer of energy. Choline is a marker of cellular membrane turnover. The ratio between these metabolites is also often examined. There are additional chemicals such as glutamate and glutamine that can also be examined using MRS.

Only one study thus far has used MRS to study psychopathy. Basoglu et al. (2008) examined a group of military conscripts with high psychopathy scores who had committed serious violent crimes. They examined three brain regions previously implicated in psychopathy—the amygdala/hippocampus, the dorsolateral prefrontal cortex, and the anterior cingulate. They examined the three metabolites mentioned above—NAA, Cr, and Cho. They found that the individuals with higher psychopathy scores demonstrated a reduced ratio of NAA to Cr in the anterior cingulate. This ratio is thought to be associated with decreased neuronal integrity (Bertolino and Weinberger 1999), suggesting that the integrity of the neurons in the anterior cingulate may be compromised in psychopathic individuals. The anterior cingulate is a region involved in effortful control, self-regulation, signaling errors, and affective processing.

Perfusion MRI

Perfusion MRI is a technique used to measure cerebral blood flow. Cerebral blood flow reflects neuronal functioning and is therefore indicative of the functioning of brain regions. Perfusion is typically conducted while the participant is at rest, although some forms of perfusion MRI such as arterial spin-labeling (Detre et al. 2012), can be conducted while the participant is engaged in a task, as an alternative to BOLD fMRI. Perfusion fMRI is thought to be ideal for imaging a sustained behavioral state, such as stress, in which participants do not quickly return to a "baseline" state. Perfusion MRI has not yet been implemented in the study of psychopathy, although one study used SPECT to examine regional cerebral blood flow. Soderstrom et al. (2002) found reduced perfusion in frontal and temporal regions in a group of violent offenders with high scores on the interpersonal aspects of psychopathy. Unlike SPECT, perfusion MRI has the advantage that it does not involve injection of a radioactive tracer prior to scanning.

Key Findings

Brain imaging studies of psychopathy have been conducted on a variety of samples, including undergraduates, individuals from the community, psychiatric patients, and incarcerated individuals. Studies have also been conducted in youth with callous-unemotional traits.

It is important to note that the findings of differences in the brains of psychopathic individuals do not *necessarily* reflect abnormality or impairment, although those are the terms typically used (including in our own studies). Unlike patients who incur brain damage such that the injury is noticeable and pronounced on an MRI image, the differences in the brains of psychopathic individuals are typically much more subtle. There are currently no normative standards for what is considered "normal" brain structure or functioning. With measures such as IQ, we have been able to collect data from large samples of individuals and have been able to establish agreed-on cutoffs for what we consider to be in the "abnormal" range. This determination is based on both frequencies in the population and the cognitive and behavioral consequences of an IQ below a specific level. It the future, it may be possible to build up a very large sample of brain images so that we can gain a better idea of what level of structure or functioning may be considered outside of the normal range of variation in brain structure or functioning.

Another important point is that a finding of altered structure or functioning in a particular region does not mean that all individuals with psychopathy will demonstrate this reduction or increase. The findings discussed in the following sections represent either average differences between psychopathic and nonpsychopathic individuals or correlations between psychopathy scores and brain structure/functioning; these findings refer to patterns across many individuals and do not make claims about individual subjects. Thus, it is important to remember that we cannot use an image of the brain to determine that an individual has, or is going to have, high levels of psychopathic traits.

Brain imaging findings, for the most part, have been able to confirm what has been hypothesized based on psychophysiological, neuropsychological, and behavioral data regarding the brain regions that are implicated in psychopathy. These regions include the amygdala and parts of the frontal lobe. In addition, brain imaging research has identified several additional regions that may function differently in psychopathic individuals, or that may indicate abnormal development of the brain. A summary of the brain imaging findings in psychopathy to date are listed in Table 5.1. The take-home messages from this literature are as follows:

1. The amygdala and ventromedial/orbitofrontal cortex are the brain regions most consistently associated with psychopathy.

Amygdala.
As discussed in the previous chapters, evidence from psychophysiology and neuropsychology studies suggests that the amygdala is a region that is likely altered in psychopathic individuals. This research has found

Table 5.1. *Brain Imaging Findings in Psychopathy*

Brain region	Function	Findings
Frontal lobe (general)		Reduced volume (Yang et al. 2005)
		Gray matter thinning (Yang, Raine, Colletti, et al. 2009)
Dorsolateral prefrontal cortex	Planning and organization	Gray matter reductions (Müller et al. 2008)
	Attentional set shifting and cognitive flexibility	Reduced activity when defecting in social interaction (Rilling et al. 2007)
		Increased activity during moral decision making (Glenn, Raine, Schug, Young, et al. 2009)
	Cognitive reappraisal of emotional experience	Increased activity during tasks involving emotional processing (Gordon, Baird, and End 2004, Intrator et al. 1997, Kiehl et al. 2001)
	Abstract reasoning	Increased white matter concentration in youth (De Brito et al. in press)
Orbitofrontal cortex/ventro-medial prefrontal cortex	Processing social and emotional stimuli	Gray matter reductions (de Oliveira-Souza et al. 2008)
	Self-reflection	Reduced activity during fear conditioning (Birbaumer et al. 2005)
	Guilt and embarrassment	Reduced activity during cooperation (Rilling et al. 2007)
	Cognitive appraisal of emotion	Reduced activity during evaluation of moral violations (Harenski et al. 2010)
	Emotion regulation	Reduced activity during emotional processing (Gordon, Baird, and End 2004, Kiehl et al. 2001, Müller et al. 2003, Schneider et al. 2000, Viet et al. 2002)
	Theory of mind (affective component)	Increased gray matter concentrations in youth (De Brito et al. 2009)
	Shifting behavior when rewards change	Increased activity during reversal learning (Finger et al. 2008)
Frontopolar cortex		Gray matter reductions (de Oliveira-Souza et al. 2008)

Table 5.1 (continued)

Brain region	Function	Findings
Temporal lobe (general)		Gray matter thinning (Yang, Raine, Colletti, et al. 2009)
		Reduced volume (Dolan et al. 2002, Müller et al. 2008)
		Reduced blood flow (Soderstrom et al. 2002)
		Increased gray matter concentration and volumes in youth (De Brito et al. 2009)
Amygdala	Aversive conditioning	Volume reductions (Yang, Raine, Narr, et al. 2009)
	Associating pain of others to one's own actions	Reduced activity during emotional processing (Kiehl et al. 2001; Gordon, Baird, and End 2004)
	Enhancing attention to emotional stimuli	Reduced activity during fear conditioning (Birbaumer et al. 2005)
		Reduced activity during social noncooperation (Rilling et al. 2007)
		Reduced activity during moral decision making (Glenn, Raine, and Schug 2009)
		Increased activity when viewing emotional pictures (Müller et al. 2003)
		Reduced activity to fearful faces (Marsh et al. 2008, Jones et al. 2009)
Hippocampus	Retrieval of emotional memories	Morphometric differences (Boccardi et al. 2010)
	Fear conditioning	Asymmetry (Raine et al. 2004)
		Reduced volume (posterior) (Laakso et al. 2001)
		Reduced activity during emotional processing (Kiehl et al. 2001)
Angular gyrus/superior temporal gyrus	Complex social emotion	Gray matter reductions (Müller et al. 2008)
	Linking emotional experiences to moral appraisals	Gray matter reductions (de Oliveira-Souza et al. 2008)
		Reduced activity during semantic processing (Kiehl et al. 2004)
		Reduced white matter concentrations in youth (De Brito et al. in press)
Anterior temporal cortex		Gray matter reductions (de Oliveira-Souza et al. 2008)
		Reduced activity during evaluation of moral violations (Harenski et al. 2010)

Table 5.1 (continued)

Brain region	Function	Findings
Other regions		
Anterior cingulate	Effortful control	Gray matter reductions (Müller et al. 2008)
	Self-regulation	No volumetric differences (Glenn, Yang, et al. 2010)
	Signaling conflict or error	Reduced activity during emotional processing (Kiehl et al. 2001)
	Affective processing, including empathy-related functions	Reduced activity during fear conditioning (Birbaumer et al. 2005, Viet et al. 2002)
		Reduced activity when defecting in social interaction (Rilling et al. 2007)
		Increased gray matter concentrations in youth (De Brito et al. 2009)
		Reduced white matter concentrations in youth (De Brito et al. in press)
Posterior cingulate	Recalling emotional memories	Gray matter thinning (Yang, Raine, Colletti, et al. 2009)
	Experiencing emotion	Reduced activity during emotional processing (Kiehl et al. 2001)
	Self-referencing	Reduced activity during fear conditioning (Birbaumer et al. 2005)
Ventral striatum	Reward sensitivity	Reduced activity during emotional processing (Kiehl et al. 2001)
	Persistence in repeating actions related to rewards	Increased volume (Glenn, Raine, et al. 2010)
	Enhanced learning from rewarding signals	Increased activity in anticipation of reward (Buckholtz et al. 2010)
Parahippocampal gyrus	Processing of social context	Reduced activity during emotional processing (Kiehl et al. 2001)
	Episodic memory	
Insula	Emotional processing, including social emotions	Reduced activity during fear conditioning (Birbaumer et al. 2005)
Corpus callosum	Transfer of information between left and right hemispheres of the brain	Increased volume and length, reduced thickness (Raine et al. 2003)

that psychopathy is associated with deficits in a number of processes that are thought to rely on the functioning of the amygdala, including responding to aversive stimuli, aversive conditioning, augmentation of the startle reflex, and recognizing fearful facial and vocal expressions. In addition, the amygdala is involved in the production of emotional states (Phillips et al. 2003) and the experience of moral emotions (Moll et al. 2002). The amygdala has been identified as a region important in moral judgment (Greene et al. 2004), and it has also been found to respond during one's own moral violations (Berthoz et al. 2006). Because psychopathic individuals demonstrate deficits in these processes, it has been hypothesized that deficits in the amygdala may be able to account for a wide range of features of psychopathy.

Brain imaging studies have provided support for this hypothesis, observing both structural and functional differences in the amygdala in psychopathic individuals. Reduced volume of the amygdala has been reported in psychopathic individuals, particularly in the basolateral and superficial nuclei groups (Yang, Raine, Narr, et al. 2009). In several fMRI studies, reduced activity in the amygdala has been associated with psychopathy during the processing of emotional stimuli (Kiehl et al. 2001), during fear conditioning (Birbaumer et al. 2005), during a socially interactive game (Rilling et al. 2007), and during an affect recognition task (Gordon, Baird, and End 2004). Psychopathy has also been found to be associated with reduced amygdala functioning during moral decision making about emotional moral dilemmas (Glenn, Raine, and Schug 2009); this supports the idea that dysfunction in the amygdala may partly underlie deficits in moral behavior in psychopathic individuals. One early study reported *increased* amygdala activation in criminal psychopaths while viewing negative visual content (Müller et al. 2003), but this appears to be the exception.

The amygdala is located in the temporal lobe of the brain. Several studies have also identified differences in the structure and function of this region. Reduced volume has been observed in the temporal lobe in three studies of psychopathic individuals (Müller et al. 2008, Dolan et al. 2002, Gregory et al. in press). Reduced blood flow in the temporal cortex has also been correlated with psychopathy (Soderstrom et al. 2002). Reduced activity has been observed in the anterior temporal cortex when distinguishing between moral and nonmoral violations

(Harenski et al. 2010) and in the medial temporal cortex when viewing emotional pictures (Müller et al. 2003).

Orbitofrontal/ventromedial prefrontal cortex.
The frontal lobe was one of the first brain regions to be identified in early studies of antisocial and aggressive individuals (Goyer et al. 1994, Raine, Buchsbaum, et al. 1994, Raine, Buchsbaum, and Lacasse 1997, Raine et al. 1998). Similar findings have been observed in psychopathic individuals. In the prefrontal cortex, the volume of gray matter has been found to be reduced by 22.3 percent in psychopathic individuals with prior convictions (Yang et al. 2005), and the gray matter is also thinner (Yang, Raine, Colletti, et al. 2009). Reduced gray matter volume in the prefrontal cortex has also been observed in forensic psychiatric patients with high psychopathy scores (Müller et al. 2008).

More recent studies have begun to narrow down the specific subregions of the frontal lobe that appear to be associated with psychopathy. Consistent with research from psychophysiology and neuropsychology studies, the strongest findings appear to be in the orbitofrontal/ventromedial regions of the prefrontal cortex. As previously discussed, this region is involved in several processes that are important to social behavior and may lead to psychopathic traits when disrupted. The orbitofrontal region is important in understanding the emotional states of others (Shamay-Tsoory et al. 2005) and in regulating one's own emotions (Ochsner et al. 2005). It is involved in processing reward and punishment information (Rolls 2000) and inhibiting responses (Vollm et al. 2006, Aron, Robbins, and Poldrack 2004). Unsurprisingly, the orbitofrontal cortex, along with the medial PFC, is also important in moral decision making. The orbitofrontal cortex and medial PFC have been implicated in moral tasks including viewing pictures depicting moral violations (Harenski and Hamann 2006, Moll et al. 2002), interpreting morally disgusting statements (Moll et al. 2005), making judgments about auditory moral sentences (Moll, Eslinger, and de Oliveira-Souza 2001), making moral decisions versus semantic decisions (Heekeren et al. 2003), passing judgment on moral actions (Borg et al. 2006), expressing sensitivity to moral issues (Robertson et al. 2007), interpreting difficult versus easy moral dilemmas, interpreting personal versus impersonal moral dilemmas, and making utilitarian moral decisions (e.g., sacrificing life for the greater good) versus "nonutilitarian" decisions (e.g., prohibiting a loss of life even though more lives could be saved) (Greene et al. 2004). It has been suggested that dysfunction in the orbitofrontal region results in poor response inhibition (Aron, Robbins, and Poldrack 2004) and poor decision making (Bechara 2004). This also applies to the moral domain, as patients with damage to the orbitofrontal cortex have altered patterns of moral decision making (Koenigs et al. 2007, Ciaramelli et al. 2007). In moral decision making, the orbitofrontal cortex may be important in integrating moral knowledge with emotional cues, understanding the emotional states of others, and inhibiting antisocial impulses. It has been hypothesized that the medial prefrontal cortex is important in moral judgment because it may be involved in processing the emotional and social component of moral stimuli and assessing the perspectives of the self and others (Ochsner et al. 2005).

VBM studies have found gray matter reductions in the orbitofrontal cortex in psychopathic individuals (de Oliveira-Souza et al. 2008, Yang, Raine, Colletti, et al. 2009, Tiihonen et al. 2008). One study found that the reduced thickness of the orbitofrontal cortex was associated with increased response perseveration in psychopathic individuals, confirming that the reductions in this region contribute to the neuropsychological findings in psychopathy (Yang et al. 2011). Given the multiple functions that the orbitofrontal cortex is involved in, as discussed above, reductions in this region likely contribute to a number of aspects of psychopathy in addition to response perseveration.

Reduced functioning of the orbitofrontal cortex has also been observed in functional imaging studies during both cognitive and emotional tasks. For example, in a semantic task using fMRI, Kiehl et al. (2004) found that compared to controls, psychopaths fail to show the appropriate neural differentiation between abstract and concrete stimuli in the left ventrolateral prefrontal cortex. In another study using SPECT, Soderstrom et al. (2002) found significant negative correlations between psychopathy scores (particularly the interpersonal factor) and frontotemporal perfusion. Functional brain imaging studies have also found that psychopathy is associated with reduced activity in the orbitofrontal cortex during fear conditioning (Birbaumer et al. 2005) and during a socially interactive game (Rilling et al. 2007). In addition, by using affective pictures as stimuli, a growing number of fMRI studies have reported reduced emotion-related activation in the orbitofrontal cortex and ventrolateral prefrontal cortex psychopaths (Gordon, Baird, and End 2004, Kiehl et al. 2001, Müller et al. 2003, Schneider et al. 2000, Viet et al. 2002). Reduced activity in the ventromedial prefrontal cortex has also been observed in criminal psychopaths when evaluating pictures of moral violations (Harenski et al. 2010). Overall, a recent meta-analysis of 43 structural and functional imaging studies of antisocial, violent, and psychopathic individuals revealed a significant association with structural and functional reductions in the right orbitofrontal cortex (Yang and Raine 2009).

Connectivity.
A couple of studies have examined the connectivity between the amygdala and orbitofrontal cortex. As discussed in Chapter 3, reduced connections between these regions may mean that (1) emotion-related information from the amygdala that signals cues of threat, risk, or harm to others may not be able to reach cortical areas in order to inform decision making, resulting in the callousness, lack of empathy, risk taking, and instrumental aggression observed in psychopathy, and (2) cortical regions may be less able to send inhibitory signals to subcortical regions, resulting in deficits in emotion regulation and inhibition.

Using DTI, Craig et al. (2009) found reduced microstructural integrity of the uncinate fasciculus, a major fiber tract connecting the amygdala and the orbitofrontal cortex, in adult psychopaths with criminal convictions compared to healthy controls. This study provided initial evidence that communication between these regions may be reduced because of disturbances in the white matter tract. In youth with callous-unemotional traits, Marsh et al. (2008) observed reduced functional connectivity between the amygdala and ventromedial prefrontal cortex when viewing fearful facial expressions; the severity of callous-unemotional symptoms was found to be negatively correlated with the degree of functional connectivity between these regions.

2. Regions of the "moral neural circuit" have also been implicated.

Although the amygdala and orbitofrontal cortex are the regions most consistently implicated in the development of psychopathy, research in psychopathic individuals demonstrates differential functioning in other regions as well; several of these regions have been found to be important in moral decision making, suggesting that psychopathic behavior may result from disruptions to the neural network underlying moral judgment.

Moral neural network.
In addition to the amygdala and orbitofrontal cortex, regions such as the angular gyrus (posterior superior temporal gyrus), posterior cingulate, and medial prefrontal cortex have also been associated with psychopathy. Reduced gray matter volume (Müller et al. 2008) and concentration (de Oliveira-Souza et al. 2008) in the angular gyrus (posterior superior temporal gyrus) have been observed in structural imaging studies using VBM. Reduced functioning in the angular gyrus has been observed in psychopathic individuals during a semantic processing task (Kiehl et al. 2004) and in individuals scoring high on the interpersonal aspects of psychopathy during moral decision making (Glenn, Raine, and Schug 2009).

The angular gyrus is implicated in the experience of guilt and embarrassment (Takahashi et al. 2004), which are emotions that motivate individuals to desist from future antisocial behaviors. It has also been found to be involved in reasoning about social contracts (Fiddick, Spampinato, and Grafman 2005) and is thought to be important in complex social cognition and linking emotional experiences to moral appraisals (Moll et al. 2002).

In the posterior cingulate, cortical thinning has been observed in psychopathic individuals (Yang, Raine, Colletti, et al. 2009). Reduced functioning in this region has been observed in psychopaths during an affective memory task (Kiehl et al. 2001) and during fear conditioning (Birbaumer et al. 2005). Reduced activity has also been observed in individuals scoring high on the interpersonal aspects of psychopathy during moral decision making (Glenn, Raine, and Schug 2009). The posterior cingulate is involved in the recall of emotional memories (Maratos et al. 2001), the experience of emotion (Mayberg et al. 1999), self-referencing (Ochsner et al. 2005), and reflecting on one's duties and obligations (Johnson et al. 2006). The posterior cingulate is the region mentioned in Chapter 1 in which one study found that nearly half of the genetic influences between gray matter concentration and psychopathic traits overlapped, suggesting that a subset of genes may confer risk for psychopathic traits via their effects on gray matter concentrations in this region (Rijsdijsk et al. 2010).

In the medial prefrontal cortex, reduced gray matter volume has been observed in violent offenders with psychopathic traits compared to violent offenders without psychopathic traits and nonoffenders (Gregory et al. in press). This region, along with the posterior cingulate and angular gyrus, is involved in aspects of social cognition that are important to moral decision making and has been found to be active in studies of moral judgment (Greene et al. 2001, Greene et al. 2004). Activity in the posterior cingulate and angular gyrus, in addition to the orbitofrontal cortex and the amygdala, has been found to be reduced in individuals scoring higher on the interpersonal aspects of psychopathy during moral decision making (Glenn, Raine, and Schug 2009). The interpersonal features involve manipulativeness, conning, superficial charm, and deceitfulness. Reduced functioning in these regions may indicate dysfunction of the complex social processes listed above (e.g., self-referential thinking, emotional perspective taking, recalling emotional experiences to guide behavior, and integrating emotion into social cognition), which are important for interpersonal interactions central to behaving morally. Reduced functioning in these regions may suggest a failure to consider how one's actions affect others, a failure to consider the emotional perspective of the harmed other, or a failure to integrate emotion into decision-making processes.

Anterior cingulate.
The anterior cingulate cortex is a brain region that has been implicated in a many aspects of emotion and cognition. Its dorsal subdivision is involved in processes such as effortful control, self-regulation, and signaling conflict or error, while its ventral subdivision is involved in affective processing, including empathy-related functions (Bush, Luu, and Posner 2000, Shirtcliff et al. 2009). Functional imaging studies have revealed reduced activity in the anterior cingulate region in psychopathic individuals (Kiehl et al. 2001, Müller et al. 2003, Birbaumer et al. 2005). However, a recent structural imaging study did not find volumetric differences in the anterior cingulate of psychopathic individuals

(Glenn, Yang, et al. 2010). The anterior cingulate serves as a relay station of information and is densely interconnected to regions such as the amygdala and orbitofrontal cortex, both of which are consistently implicated in psychopathy. Therefore, it is unclear whether functional imaging findings reflect a deficit within the anterior cingulate itself or whether they reflect reduced input from regions such as the amygdala and orbitofrontal cortex. Alternatively, the functioning of the anterior cingulate may in fact be reduced, but the volume of the structure may not be different. For example, there may be altered connections between the neurons within the anterior cingulate, but not necessarily fewer neurons.

Hippocampus.
The hippocampus is a region that is important in the retrieval of emotional memories and is involved in fear conditioning (Fanselow 2000, LeDoux 1998). Several studies have observed morphometric differences in the hippocampus of psychopathic individuals. Antisocial alcoholics with high psychopathy scores demonstrate reduced volume in the posterior section of the hippocampus (Laakso et al. 2001). Unsuccessful psychopaths (with criminal convictions) have an exaggerated anterior hippocampal volume asymmetry (right > left) relative to both successful psychopaths (without criminal convictions) and controls (Raine et al. 2004). Boccardi et al. (2010) found a depression in the C4 neurons of the hippocampus, which are thought to be responsible for visceral sensory and autonomic responses, and in the CA3 region, which is involved in the processing of emotional and visceral input and contextual fear conditioning. Reduced functioning has been observed in criminal psychopaths during emotional processing (Kiehl et al. 2001). Differences in the hippocampus may disrupt learning in social contexts and therefore reduce sensitivity to environmental cues of future punishment.

Dorsolateral prefrontal cortex.
Several studies have identified the dorsolateral prefrontal cortex as a region that may be altered in psychopathy. The dorsolateral prefrontal cortex is a region that is involved in processes such as planning and organization (Smith and Jonides 1999), attentional set shifting and cognitive flexibility (Dias, Robbins, and Roberts 1996), and cognitive

reappraisal of emotional experience (Ochsner et al. 2002); it is also involved in higher cognition. Thus, dysfunction in the dorsolateral prefrontal cortex may impair planning and other executive functions that may predispose to outcomes such as occupational failure, repetition of antisocial behaviors despite negative consequences, and a failure to consider alternative strategies to resolve conflict.

Two VBM studies have found reductions in the gray matter of the dorsolateral prefrontal cortex (Yang, Raine, Colletti, et al. 2009, Müller et al. 2008). However, several functional imaging studies of psychopathy have observed *increased* activation in this region during tasks that involve emotional processing (Glenn, Raine, Schug, et al. 2009, Kiehl et al. 2001, Gordon, Baird, and End 2004, Rilling et al. 2007). Since the dorsolateral prefrontal cortex is involved in higher cognition, it has been suggested that some psychopaths may use more cognitive resources to process affective information than do nonpsychopaths (Kiehl et al. 2001).

Striatum.
The striatum has been linked to traits such as reward seeking and impulsivity; it is also associated with reward sensitivity, which facilitates stimulation-seeking behavior, persistence in repeating actions related to rewards, and enhanced learning from rewarding signals (Cohen et al. 2009, O'Doherty 2004). One study found a 9.6 percent increase in the volume of the striatum of psychopathic individuals (Glenn, Raine, et al. 2010). Similarly, Buckholtz et al. (2010) found that the impulsive-antisocial traits of psychopathy were associated with dopamine release in the striatum and increased activity in the striatum in anticipation of reward. These findings suggest that hyperactivity of the striatum may contribute to features of psychopathy such as reward seeking and may also impair learning. However, one study has observed reduced functioning in this region during emotional processing (Kiehl et al. 2001).

Summary.
In sum, widespread regions have been implicated in psychopathy. In some cases it may be difficult to determine whether differences actually exist in a region, or whether reduced functioning is a result of reduced functioning in regions such as the amygdala and orbitofrontal cortex,

which are connected to it. It has also been suggested that some of the variability in brain imaging findings is attributable to the different types of samples that have been examined (e.g., undergraduates, prisoners, community members) and the variety of methodologies that have been used (Koenigs et al. 2011); some of the functional imaging findings may also be context-dependent, and not necessarily indicative of abnormal functioning in all circumstances (Newman et al. 2010).

3. The instrumental aggression in psychopathy is associated with unique neurobiological correlates.

As mentioned in the introduction, one feature that distinguishes psychopathy from other disorders is that it is associated with elevated levels of instrumental aggression, in addition to elevated levels of reactive aggression. The neural bases of reactive and instrumental aggression are thought to differ. Reactive aggression activates the basic threat system, which includes the amygdala and other regions such as the hypothalamus and periaqueductal gray. Individuals with reactive aggression have exaggerated responses in this system (e.g., Lee, Chan, and Raine 2008, Coccaro et al. 2007, Herpertz, Dietrich, and Wenning 2001). In addition, frontal regions such as the medial, orbital, and inferior frontal cortices that are thought to regulate the functioning of this system tend to be reduced, meaning that the functioning of the threat response system is unregulated.

In contrast, psychopathic individuals, who demonstrate increased instrumental aggression, exhibit reduced responding in the amygdala (Blair 2010b). This is an important difference to note because it suggests that individuals with psychopathic traits are, at least in part, qualitatively different from other aggressive individuals. Although there are commonalities in some of the brain imaging findings between psychopathic individuals and other aggressive individuals, such as reductions in the prefrontal cortex, the fact that amygdala functioning occurs in opposite directions suggests that the neurobiological causes of aggressive behavior are different for psychopathic individuals and other individuals demonstrating aggression. Whereas other individuals are aggressive due to hyperactive threat response systems, psychopathic individuals may be aggressive due to a lack of input from the amygdala, which results in a lack of fearfulness and empathy for others. The implications of this are that the development of psychopathy likely stems from a somewhat different set of genetic and environmental risk factors, and that the potential treatment of psychopathy is likely to be different from that of aggressive individuals.

>   4. Brain imaging studies suggest that brain differences are neurodevelopmental in nature.

Brain imaging studies have given some indication that there may be neurodevelopmental abnormalities associated with psychopathy. Raine et al. (2010) reported that individuals with cavum septum pellucidum, a marker for fetal neural maldevelopment, exhibited higher levels of psychopathy than did those without cavum septum pellucidum. The septum pellucidum is one component of the septum and consists of a deep, midline limbic structure made up of two translucent leaves of glia separating the lateral ventricles, forming part of the septo-hippocampal system. During gestation, a space forms between the two laminae—the cavum septum pellucidum—and then is gradually fused back together upon development of the alvei of the hippocampus, amygdala, septal nuclei, fornix, corpus callosum, and other midline structures. Lack of such limbic development interrupts the closure of the cavum, resulting in the preservation of the cavum septum pellucidum into adulthood. The finding of higher levels of psychopathy and antisocial personality in individuals with cavum septum pellucidum in adulthood provides initial evidence for a neurodevelopmental abnormality in antisocial individuals.

Another finding that suggests that neurodevelopmental abnormalities may exist is that of increased white matter volume and length, but reduced thickness, in the corpus callosum of psychopathic individuals (Raine et al. 2003). The corpus callosum is a white matter tract that connects the two hemispheres of the brain. This finding suggests that there may be a disturbance in the normal neurodevelopmental process of hemispheric specialization. The fact that morphological changes to the corpus callosum are complex and involve both thinning and lengthening, as well as an increase in white matter volume, tends to dictate against simple, nondevelopmental processes such as discrete trauma or degenerative disease processes. These alterations in psychopathic individuals may instead reflect atypical neurodevelopmental processes involving a disruption in early axonal pruning or increased white matter myelination. Future studies examining markers for neurodevelopmental abnormalities will help to improve our understanding of how the differences in brain structure and functioning mentioned in the previous sections may arise.

> 5. Studies of youth with callous-unemotional traits tend to implicate similar brain regions, but findings are not always in the same direction.

Although several brain imaging studies have examined youth with conduct disorder, only a few have examined youth with callous-unemotional traits. In general, these studies identify similar brain regions to adult studies—regions of the temporal cortex, including the amygdala, and regions of the prefrontal cortex, including the orbitofrontal/ventromedial prefrontal cortex. Using fMRI, Finger et al. (2008) found that children and adolescents with callous-unemotional traits and disruptive behavior disorders demonstrated different patterns of functioning in the ventromedial prefrontal cortex compared to healthy controls during a reversal learning task. In the same sample, Marsh et al. (2008) reported reduced amygdala responding to fearful expressions in youth with callous-unemotional traits compared to healthy controls. As mentioned above, these children also demonstrated reduced connectivity between the amygdala and ventromedial prefrontal cortex. Jones et al. (2009) also found that boys with conduct problems and callous-unemotional traits demonstrated reduced activity in the amygdala when viewing fearful faces compared to control participants.

The brain undergoes substantial structural development throughout childhood and adolescence, making it difficult to directly compare brain imaging findings from children with psychopathic traits to those of adults. Studies of the brain structure of youth with callous-unemotional traits have produced different results from studies of adults. In a VBM study, De Brito et al. (2009) found that youth with callous-unemotional traits demonstrated *increased* gray matter concentration in the medial orbitofrontal cortex and the anterior cingulate. Gray matter volume and concentration was also increased in the temporal lobes and in the superior temporal gyrus (angular gyrus), a region identified as being reduced in three VBM studies of adult psychopathic individuals. The authors suggest that these findings may represent a delay in cortical maturation in these regions. These youth also demonstrated reduced white matter concentration in the superior frontal lobe, anterior cingulate, right superior temporal gyrus, and precuneus. Again, this may reflect delayed maturation, as white matter in the brain increases from childhood to adulthood. However, *increased* white matter concentration was observed in one region, the dorsolateral prefrontal cortex, suggesting possible advanced development. Interestingly, this is the region discussed above in which some studies of adult psychopathy have found increased functioning. This suggests that the dorsolateral prefrontal cortex is a region that may develop more quickly in psychopathic youth, and may be a region that compensates for deficits in other brain regions.

Thus, whereas functional imaging studies of youth with callous-unemotional traits have produced relatively similar findings to adult samples, structural imaging studies have observed different findings, which are possibly indicative of delayed maturation of the brain regions that are found to function differently in psychopathic adults. Longitudinal studies examining the brain at multiple time points will help to clarify how the patterns of functioning observed in adults develop.

Conclusions

As brain imaging methods advance, researchers will be able to examine the structure and function of the brain of psychopathic adults and youth with more precision. Despite an exponential increase in brain imaging research on psychopathy implicating multiple brain systems, neuroscience research on this important social and clinical construct is far from complete. With the continual development of imaging techniques, as well as unique paradigms from social neuroscience, our understanding of the neurobiological bases of psychopathy will become more sophisticated. Many discrepancies remain in the literature that will need to be clarified in future studies. Different inventories for assessing psychopathy, different cutoff scores, and different populations for recruiting participants all likely contribute to the variability in findings (Patrick, Venables, and Skeem 2012).

A future direction that holds promise is the delineation of the specific genes that give rise to the brain abnormalities found in psychopathic individuals. For example, a common polymorphism in the MAOA gene has been implicated in antisocial behavior (Caspi et al. 2002); in males this same polymorphism is associated with an 8 percent reduction in the volume of the amygdala, anterior cingulate, and orbitofrontal cortex (Meyer-Lindenberg et al. 2006), which are regions implicated in psychopathy.

6

Biosocial and Environmental Influences

In the preceding chapters, we reviewed evidence of the biological markers that have been associated with psychopathy. As discussed in Chapter 2, behavioral genetics studies estimate that 40 to 60 percent of the variance in psychopathy is genetic in origin. This suggests that the "nurture" part of the picture is just as important as "nature." Environmental factors *do* significantly contribute to the development of psychopathy. Compared to research on the environmental factors that contribute to crime in general, very little research has examined these factors in relation to psychopathy. However, emerging research suggests that environmental factors such as parenting, abuse, poverty, head injury, birth complications, nutrition, toxins, and a variety of other factors both within and outside the home may be associated with psychopathy. Thus, there are numerous areas that could be targeted with prevention and intervention efforts.

The idea that genes still contribute to approximately half of the risk for psychopathy may at first seem discouraging, as it suggests that we may be able to solve only part of the problem. However, as discussed in

Chapter 2, environmental factors have the ability to change gene transcription, or the way in which a gene's DNA sequence produces proteins. This may, in turn, alter neurochemical signaling mechanisms and/or the way that the brain develops. Environmental factors can also alter levels of neurochemicals such as hormones. For example, trauma or chronic stress can alter cortisol levels and thus change the way the brain responds to stress in the future. Finally, environmental influences in the womb or in early childhood can alter the way that the brain develops, leading to differences in structure and functioning. Thus, the environment can influence how an individual's biological systems develop, and can continue to produce changes in structure and functioning of these systems throughout the life span.

As discussed in Chapter 1, although we tend to categorize hormones, neurotransmitters, and brain structure/functioning as "biological" risks, in reality these abnormalities may have either environmental or genetic origins. For example, reduced cortisol levels could result from a particular gene or set of genes, and may be present regardless of the environment in which the individual develops. Alternatively, an individual may not carry *any* genes that predispose for reduced cortisol levels, but may develop reduced levels due to an environmental influence such as exposure to toxins in utero or trauma in early childhood. In most cases, cortisol levels likely reflect an *interaction* between genetic and environmental factors, or what we refer to as a biosocial interaction. In this case, the individual may carry some risk genes, but these may confer little risk unless triggered or "switched on" by an environmental influence. Thus, it is important to keep in mind that the "biological" findings reviewed in the preceding chapters could result from genes, environmental factors, or a combination of both. For the most part, studies have not yet investigated the source of specific biological differences in psychopathy. If we want to gain a complete understanding of psychopathy, we must understand how environmental factors interact with biological factors.

Challenges in Studying Environmental Factors

One major challenge in studying environmental factors is that it is often difficult to determine which factors actually play a causal role in the development of psychopathy (or any disorder) and which factors may only be correlated. This is because many environmental factors tend to be related to each other. For example, poor parental supervision is a potential environmental risk factor, but poor parental supervision may also be related to low family income, poor housing, a more antisocial or drug-abusing parent, and large family size, each of which may also be a risk factor. Thus, it is difficult to determine what the key underlying factor is. Oftentimes there may be sequential effects of risk factors, such that one risk factor such as socioeconomic status is associated with antisocial behavior because of its influence on family factors such as parental supervision.

In addition, many potential environmental factors may be difficult to distinguish from genetic factors. For example, having an antisocial parent has been found to be a significant predictor of psychopathy. This may be due to the nature of the environment (e.g., the child may learn antisocial behaviors from the parent, may receive less supervision from an antisocial parent, and may grow up with less stability and resources) or to the fact that several of the genetic risk factors for antisocial behavior have likely been passed on from parent to child. It is very difficult to disentangle these elements when examining factors of the family environment. The behavioral genetics studies discussed in Chapter 2 can give us an estimate of the overall contributions of genes versus environmental factors, but they do not provide information about specific environmental factors.

It is important to keep in mind that the estimates of the contribution of environmental factors generated by behavioral genetics studies represent averages, meaning that in some individuals the contribution of biological factors may be stronger, and in other individuals the contribution of environmental factors may be stronger. There also may be sex differences. For example, Fontaine et al. (2010) found that in youth with stable, high levels of callous-unemotional traits, boys demonstrated stronger genetic influences, whereas girls demonstrated stronger shared environmental influences.

Because of the above issues, most studies are not able to distinguish between related environmental factors, or between genetic and environmental factors, so we cannot draw firm conclusions about which factors are actually causal. In addition, the mechanisms by which environmental factors influence the brain are largely unknown.

Environmental Factors

For years, researchers in the field of criminology have conducted extensive research on social factors associated with crime in general. However, surprisingly little research on psychopathy has focused on environmental factors. One of the most comprehensive studies to date examining the influence of family-related environmental factors on psychopathic traits is the Cambridge Study in Delinquent Development. This is a 40-year prospective longitudinal survey of the development of antisocial behavior. The researchers followed 411 boys from age 8 to age 48 (Farrington et al. 2006). Various individual, family, and socioeconomic risk factors were measured at ages 8 to 10. At age 48, 304 men completed the Psychopathy Checklist: Screening Version (PCL:SV), along with other measures. Scores on the PCL:SV ranged from 0 to 17; the researchers determined that there were qualitative differences in the individuals scoring 10 or higher on the measure and the remainder of the sample—nearly half of the men scoring 10 or more were chronic offenders, compared with 1 percent of the remainder. Table 6.1 shows the odds ratios that individuals scoring 10 or more had a particular risk factor. Generally, an odds ratio of 2.0 or greater indicates a strong relationship.

As shown in the table, some risk factors were associated more strongly with one factor of psychopathy than the other, meaning that some factors may confer risk for antisocial behavior more generally, rather than for the core features of psychopathy. Data from the Cambridge Study are particularly valuable because they are not from retrospective reports, which can introduce some bias.

Parenting and Family Factors

Many are curious to know how important parenting is in the development of psychopathy. Numerous studies of antisocial behavior and crime have identified parenting practices such as harsh or erratic discipline, poor parental supervision, and distant, cold, and rejecting parenting styles as risk factors for antisocial behavior. In the Cambridge Study, poor parental supervision in youth significantly predicted psychopathy scores in adulthood, but this was true only for the Lifestyle-Antisocial

Table 6.1. Psychosocial Predictors of Psychopathic Traits at Age 48

Risk factor at ages 8–11	% PCL: SV 10+		OR	Affective OR	Antisocial OR
	No	Yes			
Poor supervision	8	24	3.6*	1.9	3.9*
Harsh discipline	8	19	2.6*	2.3*	2.0*
Father uninvolved	4	23	6.5*	4.7*	2.7*
Physical neglect	8	34	5.9*	4.8*	5.2*
Disrupted family	7	25	4.3*	1.9*	4.6*
Large family size	7	22	3.5*	3.0*	3.8*
Convicted father	6	25	5.1*	4.4*	3.8*
Convicted mother	9	30	4.5*	3.2*	4.7*
Delinquent sibling	9	28	4.0*	3.6*	4.2*
Young mother	9	19	2.4*	1.4	2.6*
Depressed mother	8	18	2.7*	2.1*	3.3*
Low social class	8	22	3.1*	2.5*	2.8*
Low family income	7	25	4.6*	3.9*	3.6*
Poor housing	7	18	3.0*	1.7	2.9*
Unpopular	7	18	2.9*	2.9*	1.5
Delinquent school	7	24	3.9*	2.9*	2.7*
Low nonverbal IQ	8	18	2.4*	2.4*	1.9
Low verbal IQ	8	19	2.3*	3.5*	1.3
Low school track	7	19	3.0*	3.0*	2.1*
High daring	7	21	3.6*	2.0*	2.6*
Lacks concentration	8	23	3.6*	2.5*	2.8*
High impulsivity	8	18	2.4*	2.7*	1.9
Dishonest	7	22	4.1*	2.0	4.4*
Troublesome	8	23	3.4*	2.0*	2.7*

Note: The figures show the percentages of those without the risk factor (No) and with the risk factor (Yes) who scored 10+ on the PCL:SV. OR, odds ratio; Affective OR, OR for Factor I; Antisocial OR, OR for Factor 2. Nonsignificant predictors: authoritarian parent, parental conflict, depressed father, low junior school attainment. *p < .05, one-tailed.

Source: Reprinted from Farrington (2006). Reprinted with permission.

features (Factor 2). Harsh and erratic parental discipline predicted both factors of psychopathy. One of the strongest predictors of the affective features of psychopathy was having an uninvolved father, although this is likely to be mediated by a number of other factors. A comparison of psychopathic and nonpsychopathic offenders in Scotland found that psychopathic prisoners were significantly more likely to report that they had experienced parental indifference or neglect, poor parental supervision, and poor parental discipline as children (Marshall and Cooke 1999). In a sample of 10-year-old boys, physical punishment and inconsistent discipline were associated with psychopathy scores. Lax supervision was also associated with the interpersonal Facet 1 (Vachon et al. 2012). Although more research needs to be conducted to determine to what degree parenting styles are related to the development of psychopathic traits, one theory is that proper socialization depends on parental rewards and punishments, and that children may become antisocial if parents do not respond consistently and contingently to their child's behavior.

However, it is difficult to establish a causal link between parenting behaviors and psychopathic traits because genetic factors may influence parenting behaviors and also the child's behavior. In addition, the child's behavior may also influence the parent's behavior. For example, a child with a difficult temperament may elicit harsher parenting behaviors. Indeed, a short-term longitudinal study of parental monitoring in adolescents found evidence of child-driven changes in parents' monitoring behaviors over time in adolescents with callous-unemotional traits (Muñoz, Pakalniskiene, and Frick 2011).

Family conflict is another factor that has been associated with psychopathy. The Cambridge Study found a significant relationship between having a disrupted family at age 8 and psychopathy scores at age 48; relationships were strongest with the Lifestyle-Antisocial Factor 2. Similarly, psychopathy scores in adolescence have been associated with family conflict during childhood (five years earlier), though not with concurrent family conflict during adolescence (Fowler, Langley, Rice, Whittinger, et al. 2009). Koivisto and Haapasalo (1996) found a significant correlation between psychopathy and family conflict, but Patrick, Zempolich, and Levenston (1997) did not. Large family size may also be related to increased family conflict. This was found to be a predictor of psychopathy scores, particularly the Lifestyle-Antisocial Factor 2, in the Cambridge Study. However, large family size and marital status were not associated with psychopathy scores in adolescents (Fowler, Langley, Rice, Whittinger, et al. 2009).

Farrington (2000) found that being separated from a parent before age 10 predicted higher Lifestyle-Antisocial Factor 2 scores in adulthood, but not Interpersonal-Affective Factor 1 scores. Two additional studies have found that nonparental living arrangements (e.g., foster care) predicted higher psychopathy scores in incarcerated adolescent offenders (Campbell, Porter, and Santor 2004) and in delinquent girls but not boys (Krischer and Sevecke 2008). Koivisto and Haapasalo (1996) found that adult offenders with higher psychopathy scores were more likely to have experienced parental absence or death.

Another hypothesis for why these types of family factors may be associated with psychopathy is that individuals may not develop proper attachment; they may not become emotionally attached to warm, loving, prosocial parents. For example, Gao, Raine, Chan, et al. (2010) found that individuals with higher psychopathy scores at age 28 reported that as children they experienced poor parental bonding (lack of maternal care and low paternal overprotection). They also found in a prospective study that children separated from their parents in the first three years of life were more likely to have a psychopathic personality in adulthood. Parental deprivation or loss of a parent may result in changes in the stress response system. Studies have found that young children who experience parental desertion or very low levels of care demonstrate abnormal cortisol levels (Tyrka et al. 2008, Kertes et al. 2008). Having a depressed mother may also impair attachment between mother and child; this was linked to psychopathic traits in the Cambridge Study.

Finally, studies have also shown that having a parent who has been convicted of a crime or having a delinquent older sibling are predictors of psychopathy. The Cambridge Study found these risk factors to be strongly related to both Factor 1 and Factor 2 scores at age 48. Similarly, Krischer and Sevecke (2008) found that parental criminal record showed the strongest relationship with psychopathy scores in delinquent boys and girls. This is likely due to a combination of genetic and environmental factors. In addition to the shared genes within a family, there may be intergenerational continuities in the exposure to multiple risk factors such as poverty, disrupted families, and living in deprived neighborhoods. Furthermore, the child may also learn anti-social behaviors from antisocial parents and older siblings. The child with an antisocial parent may also have poor parental supervision and inconsistent discipline (Farrington 2006).

Abuse and Neglect

Prospective longitudinal studies have also found evidence of a link between childhood abuse and neglect and psychopathy scores in adult-hood. In the Cambridge Study, physical neglect measured at age 8 pre-dicted high scores on both psychopathy factors. Weiler and Widom (1996) found that victims of childhood abuse and/or neglect before age 11 displayed high psychopathy scores in adulthood, despite con-trols for demographic characteristics and criminal history. Similarly, Lang, af Klinteberg, and Alm (2002) found that boys who were abused or neglected at ages 11 to 14 had higher psychopathy scores at age 36. Retrospective studies of offenders have also found correlations between early child abuse and high psychopathy scores in adulthood (Koivisto and Haapasalo 1996, Patrick, Zempolich, and Levenston 1997, Gao, Raine, Chan, et al. 2010) and adolescence (Campbell, Porter, and San-tor 2004). Krischer and Sevecke (2008) found that adolescent criminal boys who had been abused tended to have higher psychopathy scores, although this was not the case for girls.

Other studies have failed to observe relationships between early abuse and psychopathy (Marshall and Cooke 1999). One idea is that these relationships may vary depending on the subtype of psychopa-thy. Kimonis et al. (2012) found that childhood abuse was linked to the secondary (high-anxious) subtype of psychopathy, but not to the pri-mary (low-anxious) subtype. Similarly, youth with secondary psychop-athy have been found to report a greater history of traumatic experi-ences and past posttraumatic stress disorder symptoms than youth with primary psychopathy (Tatar et al. 2012). In a study of female psycho-paths, Hicks, Vaidyanathan, and Patrick (2010) found that secondary psychopathy was more likely to be associated with childhood *physi-cal* abuse, whereas primary psychopathy was more likely to be associ-ated with childhood *sexual* abuse. Interestingly, primary psychopaths exhibited fewer mental health problems as adults, suggesting that the two groups may react differently to traumatic experiences.

Finally, another study found that unsuccessful, but not successful, psychopaths were more likely to have been physically abused by a caregiver at an early age than nonpsychopathic controls. However, the differences between the two psychopathy groups were not significantly different (Gao, Raine, and Schug 2011).

There are several ways in which abuse could potentially lead to the development of psychopathy. In the most direct sense, physical assault may lead to actual damage to the brain. Particularly if the abuse occurs early in life, this may disrupt the child's ability to learn and be socialized. Physical abuse may also affect emotional reactivity. Physically abused children have been found to show exaggerated emotional reactivity and increased vigilance to threat-related cues (Dodge and Pettit 2003). Abuse may also affect the way that children process information and cope with problems. Children may become less sensitive to violence and pain, and less able to form secure attachments with others (Farrington 2006).

Socioeconomic Status

Findings regarding the relationship between socioeconomic status and psychopathy appear to be inconsistent. In the Cambridge Study, low family income, low social class, and poor housing at ages 8 to 10 were found to predict psychopathy scores at age 48, with the strongest factor being low family income. Frick et al. (2003) found socioeconomic status (SES) to be a significant predictor of the stability of psychopathic traits over a four-year period in youth. Pardini and Byrd (2012) found an association between family income and callous-unemotional traits in fourth and fifth graders. Vachon et al. (2012) also found that SES was associated with psychopathy in 10-year-old boys, but this was primarily driven by the Lifestyle-Antisocial (Factor 2) features.

Other studies have not observed significant relationships between SES and psychopathy scores in adults (Patrick, Zempolich, and Levenston 1997) and adolescents (Fowler, Langley, Rice, Whittinger, et al. 2009). Sadeh et al. (2010) found that SES was significantly related to scores on the Impulsivity subscales of a psychopathy measure (the

Antisocial Process Screening Device) in adolescents, and that it was related to the Callous-Unemotional and Narcissism subscales, but only in youth with a specific genetic polymorphism.

Head Injury, Birth Complications, Toxin Exposure, Nutrition

Other types of environmental factors may have more direct influences on the biological pathway, and may be considered biological adversity. For example, head injury specifically affects the brain. Exposure to neurotoxins such as lead can affect the development and functioning of the brain. Birth complications also represent an environmental hazard, although they also may be partly genetically determined.

Fowler, Langley, Rice, Whittinger, et al. (2009) examined pre- and perinatal factors in relation to psychopathic traits in adolescents with ADHD and found that psychopathic traits were associated with maternal smoking during pregnancy. The authors acknowledge that this association could be an artifact due to the mother's own antisocial behavior, which may be associated with smoking during pregnancy. As stated earlier, having an antisocial parent may increase the likelihood of developing psychopathic traits both because of the genetic risk factors that may be passed on, and because of the antisocial influences from parent to child. A behavioral genetics study published in 2004 examined these issues. Maughan et al. tested the possibility that maternal smoking may be primarily an index for genetic risk for antisocial behavior. They found that approximately half of the association between maternal smoking and child conduct problems was due to correlated genetic influences (Maughan et al. 2004). They also found that mothers who smoked during pregnancy differed from other mothers in a number of ways, including the fact that they were more likely to be antisocial, to have children with more antisocial partners, to bring up their children in more disadvantaged circumstances, and to have had depression. Controlling for these factors, in addition to genetic factors, the effects of maternal smoking were reduced by between 75 percent and 100 percent. Thus, it is not clear whether maternal smoking itself (as a toxin that may damage the fetus) actually predisposes for psychopathic traits.

Only one study has examined birth complications in relation to psychopathic traits specifically. Birth complications such as forceps delivery, ventouse delivery, breech birth, and emergency Caesarean section were found to be associated with the emotional dysfunction features of psychopathy (Fowler, Langley, Rice, Whittinger, et al. 2009). Psychopathic traits in adolescence were not found to be associated with birth weight or prematurity.

Biological Mechanisms

In addition to considering the psychological processes such as attachment and socialization that may be affected by environmental factors, thus conferring risk for the development of psychopathy, we can also consider the ways in which environmental factors may alter biological systems to confer risk. There are several mechanisms by which parenting and family factors may alter biological systems to lead to the development of psychopathy. Negative experiences early in life may alter the functioning of biological systems involved in regulating behavior. For example, in the animal literature, studies have shown that separating rat pups from the mother in the first three weeks of life results in fearlessness and reduced stress responsivity in adulthood and alters gene expression in the hippocampus and prefrontal cortex, two brain areas critically involved in regulation of the stress response (Weaver, Meaney, and Szyf 2006). Del Giudice, Ellis, and Shirtcliff (2011) proposed a model outlining the ways in which the stress response may be regulated according to different environmental conditions.

Environmental factors may also affect the development of other brain regions. For example, using diffusion tensor imaging to examine white matter tracts, researchers have found that adolescents who suffered birth complications and low birth weights have structural differences in the white matter of the corpus callosum (Constable et al. 2008, Skranes et al. 2007), one of the regions that is structurally different in psychopathic individuals (Raine et al. 2003). Similarly, evidence suggests that environmental factors from the prenatal period to adolescence may affect the striatum, a brain region important in reward processing and learning, which is associated with traits such as impulsivity, reward seeking, and poor decision making (discussed in Chapter 6; Glenn and Yang 2012). Qiu et al. (2012) examined the shape and volume of the striatum in a sample of healthy 6-year-old boys born at term and within the normal range for birth weight. They found that boys with lower birth weight and shorter gestation had smaller volumes and altered shape of the striatum, suggesting that subtle variations in fetal development may alter the structural development of this region.

Animal studies have demonstrated the effects of early environmental enrichment and stress on the development of the striatum. One study examined the effects of tactile stimulation as a form of environmental enrichment. In male rats, tactile stimulation early in life (postnatal to weaning) resulted in enlargement of the striatum in adulthood and decreased novelty-seeking behavior (Muhammad et al. 2011). It was suggested that the reduced novelty seeking observed in rats receiving tactile stimulation could serve as a protective factor against drug abuse propensity. In support of this hypothesis, male rats that received tactile stimulation postnatally were found to be less behaviorally sensitive to amphetamine exposure in adulthood. In addition, they did not show the same postamphetamine enlargements in the striatum as rats that did not receive tactile stimulation. This suggests that environmental enrichment may alter the structural organization of the striatum in a way that allows it to be buffered against drug-induced structural changes. In other words, the early environment may affect the development of the striatum in a way that alters future susceptibility to drug addiction and possibly impulsive, antisocial behavior.

Regarding early life stress, animal studies have also shown that rat pups that were isolated from the mother for one hour per day during the first week of life showed much greater activity in the striatum after an amphetamine challenge than those who were not isolated (Kehoe et al. 1996). This suggests that early life stress may be a risk factor for drug addiction and antisocial behavior because it sensitizes the striatum. Chronic lead exposure postweaning in rats has also been found to affect neurotransmitters in the striatum (Pokora, Richfield, and CorySlechta 1996).

During adolescence, exposure to social stress has been found to cause changes in the striatum. Rats exposed to repeated social defeat during adolescence demonstrated altered neurotransmitters in the striatum in response to amphetamine exposure in adulthood. Rats exposed to the social stress also exhibited increased seeking of amphetamine in adulthood. These effects were not observed in rats that received nonsocial (foot-shock) stress in adolescence, suggesting that it is specifically social stress during adolescence that may predispose for drug-related behaviors later in life (Burke, Watt, and Forster 2011). These studies suggest that a number of environmental factors throughout development may contribute to abnormalities in the brain. The striatum is just one example of a brain region that is affected by environmental influences.

Biosocial Interactions

As evidenced thus far in this book, individual differences in psychopathic traits are linked to a large number of factors—for example, to differences in the coding of the serotonin transporter gene (Glenn 2011), cortisol levels (Cima, Smeets, and Jelicic 2008), amygdala functioning (Birbaumer et al. 2005), or environmental factors such as parental care (Farrington et al. 2006), abuse and neglect (Lang, af Klinteberg, and Alm 2002), and birth complications (Fowler, Langley, Rice, Whittinger, et al. 2009). Individual differences in psychopathic traits over time are likely due to interactions between biological and environmental factors.

We know very little about the interactions between environmental factors and the biological factors that predispose to antisocial behavior. In fact, across the literature, it is noticeable that criminology researchers rarely employ methods to measure the biological variables in their antisocial samples, while biological researchers often use social factors as covariates (factors to hold constant) instead of examining how social factors may interact with biological factors. However, both types of factors contribute to the development of psychopathy. A multidisciplinary approach that takes both environmental and biological factors into account may be critically important in furthering our understanding of the underlying mechanisms of the disorder. By neglecting to examine biosocial interactions, studies may underestimate the influence of either biological or social markers of psychopathy.

Many challenges make the quest to examine the interaction between biological and social factors extremely difficult. As mentioned early in the chapter, one of the main challenges is that biological risk factors tend to correlate significantly with social factors; this reduces the statistical power to detect interaction effects, meaning that researchers may not see an effect even if one is present. However, the innovative behavioral genetics techniques discussed in Chapter 2 involving twin and adoption samples are able to disentangle the proportion of the variance in psychopathy that can be attributed to genetic versus environmental factors. Findings from these studies suggest that biosocial interactions may indeed contribute to the development of psychopathy.

There are two general theories regarding the way that the social environment may interact with genetic and biological risk factors. One theory suggests that antisocial behavior may be exponentially increased when social and biological risk factors combine. This is because adverse social environments exacerbate genetic and biological risks. Studies from several countries have shown that birth complications (including anoxia, known to particularly damage the hippocampus) interact with negative home environments (e.g., early maternal rejection of the child) in predisposing to adult violent offending (Raine, Brennan, and Mednick 1994). In other words, individuals with biological risk factors such as birth complications may be at lower risk for developing antisocial behavior if they are protected by a good home environment, but in stressful or challenging environments, the effects of these biological risk factors may be more pronounced. Other evidence for this hypothesis comes from several studies indicating that a genetic polymorphism of the MAOA gene interacts with early child abuse in predisposing to adult antisocial behavior (Caspi et al. 2002). In nonabusive environments, this polymorphism does not appear to confer risk for antisocial behavior.

Another hypothesis is the social push perspective (Raine 2002) which argues that the association between antisocial behavior and biological risk factors will be *weaker*, rather than stronger, in adverse home environments because social risk factors for crime camouflage the biological contributions. For example, in adverse social environments, individuals may develop antisocial behavior regardless of whether they have genetic or biological risk factors. However, if an individual from a benign home environment is antisocial, then biological risk factors are more likely to play a role.

Only a few studies have examined biosocial interactions in relation to psychopathic traits. A study from our laboratory found that poor performance on the Iowa Gambling Task, which is associated with functioning in the ventromedial/orbitofrontal cortex, predicted psychopathic tendencies only in adolescents from benign home environments, but not in those from low socioeconomic backgrounds (Gao et al. 2009). These findings are consistent with the "social push" hypothesis, which states that in environments that lack social risk factors, biological factors are more likely to explain antisocial behavior.

Another study may also provide evidence of the "social push" hypothesis. Beaver, DeLisi, and Vaughn (2010) found an interaction between maternal smoking and family structure in predicting psychopathic traits. They found that maternal smoking was associated with higher psychopathy scores at age 15 in adolescents who live in a two-parent household, but not in those who live in single-parent homes. In other words, in a presumably more stable and benign (two-parent) home environment, maternal smoking, a factor that may affect biological development, is associated with psychopathic traits. The authors speculate that single-parent households may be proxy indicators for other environmental and genetic risk factors, and that exposure to maternal smoke may be trumped by these other, more potent risk factors. However, in two-parent households, where genetic and environmental risk factors may not be as saturated, maternal smoking may emerge as one of the more powerful predictors of psychopathy.

Some studies demonstrating biosocial interactions suggest that environmental factors may act as protective factors against the development of psychopathic traits. For example, a molecular genetics study by Sadeh et al. (2010) found that low SES was associated with callous-unemotional and narcissism traits of psychopathy only in youth with two long alleles of the serotonin transporter gene. This gene variant, discussed in Chapter 2, is hypothesized to confer risk for psychopathic traits (Glenn 2011). Findings from the study by Sadeh et al. (2010) suggest that higher SES may be one factor that protects individuals with this genetic polymorphism from developing psychopathic traits.

Epigenetics

In addition to behavioral genetics studies, which assess the relative contribution of genetic versus environmental factors, and molecular genetics studies, which compare differences between individuals with different genetic polymorphisms, there is a third approach to understanding gene-environment interactions—epigenetic studies. Epigenetic studies attempt to understand the physiological mechanisms that can change the way that genes are expressed. Numerous studies have shown that developmental, physiological, and environmental signals lead to changes in gene expression. In order to be able to explain and prevent psychopathy, it will be important to determine at what point specific environmental factors may alter gene expression, and the mechanisms by which this occurs.

For example, the serotonin transporter gene is hypothesized to be linked to psychopathy, in part, because it is associated with reduced biological responsivity to stress and threat. An interaction between the serotonin transporter polymorphism and aversive environmental factors may have the most impact during early childhood, when individuals are learning to consider the emotions of others and learn from punishment. Understanding when and how aversive environmental factors interact with biological factors can be useful in the development of preventive interventions. For example, interventions that are administered after an environmental factor has already altered gene expression may be less effective than interventions designed to eliminate or reduce the impact of environmental factors before they have a significant effect on biology.

Knowledge of gene-environment interactions may also help to design preventions that are more targeted toward individuals at risk. For example, consider the interaction reported by Sadeh et al. (2010), discussed above, between the serotonin transporter gene and SES. One prevention strategy may be to provide interventions for youth with long alleles of the serotonin transporter genes who are born into families with low SES.

Studies examining the effects of environmental factors on brain functioning suggest that many changes to the brain take place because of the environmental influence on gene expression. For example, in the study by Weaver, Meaney, and Szyf (2006), discussed above, maternal licking of rat pups had long-term effects on brain functioning because it regulated the expression of genes that influence the development of the stress response system. Early aversive environments may negatively affect gene expression in a way that disturbs brain development and thus predisposes to psychopathic traits.

Tremblay (2008) suggests that in order to actually test causal mechanisms that contribute to aggression, we need the type of true experiments that are regularly done with rats and monkeys. Since we cannot experimentally introduce stressors to the environment, the alternative is to manipulate the environment by providing an intervention. He states, "[E]xperimental preventive interventions can kill two birds with one stone: identify basic mechanisms leading to [aggression] and identify effective preventive interventions" (p. 2618). Randomized controlled trials, which monitor effects of the intervention on gene expression, brain functioning, and behavior, will be extremely useful in improving our understanding of how environmental factors contribute to the development of psychopathy.

Conclusions

A common misunderstanding is that biological factors are determined by genetics alone. Many do not consider the possibility that many *biological* correlates of psychopathy or criminal behavior can be the result of environmental influences. Even Cleckley argued, "Such biologic deficiencies are not necessarily hereditary" (Cleckley 1976, p. 116). By influencing gene expression, the environment can change the brain. Environmental stressors may alter the brain in a way that increases risk for the development of psychopathy. However, environmental enrichment may alter the brain in ways that may buffer the individual from the development of these traits. Because an individual's DNA sequence cannot be altered, changing the environment is the key to solving the problem of psychopathy. It is important to remember that biology is not destiny, and that many risk factors can be avoided or reduced by environmental modifications. Environmental influences can modify the way that genes are expressed, thus altering the effects that genes have on the brain, and, in turn, psychopathic traits.

7

Successful Psychopaths

Although psychopathy is overrepresented in the prison population, it has long been argued that not all psychopaths engage in criminal behavior (Cleckley 1941, Hare 1978). Instead, psychopaths are thought to be found in all walks of society, and may include individuals of high social status such as businessmen, physicians, scientists, and politicians, who are characterized by traits of egocentricity, superficial charm, manipulativeness, lack of emotion, impulsivity, and irresponsibility, but may not have had any arrests or convictions. Cleckley describes a middle-aged man who came from a well-regarded family and who made his way through three years at a prestigious university by utilizing the work of his friends and cheating on exams. He dressed in nice clothes and was popular at social gatherings. Although he had not paid his fraternity fees, he was tolerated because of his entertaining style and his ability to easily recruit new freshmen to join. By age 50, a survey of his life revealed that he had consistently been supported by wealthy women who repeatedly loaned him money and would help him find new positions when he lost a job. He had no difficulty having several women at his beck and call. When one relationship would go sour, he had no trouble finding another woman to raise money for a new venture or find him a new position. He was also able to make valuable business associations by loitering at the country club, and these associations enabled him to make a good living for brief periods, but his ventures always failed. Such individuals are sometimes referred to as successful psychopaths—individuals with high levels of psychopathic traits who are able to get by in society, often taking advantage of others, without ever coming into contact with the law.

Inevitably, there will be differences between individuals with psychopathic traits who achieve high status in society and are successful in many aspects of their lives, and those who are repeatedly incarcerated and cannot maintain a steady job. Much of the research we have discussed thus far has focused on psychopathic individuals in forensic populations and may not be generalizable to psychopaths in the general population. However, noninstitutionalized individuals with psychopathic traits not only may outnumber the institutionalized psychopathic population, but also may in the long run be more dangerous and destructive to society (Gao and Raine 2010). Exploring the differences between successful and unsuccessful psychopaths may help us to understand the factors that prevent some individuals from pursuing a more overt criminal lifestyle.

Definition of Successful Psychopath

There are several ways that successful psychopathy has been defined, and different studies have used different criteria. The following definitions have been used:

1. Individuals scoring high in psychopathy who have never been convicted of a crime
2. Individuals scoring high in psychopathy who are not incarcerated
3. Individuals with psychopathic traits and high social status
4. Serial killers who have escaped detection for a significant period

Thus, the definition of "successful" varies widely. Methods for recruiting successful psychopaths have also varied. For example, Widom

(1977) used newspaper advertisements to recruit individuals in the community with psychopathic traits. The advertisement read, "Wanted: charming, aggressive, carefree people who are impulsively irresponsible but are good at handling people and looking after number one" (Widom 1977). Among the sample that was recruited, 64 percent had adult arrest records, though only 18 percent had convictions. Raine and colleagues have recruited participants from temporary employment agencies wherein the proportion of psychopaths has been found to be relatively higher. Many studies have also examined psychopathic traits within college student samples—a population that assumes some degree of success. Thus, there is heterogeneity in what is considered "successful" psychopathy. Overall in the literature the term "successful psychopath" is used loosely. Future research on this topic may benefit from an agreed upon standard for what should be considered successful versus unsuccessful psychopathy.

It should be noted that successful psychopathy does not necessarily mean noncriminal, even when studies eliminate those who have been convicted of a crime. Studies have found that self-report measures of psychopathy in nonincarcerated populations are predictive of individual variation in self-reported antisocial behavior (Levenson, Kiehl, and Fitzpatrick 1995, Lynam, Whiteside, and Jones 1999). For example, in a large sample of undergraduates, Lynam, Whiteside, and Jones found that psychopathy was associated with higher scores on the Antisocial Behavior Inventory, a questionnaire that assesses behaviors such as alcohol and drug use and relatively serious delinquent acts such as stealing something worth more than $50 or attacking someone with a weapon.

Similarly, some studies recruiting participants from the community have found significant rates of antisocial behavior in these populations. In the study by Widom (1977), 65 percent of the sample reported having an arrest record, and nearly 50 percent reported some incarceration. In a study by Belmore and Quinsey (1994), which used the same recruitment strategy as Widom (1977), a large proportion of the nonincarcerated participants had previously been incarcerated (93 percent), meaning that these findings may not be representative of successful psychopaths who escape detection.

Biological Findings

It has been hypothesized that intact or enhanced neurobiological processes, including better executive functioning, increased skin conductance reactivity, and normative volumes and functioning of the prefrontal cortex and amygdala, may serve as factors that protect some individuals with psychopathic traits from being convicted of crimes; they may be able to attain their life goals using more covert and nonviolent approaches (Gao and Raine 2010). In contrast, unsuccessful psychopaths may have a greater number and/or severity of neurobiological risk factors, including structural and functional brain deficits, reduced skin conductance responding, and impaired executive functioning, which may predispose the unsuccessful psychopath to more extreme antisocial behavior and a reduced ability to detect cues of future punishment.

Neuropsychological Measures

Studies of successful psychopaths (broadly defined) that have employed neuropsychological testing have provided evidence for the following:

> 5. On tasks that that rely on the functioning of the orbitofrontal cortex or amygdala, successful psychopaths demonstrate similar deficits as criminal psychopaths.

In a study using the same community recruitment strategy as Widom (1977), Belmore and Quinsey (1994) found that community individuals scoring higher in psychopathic traits were more impulsive and performed worse in a card playing game involving reward and punishment than did community individuals scoring lower in psychopathic traits. Similarly, Dinn and Harris (2000) found that individuals scoring high in psychopathic traits demonstrated deficits on an object alternation task and the Stroop Color-Word Inference task, two tasks that are thought to index functioning of the orbitofrontal cortex. In a sample of university students, Mahmut, Homewood, and Stevenson (2008) found that individuals scoring higher in psychopathy performed significantly worse on the Iowa Gambling Task, paralleling results from criminal populations (Mitchell et al. 2002).

One study directly compared four groups: criminal psychopaths, noncriminal psychopaths (i.e., successful), criminal nonpsychopaths, and noncriminal nonpsychopaths. Iria and Barbosa (2009) examined fearful facial expression recognition in a go/no-go paradigm in which fearful faces were the "go" stimuli and all other facial expressions were the "no-go" stimuli. They found that both criminal and noncriminal psychopaths committed more omission errors (i.e., they did not recognize the fearful face [go stimulus] and respond accordingly). These findings suggest that psychopathy is related to poor ability to identify facial expressions of fear, regardless of the presence of (overt) criminal behavior. The ability to recognize fearful facial expressions is thought to rely on the functioning of the amygdala (Adolphs et al. 1999).

Lynam, Whiteside, and Jones (1999) assessed passive avoidance learning and response modulation in relation to psychopathy in a sample of undergraduates. They found that, similar to criminal psychopaths (Newman and Kosson 1986), participants who scored high on a self-report measure of psychopathy demonstrated more errors of commission on a successive go/no-go task involving monetary reward and punishment (passive avoidance learning task). Widom and Newman (1985) also observed errors on this task in a community sample. In the study by Lynam, Whiteside, and Jones (1999), those scoring higher in psychopathy also demonstrated more errors on the Q-task, which is designed to assess the ease with which an association between a stimulus and punishment is formed, and whether these cues are effective in interrupting ongoing behavior. Deficits on this task have also been observed in criminal psychopaths (Patterson and Newman 1993). As discussed in Chapter 4, the ability to form the stimulus-reward and stimulus-punishment associations required for these tasks is thought to depend on amygdala functioning (Baxter and Murray 2002).

6. On tasks assessing executive functioning, successful psychopaths do not demonstrate deficits and show either equivalent or better performance than nonpsychopathic control participants.

In the sample recruited from the community by Widom (1977), the authors failed to find deficits in delay of gratification or deficits on the Porteus Maze Test, a measure of executive functioning. In the study by Belmore and Quinsey (1994), community individuals scoring higher in psychopathy performed *better* than nonpsychopathic controls on a divergent thinking task, another measure of executive functioning. In a sample of individuals scoring high in psychopathy, but who had never been convicted of a crime, Ishikawa et al. (2001) found that performance on the Wisconsin Card Sorting Test was *better* than that of nonpsychopathic control participants. In contrast, unsuccessful, convicted psychopaths demonstrated impaired executive functioning compared to controls.

Psychophysiology

Reduced fear-potentiated startle is one of the best replicated findings in the psychopathy literature. Similar to findings in incarcerated populations, several studies examining psychopathic traits in community and student samples have found that individuals with psychopathic traits demonstrate impaired augmentation of the startle response to aversive stimuli (Benning, Patrick, and Iacono 2005a, Vanman et al. 2003, Justus and Finn 2007).

In contrast, evidence from ERP studies suggests that there may be differences between successful and unsuccessful psychopaths, specifically on the P300, which is thought to reflect attentional processes related to the orienting ("what is it?") response, described in Chapter 3. In a sample of individuals recruited from temporary employment agencies, Gao, Raine, and Schug (2011) found that unsuccessful psychopaths (psychopathic individuals with at least one criminal conviction) demonstrated reduced P300 amplitudes during an auditory oddball task compared to nonpsychopathic controls. In contrast, successful (unconvicted) psychopaths did not differ from controls, suggesting that they have intact orienting capabilities. Similarly, in a study of male students, of whom those with psychopathic traits would be presumed successful, no relationships between psychopathy and the amplitude of the P300 were observed. When examining the two factors of psychopathy in a sample of undergraduate students, Carlson, Thai, and McLarnon (2009) found that the impulsive features were associated with reduced P3 amplitudes, whereas the fearless dominance features were associated with increased P3 amplitudes. This suggests that within successful psychopaths there may be divergent patterns of effects for the different factors. This may account for the null findings observed in other studies (Gao, Raine, and Schug 2011, Campanella, Vanhoolandt, and Philippot 2005). However, in a sample of undergraduate females, Anderson et al. (2011) found increased P3 amplitude in relation to *both* factors of psychopathy. In sum, studies seem to suggest that P3 amplitudes may be intact or enhanced in successful psychopaths. However, it should be noted that P300 findings in unsuccessful (incarcerated) psychopaths are also not consistent (Raine and Venables 1988a, Kiehl et al. 1999).

Another study has also suggested that there may be psychophysiological differences between successful and unsuccessful psychopaths. In a sample of individuals recruited from temporary employment agencies, Ishikawa et al. (2001) found that compared with unsuccessful psychopaths (those with at least one conviction), successful psychopaths had increased heart rate stress reactivity compared to nonpsychopathic controls. In contrast, unsuccessful psychopaths demonstrated reduced heart rate stress reactivity compared to controls. However, Dinn and Harris (2000) found reduced skin conductance responding to aversive stimuli in a community sample scoring high in psychopathy similar to that observed in criminal psychopaths (Lorber 2004).

Brain Imaging

Given that successful and unsuccessful psychopaths both suffer emotional dysfunction such as shallow affect and lack of remorse, it is plausible that similar deficits may exist in both of these groups. Indeed, several brain imaging studies in student and community populations have revealed deficits in the amygdala, similar to those that have been identified in incarcerated populations (Rilling et al. 2007, Gordon, Baird, and End 2004, Glenn, Raine, and Schug 2009, Yang, Raine, Narr, et al. 2009). However, one structural imaging study comparing unsuccessful psychopaths (those with at least one conviction) to successful (unconvicted) psychopaths in a sample recruited from temporary employment agencies found that unsuccessful psychopaths demonstrated reduced gray matter in the amygdala, whereas successful psychopaths did not (Yang et al. 2010). However, successful psychopaths did show a 9.3 percent volume reduction in the left amygdala and a 12.7 percent volume reduction in the right amygdala compared to controls, although this difference was not significant, likely due to the small sample size. This suggests that successful psychopaths may have deficits in the amygdala, but that the deficits may be less pronounced.

In the prefrontal cortex, Yang et al. (2005) found that unsuccessful psychopaths showed a 22.3 percent reduction in prefrontal gray matter volume compared to nonpsychopathic controls, whereas successful psychopaths did not differ from controls. Further localization revealed that unsuccessful psychopaths demonstrated volume reductions in the middle frontal gyrus and orbitofrontal cortex (Yang et al. 2010). Unsuccessful psychopaths also showed significant reductions in cortical gray matter thickness compared to controls in the middle frontal gyrus, bilateral orbitofrontal cortex, temporal cortex, and posterior cingulate. Successful psychopaths showed no significant overall thinning compared to controls. However, two fMRI studies conducted in undergraduate populations found reduced activity in the orbitofrontal cortex in individuals scoring higher in psychopathy (Rilling et al. 2007, Gordon, Baird, and End 2004). *Increased* functioning has been observed in the dorsolateral prefrontal cortex in undergraduates (Gordon, Baird, and End 2004) and individuals recruited from temporary employment agencies (Glenn, Raine, Schug, et al. 2009) who score higher in psychopathy.

In regard to the hippocampus, Raine et al. (2004) reported asymmetry in the volume of the hippocampus in unsuccessful psychopaths, but not in successful psychopaths or nonpsychopathic controls. For the striatum, findings from community and student populations appear to contradict findings from incarcerated samples. In a sample of individuals recruited from temporary employment agencies, Glenn, Raine, et al. (2010) found a 9.6 percent increase in the volume of the striatum of psychopathic individuals. Similarly, in a sample of undergraduates, Buckholtz et al. (2010) found that the impulsive-antisocial traits of psychopathy were associated with dopamine release in the striatum and increased activity in the striatum in anticipation of reward. However, one study of incarcerated psychopaths observed reduced functioning in this region during emotional processing (Kiehl et al. 2001).

A Neurobiological Model of Successful and Unsuccessful Psychopathy

Despite limited evidence regarding the biological features of successful psychopaths, we propose a neurobiological model that may help to explain some of the differences between successful and unsuccessful psychopaths and that may provide a framework for future hypothesis testing. This model is depicted in Figure 7.1 and is based on an earlier model by Gao and Raine (2010).

The top section of the figure outlines the hypothesized neurobiological deficits that would give rise to successful and unsuccessful psychopathy. As reviewed above, brain imaging studies suggest that successful psychopaths have deficits in the structure and functioning of the amygdala and orbitofrontal cortex, although these deficits may be to a lesser degree than those observed in unsuccessful psychopaths. This is supported by results from neuropsychological tests that assess the functioning of the orbitofrontal cortex and amygdala, showing that successful psychopaths have similar deficits to unsuccessful psychopaths. Finally, skin conductance recordings show that successful psychopaths demonstrate similar deficits in fear-potentiated startle and responding to aversive stimuli as unsuccessful psychopaths, reflecting potential deficits in the amygdala.

In contrast, in brain regions that are more involved in cognitive functioning, such as the superior parts of the frontal lobe, the parietal lobe, and the anterior and posterior cingulate, successful psychopaths do not appear to demonstrate deficits, and some evidence suggests that functioning may be enhanced. Successful psychopaths perform better on a measure of divergent thinking and on the Wisconsin Card Sorting Test, two measures of executive functioning. There is also evidence of increased P300 amplitudes to orienting stimuli, which may reflect functioning of the parietal lobe.

The middle section shows how this pattern of neuropsychological effects would result in characteristics observed in successful and unsuccessful psychopaths. Both groups demonstrate reduced emotional empathy and emotional processing, although successful psychopaths

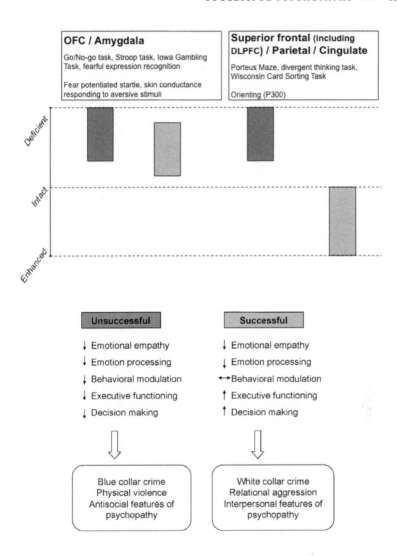

Figure 7.1. A neurobiological theoretical model on different etiologies (top) and manifestations (bottom) of successful and unsuccessful psychopathy, and the similarities between the two subtypes (middle). OFC, orbitofrontal cortex; PCL-R Facet 1, glib/superficial, grandiose, lying, and conning/manipulating; PCL-R Facet 4, poor behavioral controls, early behavior problems, and criminal versatility. Source: Modified from Gao and Raine (2010).

may demonstrate this to a lesser degree. Regarding behavioral modulation, successful psychopaths may be impaired in some contexts because of deficits in the orbitofrontal cortex but may have better abilities in other contexts because of superior functioning in regions involved in cognitive inhibition, such as the dorsolateral prefrontal cortex. Successful psychopaths are also expected to show better executive functioning and better decision making because of the increased or enhanced functioning in cognitive regions.

Finally, the bottom part of the figure shows how these features may translate into antisocial behavior. For unsuccessful psychopaths, the combination of deficits in both emotional and cognitive abilities may result in antisocial individuals who have difficulty regulating their behavior, and who are less sensitive to environmental cues predicting danger and capture. Because of poor behavior controls, we hypothesize that they would be more prone to physical violence. We also anticipate that they would score higher on the antisocial features of psychopathy (Facet 4). Scores on the Interpersonal Facet 1 may be lower because of reduced cognitive abilities necessary to con and manipulate others.

Successful psychopaths may similarly engage in antisocial behavior because of a lack of empathy and emotional responding. However, we expect this behavior to be more planned and regulated. Intact or superior cognitive functioning may mean that successful psychopaths can con and manipulate others, and plan their crimes to better escape detection. We also hypothesize that better behavioral control will result in less physical violence and more relational aggression or crimes such as white-collar crime that do not involve force.

Limitations of Research on Successful Psychopaths

Because definitions of successful psychopaths can vary widely, it is difficult to draw conclusions about this research as a whole. Some samples of successful psychopaths include individuals who have previously been convicted of crimes and/or individuals who would not be considered successful in terms of acquiring resources or social status in society. Future studies focusing on high-functioning manifestations of noncriminal psychopathy will most certainly be of interest to many in the field. Studies using self-report measures of psychopathy have the advantage of screening larger numbers of participants from the general community to identify individuals who have psychopathic traits do not come from a high-risk sample (Hall and Benning 2006). Focusing on perpetrators of white-collar crime may also be one way to recruit samples of psychopathic individuals with high social status who have successfully escaped detection for much of their lives.

Conclusions

In sum, some studies of successful psychopaths (broadly defined) demonstrate effects similar to those in incarcerated populations. For example, successful psychopaths demonstrate reduced fear-potentiated startle. Other studies have found intact or enhanced functioning in successful psychopaths in domains such as heart rate reactivity and P300 amplitudes. Brain imaging studies suggest that successful psychopaths likely have deficits in the amygdala but these deficits may not be as pronounced. Structural imaging studies have found that successful psychopaths do not appear to have deficits in the frontal lobe, whereas functional imaging studies have provided some evidence of reduced functioning in the orbitofrontal cortex and increased functioning in the dorsolateral prefrontal cortex. These latter findings appear to be in line with neuropsychological findings, which suggest that successful psychopaths have deficits on tasks that index orbitofrontal cortex functioning, but may have intact or enhanced functioning on tasks that rely on the dorsolateral prefrontal cortex. Enhanced autonomic responding and better executive functioning may protect a subgroup of psychopaths from being detected and arrested, allowing them to perpetrate significant harm to others in the community.

8

Ethical Issues

Mr. Oft is a 40-year-old man with no prior history of mental health problems or antisocial behavior. He is happily married and lives at home with his wife and stepdaughter. In 2000, he began collecting pornography, much of which was child pornography. Shortly thereafter, he began soliciting prostitution, and also started making sexual advances toward his stepdaughter. His stepdaughter reported these actions, and Mr. Oft was arrested. He was diagnosed with pedophilia and found guilty of child molestation. The judge gave him a choice of either participating in a 12-step program for sexual addiction or going to prison. He chose the 12-step program, but after entering the program, he began soliciting sexual favors from the staff at the rehabilitation center and was terminated from the program. The night before his sentencing, he began complaining of a severe headache, and then began having balance problems and became unable to control his bladder. An MRI was ordered, and it was discovered that he had a massive tumor occupying a large portion of his frontal lobe (Burns and Swerdlow 2003).

Mr. Oft received surgery to remove the tumor. After recovery, he successfully completed the 12-step program, was believed to no longer pose a threat to his family, and returned home. However, in October 2001, he began collecting pornography again. An MRI revealed that his tumor had regrown. Doctors removed the tumor again, and his behavior returned to normal.

Does learning about Mr. Oft's tumor change whether you think he is responsible for his inappropriate sexual behavior? Does knowing that a large portion of his brain was damaged change whether you think he should be punished for it? On one hand, one could argue that there is a highly visible abnormality in his brain that is affecting his behavior. The parts of his brain that enable him to control his impulses and weigh the consequences of his decisions were damaged. The fact that this behavior returned to normal after the tumor was resected and then worsened again as the tumor returned is strong evidence that the tumor was the cause of his bad behavior. If the tumor had not been present, it is very unlikely that this behavior would have emerged. Because the development of the tumor was beyond Mr. Oft's control, he should not be held criminally responsible and should not be punished.

On the other hand, one could argue that this argument is a slippery slope. In reality, *all* behavior is caused by our brains. If we declare that some individuals are not responsible for their behavior because of how their brains function, we might as well decide that *no one* can be held responsible. What will happen to society if we start letting people off the hook because "their brains made them do it"? Furthermore, until the final hours before the tumor was discovered, Mr. Oft did not have cognitive deficits that impaired his ability to distinguish between right and wrong. He was aware of the fact that his behavior was highly inappropriate, and therefore he should have been able to make the right decision.

We present this case, reported by Burns and Swerdlow (2003), to show how having information about the brain can raise a number of questions about free will and criminal responsibility. Before learning about Mr. Oft's tumor, we assume that he is making bad decisions on his own accord. In fact, Mr. Oft himself was initially unaware of the tumor in his brain and perceived himself to be acting according to his own free will. Once we learn of his tumor, we begin to question how much control he actually had over his behavior and question whether we believe he should be punished or not.

Although brain abnormalities as severe as Mr. Oft's may be quite rare, his case also leads us to question cases in which brain abnormalities are much more subtle. In most antisocial individuals, we do not observe such obvious, widespread impairments. Instead, across groups of individuals, we find relatively modest associations between the size or functioning of brain regions and the presence of antisocial tendencies. Whereas we may be inclined to excuse Mr. Oft from blame because of his pronounced brain impairment, we may be much more uneasy about the prospect of applying this same logic on a larger scale to individuals without such extreme deficits. Again, the slippery slope argument arises—since all behavior is caused by our brains, it would be impossible to draw a distinction between those who should be excused for their behavior because of a brain abnormality and those who should be held responsible. Thus, we are faced with the difficult question of whether information about the brain or any other biological measure should be used in the determination of criminal responsibility.

We argue that although it is true that all behavior is caused by our brains, the fact is that not all brains work the same way. Just like any other part of our body, our brains can become damaged or be deficient. Sometimes these abnormalities lead us to do things that are harmful to others. Sometimes these abnormalities lead us to have hallucinations or memory impairments. Current laws regarding criminal responsibility in the United States do acknowledge that individuals with severe cognitive impairments, such as some people with schizophrenia or dementia, have an impaired ability to understand the difference between right and wrong; these individuals are typically not considered criminally responsible, and, rather than being punished, they are usually admitted into psychiatric facilities. Most people feel comfortable with this idea that we should not punish individuals with severe cognitive impairments. The outward behavioral manifestation of brain dysfunction is apparent in many of these cases, and it seems clear that these individuals are not freely choosing to behave antisocially.

Opinions change, however, when arguments about brain deficits are applied to individuals who do not have obvious cognitive impairments. Psychopaths, for example, *are* aware of the differences between right and wrong. They act intentionally, with the understanding that there are rules and consequences for violating them. In light of this, it is difficult for people to justify excusing psychopaths' bad behavior. However, we argue that this cognitive capacity for rationality is not all that is required for appropriate moral behavior.

Emotion in Moral Judgment

As much as we may think that our moral judgments are the product of careful deliberation and reasoning, psychological and neuroscientific studies are providing increasing empirical evidence that our moral judgments are highly influenced by our emotions. Some suggest that moral behavior is primarily guided by spontaneous, effortless emotional responses that operate automatically and unconsciously (e.g., Haidt 2001). Whereas conscientious reasoning often fails to predict actual moral behavior, moral emotions are often found to be a powerful force behind behaving morally (Moll, de Oliveira-Souza, and Eslinger 2003, Colby and Damon 1995). Neuroimaging studies show that during the process of moral decision making, brain regions involved in emotional processing become active, particularly when individuals contemplate moral dilemmas that involve causing direct harm to another individual (Greene et al. 2001, Greene et al. 2004).

As discussed in Chapter 4, studies of individuals with brain damage find that when brain areas involved in emotional processing are compromised, moral judgment is altered (Koenigs et al. 2007, Ciaramelli et al. 2007). In these patients, judgment is impaired in moral dilemmas involving an option of causing direct harm to another individual. The patients are more likely to judge harmful acts as permissible, suggesting that they may not experience the same degree of emotional aversiveness that healthy individuals experience when considering such acts. In most individuals, the thought or the act of causing harm to others generates an aversive emotional response. We respond negatively to cues that another individual is in distress (Blair 2007). Impairments in brain regions important in generating this emotional response can significantly alter moral judgment.

The influence of emotion on moral judgment is something that is often out of our awareness, despite the fact that we perceive our judgments to be a result of deliberate, rational processes. For example, until his tumor worsened, Mr. Oft did not demonstrate cognitive impairments that led him or others to believe that his problem was neurological. Mr. Oft was aware that his behavior was inappropriate, and perceived himself to be acting according to his own free will, but was still unable to control himself. In other words, we may not be the freely choosing actors that we perceive ourselves to be. Individual differences in how our brains function can influence our judgment without our awareness.

As discussed in Chapter 5, brain imaging research suggests that psychopathic individuals have significant reductions in both the structure and functioning of regions of the brain that are important in emotion and in decision making. Notably, there is significant overlap between the brain regions implicated in psychopathy and the regions important in emotional responding during moral decision making (for a review, see Raine and Yang 2006). In a study conducted in our laboratory, we presented participants with a series of moral dilemmas that had been compiled in a previous study examining the neural correlates of moral judgment (Greene et al. 2001). The trolley problem, presented in Chapter 4, is one of these dilemmas. Another example is the crying baby scenario:

Enemy soldiers have taken over your village. They have orders to kill all remaining civilians. You and some of your townspeople have sought refuge in the cellar of a large house. Outside you hear the voices of soldiers who have come to search the house for valuables.

Your baby begins to cry loudly. You cover his mouth to block the sound. If you remove your hand from his mouth his crying will summon the attention of the soldiers who will kill you, your child, and the others hiding out in the cellar. To save yourself and the others you must smother your child to death.

Is it appropriate for you to smother your child in order to save yourself and the other townspeople?

Most people have a very uncomfortable feeling when considering the thought of causing harm to their own baby. We found that people who are more psychopathic have less activity in the amygdala, the region that is likely involved in generating this emotional response, when contemplating these types of dilemmas (Glenn, Raine, and Schug 2009).

Thus, despite the fact that psychopathic individuals can cognitively distinguish between right and wrong (e.g., they know that it is wrong to kill another person), this study and others suggest that there are likely differences in the functioning of brain regions that are critical for appropriate moral decision making. In other words, they may lack the key emotions that provide motivation for most individuals to behave morally.

In sum, although people tend to accept evidence from studies showing that specific brain regions are necessary for functions such as reading or motor skills, when it comes to decision making and morality, we may be less likely to embrace the idea that our choices are the result of how specific brain regions function, and that free will may not be as free as we may think. In addition to determining whether an individual has the cognitive capacity for distinguishing between right and wrong, we also need to consider whether people have the *emotional* ability to make appropriate decisions.

In theory, the law does consider the concept of emotion in criminal defenses. The Model Penal Code (American Law Institute 1962) states that in order to be considered blameworthy, an individual must have the capacity to *appreciate* the wrongfulness of his or her conduct. However, despite the text of this defense, determining criminal responsibility in both criminal law theory and actual practice often relies on the individual's cognitive capacity for rationality, rather than the individual's emotional capacity. The law assumes that we are "practical reasoners." Since psychopaths act intentionally, with the understanding that there are rules and consequences for violating them, the criminal law generally does not allow evidence of psychopathy, standing alone, to support the defense that the individual is not responsible. Furthermore, requirements for the insanity defense exclude mental defect that is "manifested only by repeated criminal or otherwise antisocial conduct" (American Law Institute 1962). Thus, across a wide body of somewhat idiosyncratic state criminal law, psychopathy is typically excluded as a mental disorder sufficient for an insanity defense (Maibom 2008). We suggest that the law should accommodate the increasing psychological and neuroscientific evidence that emotional capacity is an important factor for translating factual knowledge about right and wrong into moral behavior.

Individual Differences in Moral Decision Making

In addition to deficits in emotional experience, many other factors also influence our judgments, such as how much control we have over our impulses. The fact is that not all individuals have the same capacity for making decisions. As discussed throughout the book, these individual differences are the result of differences in our genes and our environments, and the interactions between the two, which in turn affect biological systems and then behavior. Thus, although individuals are subjected to the same standards for appropriate moral behavior according to the law, they have differing capabilities for behaving accordingly.

To demonstrate this concept, consider the following example provided by Eagleman (2011, p. 115):

> If you are a carrier of a particular set of genes, the probability that you will commit a violent crime is four times as high as it would be if you lacked those genes. You're three times as likely to commit robbery, five times as likely to commit aggravated assault, eight times as likely to be arrested for murder, and 13 times as likely to be arrested for a sexual offense. The overwhelming majority of prisoners carry these genes; 98.1 percent of death-row inmates do. . . . [These genes] are summarized as the Y chromosome. If you're a carrier, we call you a male.

In other words, as much as we like to believe that we all have equal capabilities for making decisions and controlling our behavior, the fact that the rates of criminal behavior differ so greatly between males and females suggests otherwise. Because individuals do not choose their genes or the environmental factors that influence neurodevelopment, we may want to reconsider whether all individuals should be held to the same standards of accountability.

The more that neuroscience progresses, the more we will be able to understand the ways in which subtle differences in the brain influence behavior, and the more we may question the concept of free will. We will also better understand how the brain structure and functioning of psychopathic individuals contributes to their antisocial behavior. Although we may currently consider individuals without obvious signs of neurological impairment to be fully responsible, we may begin to question this premise as neuroscience begins to provide us with more answers about how biology translates into behavior. It will likely become much more difficult to draw a clear line between responsibility and nonresponsibility.

Given the growing neuroscientific evidence regarding moral judgment and antisocial behavior, we and others have argued that it is likely that some people, such as highly psychopathic individuals, are not responsible and should not be punished for their criminal behavior (Glenn, Raine, and Laufer 2011, Morse 2008). Morse (2008) argues that "severe" psychopaths are neither morally responsible nor deserving of blame and punishment because they do not understand the point of morality; they lack a conscience and the capacity for moral understanding and rationality. In the absence of appropriate emotional responding, they lack the necessary motivation to behave morally.

However, attempting to draw a firm line between responsibility and nonresponsibility is likely a futile attempt. Rather than focusing on this nearly impossible challenge, it has been suggested that it may be more important to use information gained from neuroscience to try to offer better solutions to the problem of criminal behavior (Eagleman 2011). In light of the fact that our behavior is influenced by so many factors beyond our control, a focus on accountability seems less important than a more forward-thinking system that focuses on three main issues. First and foremost is the fact that society must be protected from individuals who are at increased risk for causing harm. Second, the feelings and the rights of victims must be considered. Finally, we must also consider what is fair to the offenders, who may have biological deficits that impair their ability to behave appropriately.

1. Protection of society.
If we accept the notion that neurobiological deficits beyond offenders' control may contribute to their behavior, and that therefore some individuals may not be fully responsible, the fact remains that society must be protected. Although we may not think that punishment is justified, for severe offenders, incapacitation via institutionalization may be the only viable option for minimizing the risk of reoffending. The greatest benefit to society and to the offender is if the offender can be effectively treated and released. Institutions housing convicted offenders may be

ideal settings for research on treatment and rehabilitation methods that may prove to be effective in treating these individuals and allowing them to return to society.

In less severe cases, we believe that there are other forms of social control that may be equally or more effective at reducing recidivism than incarceration, and that these options should be explored, provided that the protection of society remains a primary consideration.

2. Acknowledging the feelings and the rights of victims.

Considering the victims of crime is also extremely important in determining how we deal with offenders. One promising way of addressing the needs and worries of the victims of crime is through restorative justice programs. These programs provide the opportunity for victims to interact with the offender, in order to express the impact of the crime upon their lives and to ask questions about the incident. Offenders can also provide their side of the story, and are given an opportunity to offer compensation to the victim. In these settings, information presented about the background of the offender, such as early life adversity, may help the victims to achieve a better understanding of the factors that contributed to the offender's behavior. We suggest that in relevant cases, an expert explanation of some of the neurobiological factors that may have contributed to the offender's behavior could also help the victim to better understand the offender and may help to promote tolerance.

Beyond the needs of individuals who were directly affected by a crime, we also should consider the need for justice by society as a whole. Some have suggested that our operational legal principles exist because they more or less adequately capture an intuitive sense of justice (Greene and Cohen 2010). Even if one accepts the empirical evidence that some individuals may have deficits that impair their ability to make appropriate decisions, the idea that these individuals should not be considered responsible for their behavior can still be difficult to accept. Crime elicits very strong emotional reactions in people, particularly those who are victims of crime. Graphic depictions of serious crimes generate feelings of anger and a strong desire for retribution. People feel strongly that crime must be punished and have understandable difficulty feeling sympathy for the perpetrators of these offenses. The idea that some individuals, who may commit the most serious crimes, are not entirely responsible for their behavior, no matter how severe, is hard to acknowledge.

In the past couple of decades, public awareness of the role of biology in other mental health disorders such as schizophrenia and depression has increased dramatically. However, there is still resistance to the idea that biological factors may contribute to persistent criminal behavior in the absence of pronounced cognitive deficits. The perceived willfulness of criminal behavior is clearly an obstacle to the notion that psychopaths may not be responsible for their behavior. Unless the accused is clearly shown to be suffering from hallucinations or other mental impairment, crime is still perceived to be a choice. Education about the ways that biology can disrupt the systems necessary for empathy and decision making may help to create a better understanding among the general public of how factors beyond individuals' control influence their behavior.

3. Humane treatment of offenders.
Brain functioning is something that is the result of genetic and environmental factors, both of which are beyond the control of the individual. If these factors contribute to criminal offending, should individuals with deficits in the key brain regions that are essential for moral decision making be punished? If we decide that retribution and harsh punishment are not appropriate for these individuals, then how should we, as a society, and from an ethical point of view, deal with these individuals?

Currently, institutions that house offenders focus on severe restrictions of liberty with the goal of punishing the offender. Serving time has additional negative effects, both professionally (lack of access to training, loss of skills, limited future employment opportunities) and personally (stigmatization, reduced social and emotional support, housing opportunities). Offenders with mental health and substance abuse issues often fail to receive adequate treatment. In addition, overcrowding, boredom, and inadequate care in prisons often exacerbate mental health problems. Thus, there are a number of ways in which offenders are "punished" aside from their loss of freedom, and many of these effects have significant long-term negative consequences. Given the growing evidence that persistent antisocial behavior is associated with biological deficits (which result from either genetic or environmental factors), this type of treatment may be highly inappropriate.

For those offenders who are at continuous high risk of committing serious offenses, we advocate housing them in a location that is secure but that practices humane treatment, minimizing aspects of punishment and allowing the individuals to have as much freedom as possible given the constraints of keeping such offenders away from society (Raine 1993). As a society, we should ensure the personal, physical, and mental well-being of individuals who are incarcerated. We also propose an increased focus on developing new treatment programs.

Aside from the incarceration of the most severe offenders, we suggest that in many cases alternative measures could be implemented (Focquaert, Glenn, and Raine 2013). Adequate control could be administered through alternative sanctions such as house arrest, electronic monitoring, or supervised community service. Research has found these types of community-based sanctions to be as effective as imprisonment (Martin 2003). These types of sanctions are less likely than imprisonment to infringe on the rights of the offenders. Sanctions that include participation in treatment and rehabilitation programs and/or offer mental health and substance abuse treatment may prove to be much more effective in reducing recidivism rates and thus protecting society. As suggested by Vandevelde et al. (2011), "Mentally ill offenders are better off with a treatment model incorporating elements of security, than with a security model incorporating elements of treatment" (p. 76).

Neuroscience Evidence in Court

The extent to which biological factors should play a role in the justice system is an open and highly controversial question. One issue that has become the source of much debate in recent years is whether neuroscience evidence should be permitted in court cases when determining criminal responsibility and/or sentencing. This has become a very pressing issue, since the use of neuroscience evidence in court is on the rise (Figure 8.1). On one hand, we might argue that information about the brain is essential in order to have a complete understanding of a particular case. For example, the image depicting Mr. Oft's tumor changes how we think about his behavior and how much control he had over it. One might still argue that Mr. Oft did have some degree of free will, but many would agree that the onset of these strong urges and Mr. Oft's inability to resist them were significantly influenced by the presence of the tumor. Thus, the information about Mr. Oft's brain seems important in the justice system's decision regarding the appropriate course of action to be taken with Mr. Oft.

This was the perspective taken by Dr. Kent Kiehl, the neuroscientist and psychopathy researcher who presented fMRI evidence in the controversial case of Brian Dugan. As mentioned in the introduction, Dugan was a convicted murderer who was on trial for an additional murder in which he was accused of raping and murdering a 10-year-old girl. In 2009, Kiehl testified that the brain scan from Dugan revealed decreased levels of activity in specific brain regions, and that these decreases were similar to those observed in other psychopathic individuals (Hughes 2010). The case raised many concerns about whether fMRI evidence should be allowed in legal settings.

Many critics argued that fMRI evidence is not suitable for drawing conclusions about individual cases. For example, in the book thus far, we have reviewed evidence that psychopathic traits are associated with differential structure and functioning of the brain. However, these brain imaging studies compare *average* differences between groups, or report correlations between brain functioning and behavior/personality measures, but do not indicate that *all* individuals with psychopathy will demonstrate the same patterns of brain functioning. There is not a one-to-one relationship between the functioning of a particular brain region and psychopathy (or behavior). Furthermore, we currently have no way of determining what level of brain functioning in different regions should be considered "abnormal" and worthy of declaring that an individual's capability for behaving morally is impaired. We do not have predefined neurobiological cutoff points for determining whether someone should be held criminally responsible or not.

Another issue that was raised was that fMRI evidence may suggest that differences in some brain regions may *increase the risk for* the development of antisocial traits, but the evidence is far from establishing that any particular brain abnormality *caused one particular individual to commit one particular crime*. In the Dugan case, the brain scan was conducted 26 years after the murder took place. It was impossible to know whether this same pattern of functioning would have been observed at the time that Dugan committed the crime. Several researchers have raised concerns with the use of brain imaging in the legal system (Eastman and Campbell 2006, Mobbs et al. 2007, Garland and Glimcher 2006), arguing that in these early stages of research on the neurobiological correlates of criminal behavior, we are not able to identify truly causal factors.

Finally, some have argued that the use of brain images in the courtroom may be too influential for jurors, who may view the brightly colored images as more accurate and objective than they actually are (Farah 2004, Mobbs et al. 2007). Indeed, studies have found that people rate information presented in the form of brain images to be more scientifically sound than information presented with other types of graphs or without an image (McCabe and Castel 2008). In the case of Brian Dugan, the judge acknowledged this point and ruled that the jury would not be allowed to see the actual brain images, but that Kiehl would be allowed to provide a description of them.

A counterargument to these concerns is that by not allowing brain imaging evidence in court we may be punishing individuals who do have brain deficits that significantly impair moral decision-making abilities. Information about Mr. Oft's brain tumor influences our judgments of how much control he had over his behavior and how much he should be punished. What about cases in which neurobiological impairments are very small? It is possible that what appear to be very subtle differences in the brain may nonetheless have a dramatic effect on behavior. For example, as mentioned in the introduction, Charles Whitman, the man who killed 13 people and wounded 32 more in a shooting rampage at the University of Texas in 1966, was found to have a tumor with a diameter the size of a nickel that impinged on the hypothalamus and amygdala. While not nearly as widespread as Mr. Oft's tumor, this abnormality, located in a critical brain region, produced drastic behavioral changes.

Although it will never be possible to identify one particular neurobiological deficit as the definitive cause of a criminal act, it may still be possible to establish reasonable criteria for what could be considered a significant biological risk factor. As Kiehl has pointed out, brain imaging evidence may be just one piece of information that may help us to understand these cases. We suggest that eventually brain imaging evidence could be treated in the same way as other forms of evidence that are presented in court—as one factor among many that may influence behavior. Evidence of environmental risk factors such as child abuse or neglect is often introduced in court cases as a factor that may have increased the risk for violence in a specific individual, but it does not imply the existence of a one-to-one causal relationship. Information from brain imaging studies could be treated similarly. Using normative databases, it may be possible to create objective measures of brain structure or functioning that indicate a particular level of abnormality. If that were possible, evidence from brain imaging would possibly be considered more objective than psychiatric diagnoses and could provide more information about the causal mechanisms that influenced an individual's behavior.

At this time, it is likely premature to use fMRI evidence in court cases, but as the technology improves, this may change. Although the presentation of brightly colored images may potentially influence jurors, we believe that just as other forms of evidence may require expert interpretation, brain imaging evidence will require an expert to explain the evidence in a clear, unbiased manner. It is the responsibility of scientists to communicate what can and cannot be concluded from the data. We suggest that biological evidence should not replace other forms of evidence, but should be considered an additional source of information that helps us to gain a more comprehensive picture of the source of the problem, which in some cases, such as Mr. Oft's, may be largely biological.

Another advantage of considering this type of information is that in some cases, we may gain information about what would be the best way to deal with the offender. For example, without the information about Mr. Oft's tumor, the best "solution," according to the law, was for Mr. Oft to participate in the 12-step program. However, given the information about his brain, it becomes apparent that a behaviorally based treatment is unlikely to be effective, and that the biological deficit must first be addressed in order for any improvement to occur. Again, Mr. Oft's case represents a more extreme example, but the hope is that with additional research, we will be able to use biological information in more subtle cases more effectively. Despite the fact that we believe that neuroscience evidence could ultimately be very useful, there are still many uncertainties regarding the accuracy and interpretation of brain imaging evidence, particularly in individual cases. Given the present state of research, there may currently be very few cases in which the presentation of brain imaging evidence is appropriate (e.g., in cases of obvious damage). However, we believe that taking into account documented neurobiological risk factors for violence in some specific cases does not mean that we have to abandon our general concepts of rationality, personhood, and responsibility (Yang, Glenn, and Raine 2008).

The Use of Biological Factors in Crime Prediction

The biological basis of crime has a grim history. In the first half of the 20th century, the idea that crime may have a biological basis was touted by phrenologists, eugenicists, and other "criminal anthropologists" such as Lombroso, Sheldon, Hooton, McKim, and the Glueks (Rafter 2008). A common concern that still persists is that we will end up using biological information to try to predict which individual is going to commit a crime and limit the person's freedom beforehand.

In the previous chapters, we hope to have clarified that biological research on antisocial behavior is not the equivalent of biological determinism, as many biological factors are the result of environmental factors, and that even genes are influenced by environmental factors. It is also important to keep in mind that many of the findings reported in this book demonstrate small associations between biological factors and psychopathic traits. It is not established that these risk factors are causal, and none of them produce large enough effects that we could accurately predict who will grow up to be an offender. Furthermore, most individuals who are delinquent as adolescents do not continue to offend in adulthood.

Rather than being used to try to predict which individuals will become criminal, much of the work on early risk factors attempts to identify which individuals may be at greatest risk for the development of psychopathic traits so that environmental interventions can be implemented at an earlier age. These interventions often have benefits that extend beyond the goal of preventing antisocial behavior, and include improvements in school performance, improvements in social adjustment, and reduced risk of substance abuse and other mental health problems.

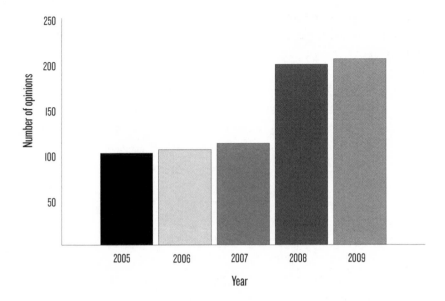

Figure 8.1. Distribution of cases by year, from a sample of 722 from 2005 to 2009 in the United States, in which neurological or behavioral genetics evidence was introduced on behalf of a criminal defendant. Reprinted from the Royal Society (2011).

Conclusions

When considering the ethical challenges that neuroscience presents for the criminal justice system, people often think of the extremes. We can continue to punish criminals for their behavior, regardless of any information about how their brains function, or we can let all criminals off the hook because all behavior is caused by our brains, and brain functioning is beyond the individual's control. As an alternative to these two extremes, we agree with the following vision:

> [W]e can build a legal system more deeply informed by science, in which we will continue to take criminals off the streets, but we will customize sentencing, leverage new opportunities for rehabilitation, and structure better incentives for good behavior. Discoveries in neuroscience suggest

a new way forward for law and order—one that will lead to a more cost-effective, humane, and flexible system than the one we have today. (Eagleman 2011, p. 115)

Just as the functioning of our brains underlies our ability to read and write, it also underlies our moral behavior. Although we perceive ourselves to be making free choices about our own behavior, research on individuals with damage to specific regions of the brain suggests that this may simply be an illusion. Damage to regions involved in emotion, inhibition, and decision making can alter our judgment without our awareness. Growing research suggests that psychopathic individuals have deficits in some of these brain regions that are important for appropriate moral behavior, suggesting that not everyone has equal capability for making appropriate choices.

Advances in biological research on criminal behavior and psychopathy are likely to continue to stimulate debate over the use of biological evidence in the determination of criminal responsibility and punishment. Ultimately, a high level of communication between scientists and legal scholars will be critical for determining how new and potentially important findings from brain imaging and other biological research should and should not influence how we deal with criminal behavior. We can do our best to make informed decisions—that are informed by both psychology and neuroscience—to decide what we think is fair.

9

Prevention, Intervention, and Treatment

The ultimate goal of biological research on antisocial behavior and psychopathy is to be able to better prevent and treat the disorder. Biological research on problem behaviors such as addiction, schizophrenia, depression, autism, and dementia has proven to be extremely beneficial in the development of treatments and methods for preventing these conditions. Although biological research on antisocial behavior is a much smaller field by comparison, the hope is that the information gained from this area can similarly enable us to develop more effective methods for prevention and intervention. Ideally, these would be methods that could be implemented in early childhood, in infancy, or even prenatally, to reduce the risk of antisocial behavior (and other negative outcomes) from a very early age.

Research examining potential treatments for individuals with psychopathic traits is growing, but is still limited. In this chapter we review some of this research and then present some promising ideas for prevention and intervention that take biological factors into consideration. When considering biologically based treatments, most people think of medication. However, treatments and interventions that target biological factors may also include modifications in nutrition, reducing exposure to toxins and promoting improvements in other health factors that affect relevant biological systems. In addition, research has begun to demonstrate the biological changes that can result from psychosocial interventions, suggesting that biological factors can be targeted through traditional forms of therapy. Thus, ultimate solutions to the problem of psychopathy could be both natural and, in some cases, surprisingly simple.

The gold standard for prevention and treatment studies is the randomized controlled trial, in which participants are randomly allocated to treatment or control groups and the groups are treated identically except for the experimental treatment. Less controlled study designs may be able to detect associations between an intervention and an outcome, but they cannot rule out the possibility that the association may have been caused by a third factor. Randomizing participants into groups ensures that there are no systematic differences in other factors (e.g., willingness to participate in the intervention) that may affect outcomes. With some forms of intervention, it is possible for both participants and clinicians to be blinded as to group status. This ensures that the results will not be affected by the participants' or clinicians' knowledge of the treatment group. When evaluating treatment research it is important to carefully consider the design of the study.

As mentioned in Chapter 8, randomized controlled trials are beneficial for two reasons: (1) we make progress in understanding what forms of interventions are effective and (2) we are able to test cause-and-effect relationships (Tremblay 2008). Randomized controlled trials are one of the most rigorous ways of determining whether a particular factor plays a causal role in the development of an outcome. For example, consider an intervention in which pregnant women are randomly assigned to a group that participates in a smoking cessation program (that is effective in reducing maternal smoking) or a control group that does not participate. If rates of antisocial behavior are lower in the offspring of those who reduced their smoking habits during pregnancy, we can conclude that prenatal smoking is causally related to antisocial behavior in offspring. However, a study in which pregnant women are not randomly assigned to groups but choose whether to participate in the program or not is subject to self-selection bias, meaning that there may be differences between women who choose to participate and those who do not, and potential effects may be due to these external factors rather than to differences in smoking behavior. Future studies implementing the more rigorous approach of the randomized controlled trial will undoubtedly be beneficial in both furthering our understanding of psychopathy and making progress toward solving the problem.

Prevention

The optimal solution to the problem of psychopathy is to develop methods that prevent the initial development of these traits. An important advantage of early prevention measures that reduce prenatal or early life risk factors is that they have the potential to prevent negative outcomes in a variety of domains, not just antisocial behavior. For example, risk factors such as child abuse and neglect or maternal depression have been found to be linked to a number of different mental health disorders. The term "multifinality" is used to describe the concept that one etiological factor can lead to a number of different pathological outcomes. The development of one disorder over another likely depends on additional genetic and environmental factors.

Research suggests that the prenatal period and early childhood years are key developmental periods. The prenatal period in particular is an important time in which to focus on preventive measures because the developing fetus is highly vulnerable to influences from the environment (Liu 2011). By targeting risk factors during pregnancy and early childhood, we may be able to significantly reduce the risk for developing psychopathic traits. These may be factors that directly influence neurodevelopment, such as nutrition, or they may be factors that have an indirect effect on biology via psychological processes. For example, postnatal maternal depression results in reduced maternal responsiveness and lower warmth, which have psychological effects on the offspring and, in turn, may alter stress hormones such as cortisol. Indeed, postnatal maternal depression has been associated with increased cortisol levels in infants (Hessl et al. 1998). Altered cortisol levels can even be observed 13-year-old adolescents whose mothers experienced depression after giving birth (Halligan et al. 2004).

Toxin exposure is one source of preventable risk that likely has direct effects on neurodevelopment and that has been found to confer risk for antisocial behavior. Prenatal bone lead concentrations have been associated with higher rates of criminal arrests in early adulthood (Wright et al. 2008). Higher levels of lead have also been associated with antisocial behavior in childhood (Needleman et al. 1996). As mentioned in Chapter 8, lead exposure postweaning has been found to affect neurotransmitters in the striatum of rats (Pokora, Richfield, and CorySlechta 1996), which may sensitize this region to rewarding stimuli. A brain imaging study in humans found that childhood blood lead concentrations were associated with a 1.2 percent reduction in total gray matter volume and that the most affected regions were in the medial prefrontal cortex, including the anterior cingulate (Cecil et al. 2008), a region that may be deficient in psychopathy. Thus, exposure to lead may increase the risk for antisocial behavior via its effect on the structure and functioning of the brain.

Ideally, initial exposure to lead would be prevented via education of future parents on the sources of lead and by conducting risk assessments of homes. However, once exposure occurs, there may be methods for reducing its negative effects on biological systems. Liu et al. (2011) found that regular breakfast intake was associated with a reduction in blood concentrations of lead in youth, likely because the presence of food reduces the absorption of lead in the gastrointestinal tract. Thus, relatively simple interventions may be able to reduce the effects of toxin exposure.

Another form of toxin exposure results from maternal smoking during pregnancy. Several studies have found maternal smoking to affect hormone and neurotransmitter levels of the offspring. Prenatal exposure to tobacco has been associated with reduced alpha-amylase levels and reactivity in 10-year-old offspring (Huijbregts et al. 2011), and the number of cigarettes the mother smokes per day is significantly related to cortisol concentrations in cord blood (Varvarigou et al. 2009). In rats, prenatal nicotine exposure affects neurotransmitters such as norepinephrine, dopamine, and serotonin (Muneoka et al. 1997). Disruptions in hormones and neurotransmitters of the fetus induced by maternal smoking may have adverse consequences on the development of the brain. Indeed, maternal smoking has been found to affect the volume and thickness of brain regions such as the corpus callosum (Bublitz and Stroud 2012), a region that is implicated in psychopathy (Raine et al. 2003), and results in a lack of coordination across brain regions during information processing (Bublitz and Stroud 2012).

The use of alcohol and other substances during pregnancy also has clear negative effects on brain development. Children with heavy prenatal alcohol exposure exhibit functional abnormalities in the medial temporal cortex and dorsal prefrontal cortex (Sowell et al. 2007) and demonstrate cortical thinning in large areas of the frontal, temporal, and occipital lobes (Zhou et al. 2011). It has been suggested that these negative effects may be partially caused by nutritional deficiencies that accompany alcohol use, in addition to direct alcoholic neurotoxicity (Ballard, Sun, and Ko 2012). The neurobiological risks of maternal substance use may be reduced by screening prospective and expecting mothers for drug use, providing abuse cessation education, providing treatment and support, and providing drug counseling (National Institute on Drug Abuse 2011). It may also be possible to reduce the neurodegenerative effects of maternal substance use by providing interventions for the offspring. For example, it has been hypothesized that supplementing the offspring with the nutrients choline, folate, and vitamin A may mitigate the effects of alcohol consumption during pregnancy (Ballard, Sun, and Ko 2012). Future research examining the effectiveness of nutritional supplementation, as well as the period of effectiveness, will be extremely valuable in the development of preventive interventions.

Nutrition plays a critical role in brain development during pregnancy and early childhood. Several studies have found that nutritional deficiencies predispose for antisocial behavior. Neugebauer, Hoek, and Susser (1999) found that male offspring of mothers who were severely malnourished during the first and second trimesters of pregnancy had 2.5 times the normal rate of antisocial personality disorder in adulthood. Poor nutrition in the first three years of life has also been associated with long-term antisocial behavior throughout childhood and late adolescence (Liu et al. 2004). In rats, prenatal malnutrition has been associated with reduced volume of the corpus callosum (Olivares et al. 2012) and alterations in the noradrenaline system in the prefrontal cortex (Flores et al. 2011).

Specific nutrients that have been linked to antisocial behavior include protein, zinc, iron, and vitamin B (Liu et al. 2004). Zinc deficiency has been associated with greater violence and aggression (Liu et al. 2004), and low levels of iron have been linked to aggression, conduct disorder, and juvenile delinquency (Rosen et al. 1985). In rhesus monkeys, Golub, Hogrefe, and Germann (2007) found that iron deficiency during infancy was associated with attenuated inhibitory responses and less emotional responsiveness to novel or threatening environments and stimuli (Golub et al. 2009), features that are observed in psychopathic individuals. Programs designed to ensure adequate intake of vitamins such as zinc and iron, both by the mother during pregnancy and by the infant during the first few years of life, may reduce the risk for the development of antisocial behavior.

Omega-3 fatty acids may also be particularly important in brain development and may be related to antisocial behavior. A correlational study indicated that increased national consumption of fish rich in omega-3 fatty acids is associated with lower levels of homicide rates, even when controlling for a number of other potentially confounding factors (Hibbeln 2001). Omega-3 (specifically docosahexaenoic acid or DHA) makes up approximately 6 percent of dry cerebral cortex; it influences the functioning of the blood-brain barrier, enhances synaptic functioning, regulates the activity of membrane enzymes, protects neurons from cell death, influences cell size, stimulates the growth of neurons, regulates serotonin and dopamine neurotransmission, and regulates gene expression (Kitajka et al. 2004). Prenatal intakes of omega-3 have been found to affect psychophysiological responding and improve performance on neurobehavioral assessments of memory in school-age children (Boucher et al. 2011). Concentrations of DHA in cord blood serum have been associated with lower rates of behavioral difficulties in children at age 10 (Kohlboeck et al. 2011). In addition, low consumption of fatty acids during pregnancy has been associated with preterm delivery and low birth weight (Olsen and Secher 2002), which negatively affect brain development. Thus, adequate intake of omega-3 fatty acids may aid in preventing a number of negative behavioral outcomes.

Finally, maternal stress and depression are factors that have been found to affect the developing brain and that are associated with psychopathic traits. Barker et al. (2011) found that maternal psychopathology from 0 to 2 years was associated with the development of callous-unemotional traits children at age 13. As mentioned above, maternal stress has an effect on hormone levels of the offspring (Hessl et al. 1998). Importantly, these changes in hormones have the potential to alter gene expression. Salaria et al. (2006) found that increased cortisol exposure in utero affects the expression of over 1,000 genes in fetal brain cells. Another form of maternal stress is disrupted sleep patterns that result from shift work. Ramlau-Hansen et al. (2011) found that maternal shift work was associated with an 11 percent increase in testosterone levels in male offspring at ages 18 to 21. One study found that omega-3 supplementation during pregnancy and lactation decreased postpartum anxiety-like behavior in rats (Chen and Su 2012). Thus, in addition to behaviorally based forms of intervention designed to reduce maternal stress and psychopathology, nutritional supplementation may also prove to be effective.

To a large extent, prevention programs have focused on reducing psychosocial factors. The Nurse-Family Partnership is one example of a treatment program that may operate, in part, through biological mechanisms. In this program, nurses pay home visits to low-income first-time mothers during pregnancy and during the first two years of life. The goals of the program are to improve the outcomes of pregnancy by helping women to improve prenatal health, to improve the child's health and development by helping parents provide more sensitive and competent care of the child, and to improve the parental life course by helping parents plan future pregnancies, complete their educations, and find work (Olds 2008). By offering counseling on pre- and postnatal nutrition and attempting to reduce maternal stress substance use during pregnancy, the program may be able to improve the neurodevelopment of the child. Programs such as these, which promote proper prenatal care, including regular physical examinations, proper nutrition, a generally healthy lifestyle, avoidance of toxins, including tobacco and substance use, and strong parental bonding, are essential for reducing exposure to risk and preventing the development of psychopathic traits and other negative outcomes (Liu 2011).

In addition to reducing risk factors, early environmental enrichment has also been found to have positive effects. Preschool-aged children who participated in a two-year enrichment program that included nutrition, physical exercise, and educational activities were found to show indications of better neurodevelopment and were 36 percent less likely to engage in criminal behavior in adulthood than those who had not participated. Tackling early health risk factors that have neurobiological effects may effectively reduce the development of psychopathic traits.

Treatment and Intervention

Overall, well-designed treatment studies using standardized measures of psychopathy are limited, but there are indications that some types of treatment may work. Salekin (2002) reviewed 42 treatment studies of adult psychopathy. In these studies, psychopathy was defined in various ways and the types of therapy included psychoanalytic, cognitive behavioral therapy, and eclectic. He found that 62 percent of patients benefited from psychotherapy, and that more effective treatments involved intensive individual sessions for an extended period and incorporated family members. However, the number of randomized controlled trials and studies utilizing modern assessments of psychopathy was limited. A subsequent review, limited to studies utilizing PCL-R-based measures of psychopathy, found that treatment results for adult psychopaths range from low-moderate to poor with three of eight studies demonstrating that psychopathic individuals benefitted from treatment (Salekin, Worley, and Grimes 2010). More controlled studies will be needed to gain a better understanding of what works and what does not. It is also likely that forms of treatment that have been found to be effective in reducing antisocial and criminal behavior are similarly effective in treating individuals with psychopathic traits, but psychopathic traits have simply not been examined in these studies.

An important reason for measuring psychopathic characteristics in youth is the hope that we may be able to identify and treat individuals with these features early in life. In recent years, several studies have examined the effectiveness of different forms of treatment for youth with callous-unemotional traits. Results from these studies have been mixed. A few studies have found that intensive inpatient treatment programs are effective for severely behaviorally disordered youth with psychopathic traits. These programs combine several approaches, including cognitive behavioral therapy, group therapy, family therapy, onsite academics, and career counseling (Caldwell et al. 2006, Rogers et al. 2004, Spain et al. 2004). One study found that this type of intensive treatment program was effective in reducing psychopathy scores over the course of 180 days. The program included school services; group treatment focused on anger management, social skills, problem solving, and substance abuse; individual counseling sessions; and unspecified pharmacological interventions (Caldwell et al. 2012). The study also included a behavioral assessment system that allowed for immediate feedback to the youth. Importantly, this study showed that the callous-unemotional traits, which are considered the core features of psychopathy, can be changed in addition to reducing the behavioral symptoms of the disorder. This study demonstrates great promise in the ability to treat psychopathy in even the most severe cases.

In an at-risk sample of youth ages 4 to 9, McDonald et al. (2011) found that a parenting intervention resulted in reductions in psychopathic traits even when controlling for behavioral symptoms. These effects were mediated by improvements in mothers' harsh and inconsistent parenting. Another study found significant reductions in callous-unemotional and narcissistic traits in 6 to 11-year-old youth who participated in either a clinic- or community based treatment program (Kolko et al. 2009). This study also implemented a comprehensive treatment approach involving cognitive behavioral therapy, parent management training, family therapy, and more. Importantly, treatment effects were maintained across a three-year follow-up period.

A less intensive intervention strategy that has recently proven to be effective in youth with psychopathic traits is a mental models intervention designed to increase motivation and raise positive emotion. Salekin, Tippey, and Allen (2012) conducted a 12-week intervention program that included 12 didactic sessions in which youth were given a motivational message that intelligence grows over time (e.g., that new neural connections can result through the process of active learning) and that the maximum benefit of treatment would be obtained by committing to the entire treatment program. The intervention also focused on generating positive emotion in youth, emphasizing positive ways of interacting with others, and asking youth to focus on their strengths. Finally, youth were asked to think about goals and mentally visualize ways of accomplishing their goals. This intervention was particularly effective in reducing the interpersonal features of psychopathy, but also resulted in decreased frequency and severity of impulsivity and decreased callousness. This intervention may work by increasing positive emotion, which may broaden cognitive networks and improve decision making in youth with psychopathic traits.

Other studies have found less promising results. Haas et al. (2011) examined the effectiveness of an eight-week summer treatment program designed to improve social skills and academic achievement and to promote prosocial behavior and decrease antisocial behavior in youth ages 7 to 12. They found that youth with callous-unemotional traits demonstrated less responsiveness to treatment, exhibited less behavioral improvement in social skills and problem solving skills, and demonstrated that punishments such as time-outs may be ineffective. Similarly, Hawes and Dadds (2005) found that although youth *without* callous-unemotional traits were responsive to a 10-week behavioral parent training intervention, youth with callous-unemotional traits had worse treatment responses.

Thus, it appears that there is evidence that some forms of treatment may be effective, whereas others may not be. One disadvantage of studies that implement comprehensive treatment approaches is that it is difficult to determine which aspects of the treatment were most effective. Most of the studies described above utilized a variety of behavioral treatment strategies. In addition, several of these studies included pharmacological interventions (Kolko et al. 2009, Caldwell et al. 2012) so it is unclear to what extent the effects are a result of medication versus the behaviorally based treatments. A study by Waschbusch et al. (2007) found that in a university-based summer treatment program, youth with callous-unemotional traits were not responsive to behavioral therapy alone, but did respond to the combination of behavioral therapy and stimulant medication (methylphenidate) used to treat ADHD symptoms. This suggests that behavioral treatments alone may not be sufficient to treat youth with callous-unemotional traits, but that medication may improve the effectiveness of these treatments. Finally, although some studies have produced significant improvements, responsiveness to treatment appears to be highly variable, with some individuals showing improvement and others not (Rogers et al. 2004). Thus, there is still much work to be done in terms of understanding which forms of treatment are most effective and in determining why some individuals may respond to treatment more than others.

Taking into consideration recent developments in understanding the neurobiology of psychopathy, it is possible that incorporating treatments that are designed to improve the functioning of biological systems may be beneficial. This might be achieved in a variety of ways, including pharmacological or psychosocial interventions that alter neurotransmitter or hormone levels or techniques that might directly alter the functioning of certain brain regions. When considering treatments that attempt to alter biological factors, our view is that it's never too early and it's never too late. Evidence suggests that hormone levels and brain structure and functioning can be changed even in adulthood (e.g., Felmingham et al. 2007).

Potential Treatments Targeting Biological Factors
Potential Targets: Hormones and Neurotransmitters

As discussed in Chapter 4, hormone levels change in response to conditions in the environment such as stressors. As such, hormone levels can also potentially be altered by treatment. Some forms of treatment may prove to be effective because they are able to restore previously disrupted hormone levels. For example, alterations in cortisol responsivity have been observed in children following a number of adverse early life experiences (Shea et al. 2005, Fisher et al. 2007). In a sample of 3- to 6-year-old foster children, Fisher et al. (2007) found that a 12-month family-based therapeutic intervention was able to restore altered diurnal cortisol patterns to a level that became comparable to the patterns demonstrated by nonmaltreated children.

Treatment-related improvements in hormone levels have also been found in antisocial youth. Brotman et al. (2007) conducted a 22-week family-based intervention in preschool children at risk for antisocial behavior. They measured salivary cortisol levels before and after a social challenge involving entry into an unfamiliar peer group. At the end of the intervention, during the social challenge, the cortisol levels of the children in the treatment group were significantly increased. A follow-up study found that the intervention's effect on aggression was largely mediated by the cortisol response (i.e., the degree to which cortisol levels increased was related to the degree to which aggression was reduced) (O'Neal et al. 2010). Like the study by Fisher et al. (2007), this study suggests that the cortisol response is malleable and that treatments may have the ability to reduce the negative effects that early life experiences or other factors may have had on hormone levels.

It is worth emphasizing that the studies discussed above involved psychosocial rather than directly biological forms of treatment. This demonstrates the significant role that the environment plays in influencing biology, and it also demonstrates that biologically based forms of treatment such as medication are not always necessary to produce lasting changes in biological systems. By understanding the effects that psychosocial treatments have on biology, we can better understand their mechanisms of action. For example, we can understand that a specific parenting intervention is effective in reducing aggression because it improves cortisol responding in the child.

Another hormone that could potentially be targeted by interventions is oxytocin. Oxytocin has been found to aid in the formation of social bonds, enhance recognition of social stimuli, and facilitate social affiliation and attachment (Lim and Young 2006). Youth with psychopathic traits have deficits in the recognition of facial expressions and emotional attachment to others. Interestingly, callous-unemotional traits have been associated with a specific polymorphism in the oxytocin receptor gene, suggesting that this system may function differently in these youth (Beitchman et al. 2012). Dadds and Rhodes (2008) have suggested that oxytocin may have therapeutic value in the treatment of youth with psychopathic traits, helping to alleviate some of the deficits in communication and emotion perception. Administration of oxytocin in healthy individuals has been found to enhance trust, improve identification of emotions from the eyes, and reduce responsiveness to social threats (Graustella and MacLeod 2012). Dadds and Rhodes suggested that oxytocin administration in combination with emotional training may improve the effectiveness of training. Administration of oxytocin in short bursts during therapeutic settings or during prescribed psychological experiences may help youth to learn to infer the emotional states of others or to develop attachment to a responsive caregiver.

Treatments may also target neurotransmitter systems. For example, as discussed above, Waschbusch et al. (2007) found that youth with callous-unemotional traits responded better to a combined treatment involving stimulant medication and behavioral therapy. Although the mechanisms for the treatment effects are unknown, the authors note that the stimulant methylphenidate targets the noradrenergic system, which has been hypothesized to be associated with the emergence of callous-unemotional traits (Blair 2006b). Understanding how hormones and neurotransmitters are altered in response to different types of treatment will undoubtedly be useful in developing better treatments that may produce larger and longer-lasting reductions in aggression and psychopathic traits.

Potential Target: Brain

Other forms of treatment may be able to affect brain structure or functioning more directly. For example, repetitive transcranial magnetic stimulation (rTMS) is a noninvasive technique that is used to stimulate the brain using very strong, pulsed magnetic fields. rTMS sessions result in changes in cortical excitability in the stimulated area. While research using the technique is still in its infancy, rTMS has been found to be an effective treatment for depression (George et al. 2010). Daily rTMS sessions over the course of several weeks on the left prefrontal cortex have been found to have antidepressant properties, even in individuals with moderately treatment-resistant depression. Treatment with rTMS over the course of several weeks may also be able to change brain structure. Peng et al. (2012) found that white matter structural integrity in the middle frontal gyrus was improved after four weeks of rTMS treatment in a sample of patients with treatment-resistant depression. This improvement was correlated with decreased severity of depressed symptoms.

Studies have also found that rTMS is capable of altering emotional processing and moral judgment (Tassy et al. 2012, Baeken et al. 2011), suggesting that it is able to affect processes relevant to psychopathy. Although the potential use of rTMS in the treatment of antisocial behavior or psychopathy has not been explored, it may be possible to use it to enhance functioning in regions of the brain that are deficient. For example, Knoch et al. (2006) found that fast rTMS applied to the right dorsolateral prefrontal cortex increases activity in the orbitofrontal cortex bilaterally. Improving functioning of the orbitofrontal cortex in psychopathic individuals could help to improve decision making and reduce impulsivity.

Similar procedures to rTMS include theta burst stimulation (TBS) and transcranial direct current stimulation (tDCS). Studies using these procedures have found that it may be possible to reduce risk taking and impulsivity in healthy participants. Cho et al. (2010) found that continuous TBS over the right dorsolateral prefrontal cortex in healthy subjects resulted in less impulsive decision making, evidenced by a preference for delayed larger rewards instead of smaller immediate rewards. Fecteau et al. (2007) found that risky decision making could be decreased using tDCS to increase excitability in the right DLPFC, while decreasing excitability in the left DLPFC. Participants in the experimental condition selected the safe option more often and appeared to be insensitive to the rewards associated with the options. Although much more research is necessary, such findings raise the possibility that manipulations of brain activity could be effective in treating some of the symptoms of psychopathy. By directly altering brain functioning or structure, these studies also provide valuable information about the role of different brain regions in processes such as decision making.

Another method for directly affecting the brain may be through dietary supplementation. For example, omega-3 supplementation has an effect on brain structure and functioning (Yehuda, Rabinovitz, and Mostofsky 2005). Randomized controlled trials of omega-3 supplementation have found significant changes in the brain in groups who receive supplementation. In a study of 8 to 10-year-old healthy boys, eight weeks of omega-3 fatty acid administration was found to significantly increase activity in the dorsolateral prefrontal cortex during a sustained attention task (McNamara et al. 2010). Omega-3 supplementation has also been found to alter the fluidity of cell membranes in the brain (Hirashima et al. 2004), suggesting that it has the potential to influence brain structure. Another study found positive associations between reported dietary omega-3 intake and gray matter volumes in the anterior cingulate cortex, hippocampus, and right amygdala (Conklin et al. 2007). As discussed in Chapter 8, each of these regions has previously been implicated in psychopathy. Thus, omega-3 supplementation may be one way to improve brain structure and functioning, thus reducing antisocial behavior. Indeed, in 231 young adult offenders, Gesch et al. (2002) found a 26 percent net reduction in reported incidents within the prison in offenders who received nutritional supplements, including omega-3 fatty acids. This finding was replicated by Zaalberg et al. (2010) in 221 young adult offenders. However, these results should be interpreted with caution, as other measures of aggressiveness were not significantly different. These studies provide some evidence that nutritional interventions can be effective even at a later age.

Research in the past decade has also begun to demonstrate how behaviorally based treatments may affect the brain. For example, studies show that cognitive behavioral therapy for treatment of posttraumatic stress disorder (PTSD) or phobias is effective in changing brain functioning. Felmingham et al. (2007) found that after eight weekly sessions of exposure-based therapy, brain functioning was changed in the anterior cingulate and amygdala in patients with PTSD. Similarly, Paquette et al. (2003) found that abnormal activity in the dorsolateral prefrontal cortex and parahippocampal gyrus was reduced to the level of controls in a sample of participants with spider phobia. These changes in the brain have also been found to mediate treatment effects. Another study of cognitive behavioral therapy for social phobia found that the degree of reduction in activity in the amygdala and hippocampus mediated the treatment-induced reduction in social anxiety during public speaking (Furmark et al. 2002). These studies suggest that the brain can indeed be changed by cognitive or behaviorally based interventions. We should note that these changes are likely the result of changes to neurotransmitters, hormones, or other factors that facilitate brain functioning, but the treatments have an effect that is large enough to be detected at the systems level via brain imaging. Understanding the biological effects of these treatments can help us to better understand how the treatments work and may aid in improving their efficacy.

Using Biological Factors to Tailor Treatments

Given that there are multiple risk factors for the development of psychopathic traits, different individuals will most certainly have different risk factors that predispose them to the disorder. In some individuals, genetic factors may have a strong influence on the development of psychopathic traits, whereas in others, environmental factors may be more important. Treatment studies may benefit by identifying subgroups of psychopathic individuals with specific risk factors and by tailoring therapies and treatments to those risk factors. Assessing biological characteristics such as brain structure and functioning, hormone levels, and the presence of particular genetic polymorphisms may aid in the designation of individuals into specific treatment programs that may offer the best chance of improvement. Several studies of treatment of other psychological conditions have shown that these types of pretreatment biological factors can moderate treatment responses.

For example, approximately half of patients with PTSD do not respond to cognitive behavioral therapy, which is the treatment of choice for the disorder. Bryant et al. (2008) found that pretreatment levels of functioning in the amygdala and anterior cingulate, as measured by fMRI, predicted which patients would respond to treatment. Greater amygdala and anterior cingulate activity was associated with poorer improvement after treatment. Similarly, a study of obsessive-compulsive disorder found that pretreatment activity in the orbitofrontal cortex predicted treatment response to both behavioral therapy and medication (Brody et al. 1998). In a sample of youth with anxiety disorder diagnoses, McClure et al. (2007) found that pretreatment activity in the left amygdala was negatively associated with symptom improvement in response to either fluoxetine (a selective serotonin reuptake inhibitor) or cognitive behavioral therapy. Finally, Kito, Hasegawa, and Koga (2012) found that responsiveness to rTMS as a treatment for depression was associated with pretreatment levels of cerebral blood flow in the ventromedial prefrontal cortex. Thus, these studies show that pretreatment levels of brain functioning can help to predict whether individuals will respond to a variety of treatments, whether behaviorally or biologically based.

The presence of specific genetic polymorphisms may also affect individuals' responses to treatment. Polymorphisms of the dopamine transporter gene have been found to moderate treatment outcomes of behavioral parent training in youth with ADHD (van den Hoofdakker et al. 2012). In children with one polymorphism, the treatment was effective, whereas it was not effective in those with the other polymorphism. In a sample of children undergoing cognitive behavioral therapy for anxiety disorders, those homozygous for the short allele of the serotonin transporter gene were significantly more likely to respond to CBT than those with the long allele (Eley et al. 2012).

In general, researchers studying psychopathy may be able to gain insight from understanding how basic neurobiological research is translated into effective treatments for other disorders. For example, depression has been linked to most of the same structures that have been implicated in psychopathy but findings occur in the opposite direction. Depression is associated with *hyper*activation in areas such as the amygdala, hippocampus, ventromedial prefrontal cortex, and anterior cingulate, and as in psychopathy, it has been proposed that the connectivity between limbic and cortical areas may be disrupted, compromising the cross-talk between regions. Future research in psychopathy may benefit from examining ongoing research on the etiology and treatment of depression. An exploration of the factors that may cause some individuals to develop *hyper*activity in certain brain regions while others experience *hypo*activity may provide essential clues to the development of psychopathy and other disorders. In addition, by examining the effects of various pharmacologic and behavioral treatments for disorders such as depression, we may be able to form new hypotheses about possible treatments for psychopathy.

Conclusions

Despite its importance, progress in developing successful programs for the prevention and treatment of psychopathic traits in youth and adults has been limited, but some studies have produced promising results. However, individuals with psychopathic traits still tend to have worse outcomes than antisocial individuals without psychopathic traits. There is a need for future research that translates the basic knowledge we have gained regarding psychopathy into full-scale treatment studies. We propose that a multisystem approach that takes both biological and environmental factors into consideration may prove to be most effective in preventing and treating psychopathy. Prevention measures in particular may be the most cost-effective way of solving the problem. By reducing the occurrence of environmental risks such as toxin exposure, poor nutrition, and maternal stress, we may in theory be able to prevent some of the brain abnormalities that are associated with psychopathy. By intervening at key points during development, we have the potential to change these biological risk factors for crime and other negative outcomes.

The consideration of treatments that have a more direct influence on biology may also prove to be beneficial. For example, if omega-3 supplementation is found to be effective in improving brain structure and/ or functioning, there could be beneficial implications for a much wider population of youth throughout the world whose adult life outcomes could be significantly improved. It will also be important to understand how traditional treatment methods may alter biological factors. By examining mechanisms of action, we can learn more about why particular treatments are effective, which will likely aid in the development of future treatments. If these treatment methods can be refined to be more effective in reducing callous-unemotional traits, they would prove to be highly cost-effective in reducing rates of antisocial behavior in childhood and ultimately crime and violence in adulthood. Finally, by examining the biological factors that may affect treatment outcomes, we can better understand why some individuals are responsive to treatment whereas others are not. This information could be used in the future to tailor treatments to individuals based on noninvasive brain scans or genetic testing.

Considering the long-term effects of continued violence and incarceration, investment in research to identify more effective methods for preventing and treating psychopathy is critical. The idea that biological factors contribute to psychopathy should not deter us from tackling the problem, but instead should spur us to think about the ways in which these biological risk factors can be prevented or ameliorated.

Conclusion

Understanding the role that biology plays in psychopathic personality will be essential both in developing solutions to reduce its occurrence and in creating public policies that are appropriate and fair. We hope to have provided the reader with a better understanding of biological research on psychopathy in several domains and to have clarified what conclusions can and cannot be drawn from the findings.

Throughout the book, we have emphasized that many of the biological factors that researchers study, including hormones, psychophysiological measures, and brain structure and functioning, reflect the combined effects of both genetics and the environment. Studying these biological mechanisms does not rule out the importance of environmental influences. Rather, these findings provide a description of the biological pathway by which both genetic *and* environmental factors—the ultimate causes of behavior—have their effects. Behavioral genetics studies suggest that, on average, approximately half of the variation in psychopathic traits is genetic and half is environmental, meaning that we need to focus on understanding both aspects in order to gain a complete picture of the causes of psychopathy.

Another point to keep in mind is that the majority of the findings we have discussed identify modest associations between psychopathic traits and biological factors. Results represent average differences between groups or correlations between biological measures and psychopathy scores; they do not indicate that every individual with psychopathic traits will demonstrate these biological differences or that all individuals with such biological differences have psychopathic traits. These findings also do not necessarily reflect "abnormality" that is outside of the range of normal variation. Finally, it has not been determined that these factors are *causally* related to the development of psychopathic traits. The finding of an association between a biological factor and a disorder does not imply that the biological factor causes the behavioral symptoms of the disorder. For example, there are many biological differences between males and females, such as differences in weight and height, but these variables do not *cause* an individual to identify with a particular gender. Similarly, the finding of a biological difference between individuals scoring high versus low in psychopathy does not necessarily indicate that this difference is a cause of the psychopathic traits.

A final point that we hope to have clarified is that *biological* is not the equivalent of *innate*. Just because researchers identify differences in the brain or in hormone levels does not mean that these factors cannot be changed. The environment influences biology throughout the life span. This provides great potential for the development of interventions. We have suggested that research focused on interventions that aim to influence biological factors may be especially helpful in improving our ability to treat psychopathy.

Biological Endophenotypes

Much of the research we have reviewed provides descriptive information about how the biology of psychopathic individuals is different. Using different methodologies, the most consistent findings are that the amygdala and ventromedial prefrontal cortex (PFC) function differently in people with higher levels of psychopathic traits. Psychophysiological research suggests that amygdala functioning may be disrupted because psychopathic individuals have reduced skin conductance responses when processing aversive stimuli, and during aversive conditioning and fear-potentiated startle paradigms, each of which is thought to rely on the functioning of the amygdala. Research in neuropsychology has provided evidence that patients with damage to the ventromedial PFC or amygdala demonstrate some of the same characteristics as individuals with psychopathy. Patients with damage to the ventromedial PFC exhibit impulsiveness, disinhibited social behavior, irresponsibility, and reactive aggression. They also demonstrate similar performance on moral decision-making tasks and gambling/risk-taking tasks. Patients with damage to the amygdala have deficits in recognizing and experiencing fear and are described as having less of a sense of "danger." They also show deficits in fear-potentiated startle and aversive conditioning similar to the deficits observed in psychopaths.

Neuropsychological research has also found that psychopathic individuals exhibit deficits on tasks that are thought to rely on the functioning of the ventromedial PFC or amygdala. The Iowa Gambling Task, for example, relies on the ability of the ventromedial PFC to facilitate reversal learning. Psychopathic individuals demonstrate deficits on this task, as well as other tasks that depend on reversal learning abilities. They also perform poorly on a variety tasks that tap into processes that are dependent on the amygdala, including emotion recognition tasks (poor recognition of fearful facial expressions and vocal cues) and tasks involving stimulus-reinforcement learning.

Brain imaging research has provided more direct evidence of differences in the amygdala and ventromedial PFC in psychopathy. Studies have observed reduced functioning in psychopathic individuals in both of these regions during a variety of tasks, most of which involve processing social or emotional information. Reduced gray matter has been observed in the ventromedial PFC and in the basolateral and superficial nuclei groups of the amygdala. In addition, both structural connectivity and functional connectivity between these regions have been found to be reduced in psychopathic individuals.

Hormones and neurotransmitters may contribute to the altered functioning of these regions. The hormone cortisol stimulates amygdala functioning, whereas testosterone inhibits it. Some evidence suggests that psychopathic individuals may have elevated testosterone to cortisol ratios, which may inhibit functioning of the amygdala. Furthermore, reduced cortisol and increased testosterone levels may also disrupt the connectivity between the amygdala and ventromedial PFC, meaning that signals from the amygdala may not be able to reach the ventromedial PFC in order to inform decision making, and that signals from the ventromedial PFC may not be able to reach the amygdala to aid in regulating emotion and inhibiting impulses.

Overall, deficits in the amygdala in psychopathic individuals may result in impairments in the process of stimulus-reinforcement learning, which allows an individual to learn the goodness and badness of objects and actions. This may mean that during development, individuals may have disrupted abilities to learn from reward and punishment. They also may not be able to learn to associate their harmful actions with the pain and distress of others, resulting in a lack of empathy. Deficits in the ventromedial PFC may similarly lead to several of the impairments observed in psychopathy. Because this region is involved in learning associations between stimuli, and anticipating and processing reward and punishment feedback, deficits may compromise decision making, social behavior, and the processing of emotional information.

Although findings regarding the amygdala and ventromedial PFC are the most consistently associated with psychopathy, other brain regions have also been implicated and may also be important. Studies of event-related potentials that occur after an error has been committed by the individual suggest that there may be deficits in the functioning of the anterior cingulate. In support of this, several functional brain imaging studies have identified reduced functioning in this region. Some neuropsychological and brain imaging studies suggest that the dorsolateral PFC, a region involved in executive functioning, may function *better* in some psychopathic individuals, which may aid in the ability of some individuals to con and manipulate others, to carefully plan crimes, and to escape detection. Other regions involved in moral judgment and in reward processing have also been implicated in psychopathy. Although research regarding some of these brain regions is less consistent, studies are attempting to clarify the role of these regions and whether they do in fact contribute to the manifestation of psychopathic traits.

The Ultimate Causes of Psychopathy

Genes and environmental factors represent the ultimate causes of the development of psychopathy. Genes guide the development of the brain and other biological systems. Initial studies have suggested that genes associated with various neurotransmitter systems may confer risk for psychopathy. Genes associated with the transmission of dopamine may alter the reward system of the brain, affecting learning and increasing susceptibility for reward seeking. Genes associated with serotonin may affect the functioning of the amygdala and alter the way that an individual responds to stress and threat.

Differences in genes mean that there is much variation in how people respond to social and environmental risk factors for crime. Individuals with more genetic risk factors are likely to be more susceptible to developing antisocial behavior in high-risk environments. However, gene expression can also be changed by the environment. Early environmental risk or protective factors may have strong influences on biological development. By identifying specific genes that are associated with psychopathy, we can improve our understanding of its developmental pathway (from genes to brain to behavior). We can also use this information to tailor treatments to the particular biological risk factors of an individual.

Environmental risk factors such as parenting, abuse, poverty, head injury, birth complications, nutrition, toxins, and a variety of other factors both within and outside the home may also contribute to the development of psychopathy. Some of these factors may confer risk for psychopathy because of their effects on biological systems. Experiences or events very early in life may alter the development of biological systems important in responding to stress and threat. They may also affect the development of brain regions. A few studies have found that psychopathy is associated with interactions between environmental risk factors and biological risk factors. Knowledge of how genetic/biological factors and environmental factors interact may be extremely helpful in designing more effective interventions.

The identification of the endophenotypes described in the previous section—differences in hormones, psychophysiology, and brain structure and functioning—will also be helpful in attempts to identify both the genetic and environmental factors that contribute to psychopathy. For example, by showing that reduced functioning of the amygdala may contribute to psychopathic traits, we can begin to explore the genetic and environmental factors that may lead to disrupted amygdala functioning (or the genetic and environmental factors that may alter hormone levels, which in turn lead to disrupted amygdala functioning).

The Goal of Biological Research

Ultimately, the goal of biological research on psychopathy is to develop prevention and intervention measures that are more targeted and effective. We argue that research on prevention and intervention should take biological factors into consideration. Because the environment has an effect on biology, including influencing gene expression, this means that the development of many biological risk factors may be preventable by changing the environment in positive ways. Modifications in nutrition, reducing exposure to toxins, and promoting improvements in other health factors may help to eliminate deficits in the brain and hormone systems that may contribute to the development of psychopathy. Cognitive and behavioral interventions are also known to have effects on biological systems. Understanding how behavioral interventions alter biology can help us to better understand how these treatments work and help us to improve their efficacy.

The prenatal period in particular is an important time in which to focus on preventive measures because the developing fetus is highly vulnerable to influences from the environment (Liu 2011). The finding that individuals with cavum septum pellucidum, a marker of fetal neural maldevelopment, have higher levels of psychopathy suggests that, at least for some individuals, disruptions in the brain, as a result of either genetic or very early environmental factors, may occur even before birth. By targeting risk factors such as nutrition and toxin exposure during pregnancy and early childhood, we may be able to significantly reduce the risk for developing psychopathic traits. Although the effectiveness of some methods may be greater the earlier they are implemented, we argue that it is never too late, as biological systems are malleable even in adulthood.

Biological research on psychopathy may also be helpful in tailoring treatments to the specific needs of individuals. Because different individuals undoubtedly have different risk factors for psychopathy, it is likely that some forms of treatment will work better for some individuals than others. Evaluating biological factors such as brain structure and functioning, hormone levels, and the presence of particular genetic polymorphisms can help us to understand why some individuals are responsive to treatment whereas others are not. This information may aid in the designation of individuals into specific treatment programs that may be the most effective for that individual. Considering the long-term effects of continued violence and incarceration, investment in research to identify more effective methods for preventing and treating psychopathy is critical.

Public Policy

The study of the biological factors associated with antisocial behavior has been the source of much controversy. The media often convey information about biological research in ways that are deceptively simple, declaring that researchers have found a particular gene or brain region that is responsible for crime. This can lead to much misunderstanding among the public and strong backlash against biologically oriented research.

It will be important for scientists to clearly communicate the purposes and limitations of this type of research, particularly when interacting with policy makers and individuals in the legal system. There are serious costs to applying this research prematurely, but also serious costs to ignoring what we do know. In a recent review of issues surrounding neuroscience and the law, the Royal Society, an international organization of distinguished scientists, put forth several recommendations for managing the inevitable intersection between these two fields. These included organizing international meetings to bring together those working across the legal system with experts in neuroscience and related disciplines; requiring neuroscience courses for those pursuing legal degrees; providing relevant training for judges, lawyers, and probation officers; and promoting additional research in areas in which neuroscience intersects with the legal system (Royal Society 2011). The authors of the report note that there is currently a big gap between research conducted by neuroscientists and the realities of the day-to-day work of the justice system, and it is important to encourage communication between the two groups.

Attempts are also being made to provide further research on the intersection between neuroscience and the law. The MacArthur Research Network on Law and Neuroscience funds research examining a number of issues, including assessing probable mental states of defendants and witnesses, assessing defendants' capacity for regulating their behavior, and assessing whether neuroscience evidence should be admitted in individual cases. It is our hope that through continued discussion and research, these issues will be handled in an informed manner that considers both the strengths and limitations of biological research.

The Next Steps

Although the field is growing, research on the biological factors associated with psychopathy has received relatively little attention compared to research on other mental health problems. It has been suggested that the biology of crime in general may be understudied for several reasons (Moffitt, Ross, and Raine 2011). Disorders such as schizophrenia, attention-deficit/hyperactivity disorder, and autism have powerful advocacy groups made up of parents and family members of patients who lobby for more funding for research, whereas no comparable group of advocates for antisocial criminal offenders exists. In addition, pharmaceutical companies may also drive support for biological research into other disorders that afflict large numbers of people who actively seek treatment. Antisocial individuals are much less likely to seek treatment or to have the financial means to pay for it. However, it is estimated that the costs to society of antisocial, violent, and criminal behavior actually surpass the costs of all other behavioral and health conditions (Anderson 1999). Our hope is that major funding agencies will recognize the burden that psychopathy bears on society and dedicate more resources to research aimed at solving the problem. If information about biology can help us to be more effective in reducing the incidence of psychopathy, it would prove to be a highly cost-effective method of reducing rates of antisocial behavior, crime, and violence in adulthood.

There are a number of avenues that are worthy of exploring in future research on the biological mechanisms associated with psychopathy. Technical advances in biological research are improving our ability to collect and analyze biological data with improved efficiency and accuracy. One of the areas that will be important for future progress is research on the connections between the different subareas of biological research covered in this book. For the most part, the relationship between psychopathic traits and factors such as genes, hormones, psychophysiological indicators, and brain structure/functioning has been examined in separate lines of research. We have limited knowledge about how these different levels of biology are connected and how environmental factors have an influence. For example, it will be important to better understand how hormones affect brain functioning, how genes affect brain development, and how environmental factors affect hormone levels. Understanding how different risk factors interact with each other will prove to be crucial in our understanding of how psychopathy develops. Many of the studies we have reviewed examine a single biological variable at one time, yet the reality is much more nuanced and complex.

Future biological research on psychopathy will also benefit from longitudinal studies that begin at an early age and follow individuals at numerous time points during development. Most studies conducted to date have examined the neurobiological basis of criminal behavior using cross-sectional data. Longitudinal studies that examine both biological and environmental factors throughout development will help to clarify the causal relationships between these factors.

Additional research is also needed to explore the biological factors associated with the different features of psychopathy. It is not clear whether psychopathy represents a unitary construct in which different features share common etiological factors, or whether psychopathy may represent separable and distinct underlying constructs that may co-occur in some individuals (Patrick and Bernat 2009). Biological research may provide insights into whether the different features of psychopathy have distinct neurobiological underpinnings. It has been suggested that studies may benefit from separately operationalizing constructs observed in psychopathy such as trait fear or externalizing tendencies in order to examine the neurobiology of a more basic process (Patrick and Bernat 2009).

Finally, as mentioned above, research furthering our ultimate goal of preventing the development of psychopathic traits is of high importance. Successful prevention and intervention efforts may be most effective when they start in early childhood or even prenatally. The consideration of individual differences in biology, in addition to the consideration of environmental factors, is likely to improve our ability to develop effective interventions.

Our hope is that we can move beyond the misunderstandings that often accompany biological research on psychopathy and that a truly biosocial perspective, examining both genetic and environmental influences, will become more mainstream. The question is no longer whether psychopathy is a result of nature or nurture, but rather how these two forces interact during development to result in psychopathic traits. Recent biological research has brought us a new understanding of how the environment is able to influence biology, not just in infancy and childhood, but throughout the life span, opening new doors to solving this complex societal problem.

Babiak, P., and R. D. Hare. 2006. *Snakes in Suits: When Psychopaths Go to Work*. New York: HarperCollins.

Cleckley, H. 1976. *The Mask of Sanity*. 5th ed. St. Louis, MO: Mosby.

Del Giudice, M., B. J. Ellis, and E. A. Shirtcliff. 2011. "The adaptive calibration model of stress responsivity." *Neuroscience and Biobehavioral Reviews* 35 (7):1562–92.

Dickerson, S. S., and M. E. Kemeny. 2004. "Acute stressors and cortisol responses: A theoretical integration and synthesis of laboratory research." *Psychological Bulletin* 130:355–91.

Eagleman, D. 2011. "The brain on trial." *Atlantic Monthly* 308:112–23.

Focquaert, F., A. L. Glenn, and A. Raine. 2013. "Free will, responsibility, and the punishment of criminals." In *The Future of Punishment*, edited by T. Nadelhoffer, 247–74. Oxford: Oxford University Press.

Gao, Y., A. L. Glenn, M. Peskin, A. Rudo-Hutt, R. A. Schug, Y. Yang, and A. Raine. 2011. "Neurocriminological approaches." In *Handbook of Criminological Research Methods*, edited by D. Gadd, S. Karstedt, and S. Messner, 63–75. London: Sage.

Gao, Y., and A. Raine. 2009. "P3 event-related potential impairments in antisocial and psychopathic individuals: A meta-analysis." *Biological Psychology* 82:199–210.

———. 2010. "Successful and unsuccessful psychopaths: A neurobiological model." *Behavioral Sciences & the Law* 28:1–17.

Glenn, A. L. 2009. "Neuroendocrine markers for psychopathy." In The *Handbook of Neuropsychiatric Biomarkers, Endophenotypes, and Genes*, edited by M. S. Ritsner, 59–70. Dordrecht, Netherlands: Springer.

Glenn, A. L., and A. Raine. 2011. "Antisocial personality disorders." In *The Oxford Handbook of Social Neuroscience*, edited by J. Decety and J. T. Cacioppo, 885–94. New York: Oxford University Press.

Granger, D. A., K. T. Kivlighan, C. Fortunato, A. G. Harmon, L. C. Hibel, E. B. Schwartz, and G. L. Whembolua. 2007. "Integration of salivary biomarkers into developmental and behaviorally-oriented research: Problems and solutions for collecting specimens." *Physiology & Behavior* 92:583–90.

Gunter, T. D., M. G. Vaughn, and R. A. Philibert. 2010. "Behavioral genetics in antisocial spectrum disorders and psychopathy: A review of the recent literature." *Behavioral Sciences & the Law* 28:148–73.

Hare, R. D. 1999. *Without Conscience: The Disturbing World of the Psychopaths among Us*. New York: Guilford.

Hariri, A. R. 2009. "The neurobiology of individual differences in complex behavioral traits." *Annual Review of Neuroscience* 32:225–47.

Koenigs, M., A. R. Baskin-Sommers, J. Zeier, and J. P. Newman. 2011. "Investigating the neural correlates of psychopathy: A critical review." *Molecular Psychiatry* 16:792–99.

Lorber, M. F. 2004. "Psychophysiology of aggression, psychopathy, and conduct problems: A meta-analysis." *Psychological Bulletin* 130 (4):531–52.

Miyake, A., and N. P. Friedman. 2012. "The nature and organization of individual differences in executive functions: Four general conclusions." *Current Directions in Psychological Science* 21:8–14.

Moffitt, T. E. 2005. "The new look of behavioral genetics in developmental psychopathology: Gene-environment interplay in antisocial behaviors." *Psychological Bulletin* 131:533–54.

Morgan, A. B., and S. O. Lilienfeld. 2000. "A meta-analytic review of the relation between antisocial behavior and neuropsychological measures of executive function." *Clinical Psychology Review* 20:113–36.

Odgers, C. L., and M. A. Russell. 2011. "What can genetically informed research tell us about the causes of crime?" In *Measuring Crime and Criminality: Advances in Criminological Theory*, edited by J. MacDonald, 141–60. New Brunswick, NJ: Transaction.

Ogilvie, J. M., A. L. Stewart, R. C. K. Chan, and D. H. K. Shum. 2011. "Neuropsychological measures of executive function and antisocial behavior: A meta-analysis." *Criminology* 49 (4):1063–1107.

Patrick, C. J. 2008. "Psychophysiological correlates of aggression and violence: An integrative review." *Philosophical Transactions of the Royal Society B—Biological Sciences* 363 (1503):2543–55.

Raine, A. 2002. "Biosocial studies of antisocial and violent behavior in children and adults: A review." *Journal of Abnormal Child Psychology* 30 (4):311–26.

Royal Society. 2011. *Brain Waves Module 4: Neuroscience and the Law*. London: Royal Society.

Salekin, R. T., and D. R. Lynam. 2010. *Handbook of Child and Adolescent Psychopathy*. New York: Guilford.

Salekin, R. T., C. Worley, and R. D. Grimes. 2010. "Treatment of psychopathy: A review and brief introduction to the mental model approach for psychopathy." *Behavioral Sciences & the Law* 28 (2):235–66.

Tremblay, R. E. 2008. "Understanding development and prevention of chronic physical aggression: Towards experimental epigenetics studies." *Philosophical Transactions of the Royal Society B* 363:2613–22.

Yang, Y., and A. Raine. 2009. "Prefrontal structural and functional brain imaging findings in antisocial, violent, and psychopathic individuals: A meta-analysis." *Psychiatry Research* 174:81–88.

Abbott, C., and J. Bustillo. 2006. "What we have learned from proton magnetic resonance spectroscopy about schizophrenia? A critical update." *Current Opinion in Psychiatry* 19:135–39.

Adolphs, R., D. Tranel, and A. R. Damasio. 1998. "The human amygdala in social judgement." *Nature* 393 (6684):470–74.

Adolphs, R., D. Tranel, A. W. Young, A. J. Calder, E. A. Phelps, and A. K. Anderson. 1999. "Recognition of facial emotion in nine individuals with bilateral amygdala damage." *Neuropsychologia* 37:1111–17.

Alexander, N., Y. Kuepper, A. Schmitz, R. Osinsky, E. Kozyra, and J. Hennig. 2009. "Gene-environment interactions predict cortisol responses after acute stress: Implications for the etiology of depression." *Psychoneuroendocrinology* 34:1294–1303.

American Law Institute. 1962. *Model Penal Code*. Philadelphia: American Law Institute.

American Psychiatric Association. 1994. *Diagnostic and Statistical Manual of Mental Disorders*. 4th ed. Washington, DC: American Psychiatric Association.

Anastassiou-Hadjicharalambous, X., and D. Warden. 2008. "Physiologically-Indexed and Self-Perceived Affective Empathy in Conduct-Disordered Children High and Low on Callous-Unemotional Traits." *Child Psychiatry & Human Development* 39 (4):503–17.

Andershed, H., M. Kerr, H. Stattin, and S. Levander. 2002. "Psychopathic traits in non-referred youths: Initial test of a new assessment tool." In *Psychopaths: Current International Perspectives*, edited by E. Blaauw, J. M. Philippa, K. C. M. P. Ferenshild, and B. Van Lodesteijn, 131–58. The Hague: Elsevier.

Anderson, D. A. 1999. "The Aggregate Burden of Crime." *Journal of Law and Economics* 42 (2):611–42.

Anderson, N. E., M. S. Stanford, L. Wan, and K. A. Young. 2011. "High Psychopathic Trait Females Exhibit Reduced Startle Potentiation and Increased P3 Amplitude." *Behavioral Sciences & the Law* 29 (5):649–66.

Anderson, S. W., A. Bechara, H. Damasio, D. Tranel, and A. R. Damasio. 1999. "Impairment of social and moral behavior related to early damage in human prefrontal cortex." *Nature Neuroscience* 2:1031–37.

Angrilli, A., A. Mauri, D. Palomba, H. Flor, N. Birbaumer, and G. Sartori. 1996. "Startle reflex and emotion modulation impairment after a right amygdala lesion." *Brain* 119:1991–2000.

Archer, J. 2006. "Testosterone and human aggression: An evaluation of the challenge hypothesis." *Neuroscience and Biobehavioral Reviews* 30:319–45.

Aromaki, A. S., R. E. Lindman, and C. J. P. Eriksson. 1999. "Testosterone, aggressiveness, and antisocial personality." *Aggressive Behavior* 25:113–23.

Aron, A. R., T. W. Robbins, and R. A. Poldrack. 2004. "Inhibition and the right inferior frontal cortex." *Trends in Cognitive Science* 8 (4):170–77.

Baeken, C., P. Van Schuerbeek, R. De Raedt, J. De Mey, M. A. Vanderhasselt, A. Bossuyt, and R. Luypaert. 2011. "The effect of one left-sided dorsolateral prefrontal sham-controlled HF-rTMS session on approach and withdrawal related emotional neuronal processes." *Clinical Neurophysiology* 122 (11):2217–26.

Ballard, M. S., M. X. Sun, and J. N. Ko. 2012. "Vitamin A, folate, and choline as a possible preventive intervention to fetal alcohol syndrome." *Medical Hypotheses* 78 (4):489–93.

Banks, T., and J. Dabbs. 1996. "Salivary testosterone and cortisol in a delinquent and violent urban subculture." *Journal of Social Psychology* 136:49–56.

Barker, E. D., B. R. Oliver, E. Viding, R. T. Salekin, and B. Maughan. 2011. "The impact of prenatal maternal risk, fearless temperament and early parenting on adolescent callous-unemotional traits: A 14-year longitudinal investigation." *Journal of Child Psychology and Psychiatry* 52 (8):878–88.

Bartels, D. M., and D. A. Pizarro. 2011. "The mismeasure of morals: Antisocial personality traits predict utilitarian responses to moral dilemmas." *Cognition* 121 (1):154–61.

Baskin-Sommers, A. R., J. J. Curtin, and J. P. Newman. 2011. "Specifying the attentional selection that moderates the fearlessness of psychopathic offenders." *Psychological Science* 22 (2):226–34.

Basoglu, C., U. Semiz, O. Oner, H. Gunay, S. Ebrinc, M. Cetin, O. Sildiroglu, A. Algul, A. Ates, and G. Sonmez. 2008. "A magnetic resonance spectroscopy study of antisocial behaviour disorder, psychopathy and violent crime among military conscripts." *Acta Neuropsychiatrica* 20:72–77.

Baucom, D. H., P. K. Besch, and S. Callahan. 1985. "Relation between testosterone concentration, sex role identity and personality among females." *Journal of Personality and Social Psychology* 48:1218–26.

Baxter, M. G., and E. A. Murray. 2002. "The amygdala and reward." *Nature Reviews: Neuroscience* 3 (7):563–73.

Beaver, K. M., M. DeLisi, and M. G. Vaughn. 2010. "A biosocial interaction between prenatal exposure to cigarette smoke and family structure in the prediction of psychopathy in adolescence." *Psychiatric Quarterly* 81:325–34.

Bechara, A. 2004. "The role of emotion in decision-making: Evidence from neurological patients with orbitofrontal damage." *Brain and Cognition* 55 (1):30–40.

Bechara, A., D. Tranel, H. Damasio, R. Adolphs, C. Rockland, and A. R. Damasio. 1995. "Double dissociation of conditioning and declarative knowledge relative to the amygdala and hippocampus in humans." *Science* 269 (5227):1115–18.

Beevers, C. G., B. E. Gibb, J. E. McGeary, and I. W. Miller. 2007. "Serotonin transporter genetic variation and biased attention for emotional word stimuli among psychiatric inpatients." *Journal of Abnormal Psychology* 116:208–12.

Beitchman, J. H., C. C. Zai, K. Muir, L. Berall, B. Nowrouzi, E. Choi, and J. L. Kennedy. 2012. "Childhood aggression, callous-unemotional traits and oxytocin genes." *European Child and Adolescent Psychiatry* 21 (3):125–32.

Belmore, M. F., and V. L. Quinsey. 1994. "Correlates of psychopathy in a noninstitutionalized sample." *Journal of Interpersonal Violence* 9:339–49.

Benning, S. D., C. J. Patrick, D. M. Blonigen, B. M. Hicks, and W. G. Iacono. 2005. "Estimating facets of psychopathy from normal personality traits." *Assessment* 12 (1):3–18.

Benning, S. D., C. J. Patrick, B. M. Hicks, D. M. Blonigen, and R. F. Krueger. 2003. "Factor structure of the psychopathic personality inventory: Validity and implications for clinical assessment." *Psychological Assessment* 15 (1):340–50.

Benning, S. D., C. J. Patrick, and W. G. Iacono. 2005a. "Fearlessness and underarousal in psychopathy: Startle blink modulation and electrodermal reactivity in a young adult male community sample." *Psychophysiology* 42:753–62.

———. 2005b. "Psychopathy, startle blink modulation, and electrodermal reactivity in twin men." *Psychophysiology* 42:753–62.

Berthoz, S., J. Grezes, J. L. Armony, R. E. Passingham, and R. J. Dolan. 2006. "Affective response to one's own moral violations." *NeuroImage* 31:945–50.

Bertolino, A., and D. R. Weinberger. 1999. "Proton magnetic resonance spectroscopy in schizophrenia." *European Journal of Radiology* 30:132–41.

Birbaumer, N., R. Viet, M. Lotze, M. Erb, C. Hermann, W. Grodd, and H. Flor. 2005. "Deficient fear conditioning in psychopathy: A functional magnetic resonance imaging study." *Archives of General Psychiatry* 62 (7):799–805.

Bjork, J. M., F. G. Moeller, D. M. Dougherty, and A. C. Swann. 2001. "Endogenous plasma testosterone levels and commission errors in women: A preliminary report." *Physiology & Behavior* 73:217–221.

Blackburn, R. 1979. "Cortical and autonomic response arousal in primary and secondary psychopaths." *Psychophysiology* 16:143–50.

Blair, K. S., J. Morton, A. Leonard, and R. J. Blair. 2006. "Impaired decision-making on the basis of both reward and punishment information in individuals with psychopathy." *Personality and Individual Differences* 41 (1):155–65.

Blair, R. J. 1999. "Responsiveness to distress cues in children with psychopathic tendencies." *Personality and Individual Differences* 27:135–45.

———. 2006a. "The emergence of psychopathy: Implications for the neuropsychological approach to developmental disorders." *Cognition* 101:414–42.

———. 2006b. "Subcortical brain systems in psychopathy." In *Handbook of Psychopathy*, edited by C. J. Patrick, 296–312. New York: Guilford.

———. 2007. "The amygdala and ventromedial prefrontal cortex in morality and psychopathy." *Trends in Cognitive Sciences* 11 (9):387–92.

———. 2008. "The amygdala and ventromedial prefrontal cortex: Functional contributions and dysfunction in psychopathy." *Philosophical Transactions of the Royal Society B—Biological Sciences* 363:2557–65.

———. 2010a. "Neuroimaging of psychopathy and antisocial behavior: A targeted review." *Current Psychiatry Report* 12:76–82.

———. 2010b. "Psychopathy, frustration, and reactive aggression: The role of ventromedial prefrontal cortex." *British Journal of Psychology* 101:383–99.

Blair, R. J. R., S. Budhani, E. Colledge, and S. Scott. 2005. "Deafness to fear in boys with psychopathic tendencies." *Journal of Child Psychology and Psychiatry* 46 (3):327–36.

Blair, R. J., E. Colledge, and D. G. V. Mitchell. 2001. "Somatic markers and response reversal: Is there orbitofrontal cortex dysfunction in boys with psychopathic tendencies." *Journal of Abnormal Child Psychology* 29:499–511.

Blair, R. J., E. Colledge, L. Murray, and D. G. V. Mitchell. 2001. "A selective impairment in the processing of sad and fearful facial expressions in children with psychopathic tendencies." *Journal of Abnormal Child Psychology* 29:491–98.

Blair, R. J., L. Jones, F. Clark, and M. Smith. 1997. "The psychopathic individual: A lack of responsiveness to distress cues." *Psychophysiology* 34 (2):192–98.

Blair, R. J., D. G. Mitchell, and K. Blair. 2005. *The Psychopath: Emotion and the Brain.* Oxford: Blackwell.

Blair, R. J., D. G. V. Mitchell, A. Leonard, S. Budhani, K. S. Peschardt, and C. Newman. 2004. "Passive avoidance learning in individuals with psychopathy: Modulation by reward but not by punishment." *Personality and Individual Differences* 37 (6):1179–92.

Blair, R. J. R., D. G. V. Mitchell, K. S. Peschardt, E. Colledge, R. A. Leonard, J. H. Shine, L. K. Murray, and D. I. Perrett. 2004. "Reduced sensitivity to others' fearful expressions in psychopathic individuals." *Personality and Individual Differences* 37 (6):1111–22.

Blake, P. Y., J. H. Pincus, and C. Buckner. 1995. "Neurologic abnormalities in murderers." *Neurology* 45:1641–47.

Blonigen, D. M., S. R. Carlson, R. F. Krueger, and C. J. Patrick. 2003. "A twin study of self-reported psychopathic personality traits." *Personality and Individual Differences* 35:179–97.

Blonigen, D. M., B. M. Hicks, R. F. Krueger, C. J. Patrick, and W. G. Iacono. 2005. "Psychopathic personality traits: Heritability and genetic overlap with internalizing and externalizing psychopathology." *Psychological Medicine* 35:637–48.

Blum, K., E. P. Noble, P. J. Sheridan, O. Finley, A. Montgomery, and T. Ritchie. 1991. "Association of the A1 allele of the D2 dopamine receptor gene with severe alcoholism." *Alcohol* 8:409–16.

Boccardi, M., R. Ganzola, R. Rossi, F. Sabattoli, M. P. Laakso, E. Repo-Tiihonen, O. Vaurio, M. Kononen, H. J. Aronen, P. M. Thompson, G. B. Frisoni, and J. Tiihonen.

2010. "Abnormal hippocampal shape in offenders with psychopathy." *Human Brain Mapping* 31:438–47.

Booth, A., and J. Dabbs. 1993. "Testosterone and men's marriages." *Social Forces* 72:463–77.

Borg, J. S., C. Hynes, J. Van Horn, S. Grafton, and W. Sinnott-Armstrong. 2006. "Consequences, action, and intention as factors in moral judgments: An fMRI investigation." *Journal of Cognitive Neuroscience* 18:803–17.

Borkovec, T. D. 1970. "Autonomic reactivity to sensory stimulation in psychopathic, neurotic, and normal juvenile delinquents." *Journal of Consulting and Clinical Psychology* 35 (2):217–22.

Bosch, J. A., E. C. I. Veerman, E. J. de Geus, and G. B. Proctor. 2011. "Alpha-amylase as a reliable and convenient measure of sympathetic activity: Don't start salivating just yet!" *Psychoneuroendocrinology* 36:449–53.

Bouchard, T. J., and J. C. Loehlin. 2001. "Genes, evolution, and personality." *Behavior Genetics* 31:243–73.

Boucher, O., M. J. Burden, G. Muckle, D. Saint-Amour, P. Ayotte, E. Dewailly, C. A. Nelson, S. W. Jacobson, and J. L. Jacobson. 2011. "Neurophysiologic and neurobehavioral evidence of beneficial effects of prenatal omega-3 fatty acid intake on memory function at school age." *American Journal of Clinical Nutrition* 93 (5):1025–37.

Boucsein, W. 1992. *Electrodermal Activity*. New York: Plenum.

Brazil, I. A., E. R. A. Bruijn, B. H. Bulten, A. K. L. von Borries, J. J. D. M. van Lankveld, J. K. Buitelaar, and R. J. Verkes. 2009. "Early and late components of error monitoring in violent offenders with psychopathy." *Biological Psychiatry* 65:137–43.

Brazil, I. A., R. B. Mars, B. H. Bulten, J. K. Buitelaar, R. J. Verkes, and E. R. A. De Bruijn. 2011. "A neurophysiological dissociation between monitoring one's own and others' actions in psychopathy." *Biological Psychiatry* 69:693–99.

Brocke, B., D. Armbruster, J. L. Muller, T. Hensch, C. P. Jacob, K.-P. Lesch, C. Kirschbaum, and A. Strobel. 2006. "Serotonin transporter gene variation impacts innate fear processing: Acoustic startle response and emotional startle." *Molecular Psychiatry* 11:1106–12.

Brody, A. L., S. Saxena, J. M. Schwartz, P. W. Stoessel, K. Maidment, M. E. Phelps, and L. R. Baxter. 1998. "FDG-PET predictors of response to behavioral therapy and pharmacotherapy in obsessive compulsive disorder." *Psychiatry Research: Neuroimaging* 84 (1):1–6.

Brotman, L. M., K. K. Gouley, K. Y. Huang, D. Kamboukos, C. Fratto, and D. S. Pine. 2007. "Effects of a psychosocial family-based preventive intervention on cortisol response to a social challenge in preschoolers at high risk for antisocial behavior." *Archives of General Psychiatry* 64 (10):1172–79.

Brown, G. L., E. L. McGarvey, E. A. Shirtcliff, A. Keller, D. A. Granger, and K. Flavin. 2007. "Salivary cortisol, dehydroepiandrosterone, and testosterone interrelationships in healthy young males: A pilot study with implications for studies of aggressive behavior." *Psychiatry Research* 159:67–76.

Bryant, R. A., K. Felmingham, A. Kemp, P. Das, G. Hughes, A. Peduto, and L. Williams. 2008. "Amygdala and ventral anterior cingulate activation predicts treatment response to cognitive behaviour therapy for post-traumatic stress disorder." *Psychological Medicine* 38 (4):555–61.

Bublitz, M. H., and L. R. Stroud. 2012. "Maternal smoking during pregnancy and offspring brain structure and function: Review and agenda for future research." *Nicotine & Tobacco Research* 14 (4):388–97.

Buckholtz, J. W., M. T. Treadway, R. L. Cowan, N. D. Woodward, S. D. Benning, R. Li, M. S. Ansari, R. M. Baldwin, A. N. Schwartzman, E. S. Shelby, C. E. Smith, D. Cole, R. M. Kessler, and D. H. Zald. 2010. "Mesolimbic dopamine reward system hypersensitivity in individuals with psychopathic traits." *Nature Neuroscience* 13:419–21.

Budhani, S., and R. J. Blair. 2005. "Response reversal and children with psychopathic tendencies: Success is a function of salience of contingency change." *Journal of Child Psychology and Psychiatry* 46 (9):972–81.

Burke, A. R., M. J. Watt, and G. L. Forster. 2011. "Adolescent social defeat increases adult amphetamine conditioned place preference and alters D2 dopamine receptor expression." *Neuroscience* 197:269–79.

Burns, J. M., and R. H. Swerdlow. 2003. "Right orbitofrontal tumor with pedophilia symptom and constructional apraxia sign." *Archives of Neurology* 60 (3):437–40.

Bush, G., P. Luu, and M. I. Posner. 2000. "Cognitive and emotional influences in anterior cingulate cortex." *Trends in Cognitive Science* 46:215–22.

Buydens-Branchey, L., and M. Branchey. 2004. "Cocaine addicts with conduct disorder are typified by decreased cortisol responsivity and high plasma levels of DHEA-S." *Neuropsychobiology* 50:161–66.

Caldwell, M. F., D. McCormick, J. Wolfe, and D. Umstead. 2012. "Treatment-related changes in psychopathy features and behavior in adolescent offenders." *Criminal Justice and Behavior* 39 (2):144–55.

Caldwell, M. F., J. L. Skeem, R. T. Salekin, and G. J. Van Rybroek. 2006. "Treatment response of adolescent offenders with psychopathy features: A 2–year follow-up." *Criminal Justice and Behavior* 33:571–96.

Campanella, S., M. E. Vanhoolandt, and P. Philippot. 2005. "Emotional deficit in subjects with psychopathic tendencies as assessed by the Minnesota Multiphasic Personality Inventory–2: An event related potentials study." *Neuroscience Letters* 373:26–31.

Campbell, M. A., S. Porter, and D. Santor. 2004. "Psychopathic traits in adolescent offenders: An evaluation of criminal history, clinical, and psychosocial correlates." *Behavioral Sciences & the Law* 22:23–47.

Canli, T., and K.-P. Lesch. 2007. "Long story short: The serotonin transporter in emotion regulation and social cognition." *Nature Neuroscience* 10:1103–9.

Cardinal, R. N., J. A. Parkinson, J. Hall, and B. J. Everitt. 2002. "Emotion and motivation: The role of the amygdala, ventral striatum, and prefrontal cortex." *Neuroscience and Biobehavioral Reviews* 26:321–52.

Carlson, S. R., S. Thai, and M. E. McLarnon. 2009. "Visual P3 amplitude and self-reported psychopathic personality traits: Frontal reduction is associated with self-centered impulsivity." *Psychophysiology* 46 (1):100–113.

Caspi, A., J. McClay, T. E. Moffitt, J. Mill, J. Martin, I. W. Craig, A. Taylor, and R. Poulton. 2002. "Role of genotype in the cycle of violence in maltreated children." *Science* 297:851–54.

Cecil, K. M., C. J. Brubaker, C. M. Adler, K. N. Dietrich, M. Altaye, J. C. Egelhoff, S. Wessel, I. Elangovan, R. Hornung, K. Jarvis, and B. P. Lanphear. 2008. "Decreased brain volume in adults with childhood lead exposure." *PLOS Medicine* 5 (5):741–50.

Chen, H. F., and H. M. Su. 2012. "Fish oil supplementation of maternal rats on an n-3 fatty acid-deficient diet prevents depletion of maternal brain regional docosahexaenoic acid levels and has a postpartum anxiolytic effect." *Journal of Nutritional Biochemistry* 23 (3):299–305.

Cho, S. S., J. H. Ko, G. Pellecchia, T. Van Eimeren, R. Cilia, and A. P. Strafella. 2010. "Continuous theta burst stimulation of right dorsolateral prefrontal cortex induces changes in impulsivity level." *Brain Stimulation* 3 (3):170–76.

Chrousous, G. P., and P. W. Gold. 1992. "The concepts of stress and stress system disorders: Overview of physical and behavioral homeostasis." *Journal of the America Medical Association* 267:1244–52.

Ciaramelli, E., M. Muccioli, E. Ladavas, and G. di Pellegrino. 2007. "Selective deficit in personal moral judgment following damage to ventromedial prefrontal cortex." *Social, Cognitive and Affective Neuroscience* 2:84–92.

Cima, M., T. Smeets, and M. Jelicic. 2008. "Self-reported trauma, cortisol levels, and aggression in psychopathic and non-psychoathic prison inmates." *Biological Psychiatry* 78:75–86.

Cleckley, H. 1941. *The Mask of Sanity*. St. Louis, MO: Mosby.

———. 1976. *The Mask of Sanity*. 5th ed. St. Louis, MO: Mosby.

Coccaro, E. F., M. S. McCloskey, D. A. Fitzgerald, and K. L. Phan. 2007. "Amygdala and orbitofrontal reactivity to social threat in individuals with impulsive aggression." *Biological Psychiatry* 62:168–78.

Cohen, M. X., J.-C. Schoene-Bake, C. E. Elger, and B. Weber. 2009. "Connectivity-based segregation of the human striatum predicts personality characteristics." *Nature Neuroscience* 12:32–34.

Colby, A., and W. Damon. 1995. "The development of extraordinary moral commitment." In *Morality in Everyday Life: Developmental Perspectives*, edited by M. Killen and D. Hart, 342–70. Cambridge: Cambridge University Press.

Comings, D. E., D. Muhleman, R. Gade, P. Johnson, R. Verde, and G. Saucier. 1997. "Cannabinoid receptor gene (CNR1): Association with I.V. drug use." *Molecular Psychiatry* 2:1611–18.

Conklin, S. M., P. J. Gianaros, S. M. Brown, J. K. Yao, A. R. Hariri, S. B. Manuck, and M. F. Muldoon. 2007. "Long-chain omega-3 fatty acid intake is associated positively with corticolimbic gray matter volume in healthy adults." *Neuroscience Letters* 421:209–12.

Constable, R. T., L. R. Ment, B. R. Vohr, S. R. Kesler, R. K. Fulbright, C. Lacadie, S. Delancy, K. H. Katz, K. C. Schneider, R. J. Schafer, R. W. Makuch, and A. R. Reiss. 2008. "Prematurely born children demonstrate white matter microstructural differences at 12 years of age, relative to term control subjects: An investigation of group and gender effects." *Pediatrics* 121 (2):306–16.

Constantino, J. N., D. Grosz, P. Saenger, D. W. Chandler, R. Nandi, and F. J. Earls. 1993. "Testosterone and aggression in children." *Journal of the American Academy of Child and Adolescent Psychiatry* 32:1217–22.

Cook, E. H., M. A. Stein, M. D. Krasowski, N. J. Cox, D. M. Olkon, and J. E. Keiffer. 1995. "Association of attention-deficit disorder and the dopamine transporter gene." *American Journal of Human Genetics* 56:993–98.

Cooke, D. J., and C. Michie. 2001. "Refining the construct of psychopathy: Towards a hierarchical model." *Psychological Assessment* 13 (2):171–88.

Cornell, D. G., J. Warren, G. Hawk, E. Stafford, G. Oram, and D. Pine. 1996. "Psychopathy in instrumental and reactive violent offenders." *Journal of Consulting and Clinical Psychology* 64:783–90.

Craig, I. W. 2007. "The importance of stress and genetic variation in human aggression." *Bioessays* 29:227–36.

Craig, M. C., M. Catani, Q. Deeley, R. Latham, E. Daly, R. Kanaan, M. Picchioni, P. K. McGuire, T. Fahy, and D. G. Murphy. 2009. "Altered connections on the road to psychopathy." *Molecular Psychiatry* 14:946–53.

Crisan, L. G., S. Pana, R. Vulturar, R. M. Heilman, R. Szekely, B. Druga, N. Dragos, and A. C. Miu. 2009. "Genetic contributions of the serotonin transporter to social learning of fear and economic decision making." *Social Cognitive and Affective Neuroscience* 4:399–408.

Dabbs, J. M., F. J. Bernieri, R. K. Strong, R. Campo, and R. Milun. 2001. "Going on stage: Testosterone in greetings and meetings." *Journal of Research in Personality* 35:27–40.

Dabbs, J. M., R. L. Frady, and T. S. Carr. 1987. "Saliva testosterone and criminal violence in young adult prison inmates." *Psychosomatic Medicine* 49 (2):174–82.

Dabbs, J. M., G. J. Jurkovic, and R. L. Frady. 1991. "Salivary testosterone and cortisol among late adolescent male offenders." *Journal of Abnormal Child Psychology* 19 (4):469–78.

Dadds, M. R., and T. Rhodes. 2008. "Aggression in young children with concurrent callous-unemotional traits: Can the neurosciences inform progress and innovation in treatment approaches?" *Philosophical Transactions of the Royal Society B—Biological Sciences* 363 (1503):2567–76.

Daitzman, R., and M. Zuckerman. 1980. "Disinhibitory sensation seeking, personality and gonadal hormones." *Personality and Individual Differences* 1:103–10.

Damasio, A. R. 1994. *Descartes' Error: Emotion, Reason, and the Human Brain*. New York: Putnam.

Damasio, A. R., D. Tranel, and H. Damasio. 1990. "Individuals with sociopathic behavior caused by frontal damage fail to respond autonomically to social-stimuli." *Behavioural Brain Research* 41 (2):81–94.

Damasio, H., T. Grabowski, R. Frank, A. M. Galaburda, and A. R. Damasio. 1994. "The return of Phineas Gage: Clues about the brain from the skull of a famous patient." *Science* 264 (5162):1102–5.

Davis, M. 1989. "Neural systems involved in fear-potentiated startle." *Annals of the New York Academy of Sciences* 563:165–83.

———. 2000. "The role of the amygdala in conditioned and unconditioned fear and anxiety." In *The Amygdala: A Functional Analysis*, edited by J. P. Aggleton, 213–87. New York: Oxford University.

Dawson, M. E., D. Filion, and A. Schell. 1989. "Is elicitation of the autonomic orienting response associated with allocation of processing resources?" *Psychophysiology* 26:560–72.

Dawson, M. E., A. Schell, and D. Filion. 1990. "The electrodermal system." In *Principles of psychophysiology*, edited by J. T. Cacioppo and L. G. Tassinary, 295–324. Cambridge: Cambridge University Press.

———. 2000. "The electrodermal system." In *Handbook of Psychophysiology*, edited by J. T. Cacioppo, L. G. Tassinary, and G. G. Berntson, 200–223. Cambridge: Cambridge University Press.

De Brito, S. A., E. McCrory, A. Mechelli, M. Wilke, A. P. Jones, S. Hodgins, and E. Viding. in press. "Small, but not perfectly formed: Decreased white matter concentration in boys with psychopathic tendencies." *Molecular Psychiatry*.

De Brito, S. A., A. Mechelli, M. Wilke, K. R. Laurens, A. P. Jones, G. J. Barker, S. Hodgins, and E. Viding. 2009. "Size matters: Increased gray matter in boys with conduct problems and callous-unemotional traits." *Brain* 132:843–52.

De Martino, B., C. F. Camerer, and R. Adolphs. 2010. "Amygdala damage eliminates monetary loss aversion." *Proceedings of the National Academy of Sciences USA* 107 (8):3788–92.

de Oliveira-Souza, R., R. D. Hare, I. E. Bramati, G. J. Garrido, F. A. Ignácio, F. Tovar-Moll, and J. Moll. 2008. "Psychopathy as a disorder of the moral brain: Fronto-temporo-limbic grey matter reductions demonstrated by voxel-based morphometry." *NeuroImage* 40:1202–13.

Deeley, Q., S. Surguladze, N. Tunstall, G. Mezey, D. Beer, A. Ambikapathy, D. Robertson, V. Giampietro, M. J. Brammer, A. Clarke, J. Dowsett, T. Fahy, M. L. Phillips, and D. G. Murphy. 2006. "Facial emotion processing in criminal psychopathy. Preliminary functional magnetic resonance imaging study." *British Journal of Psychiatry* 189:533–39.

Del Giudice, M., B. J. Ellis, and E. A. Shirtcliff. 2011. "The adaptive calibration model of stress responsivity." *Neuroscience and Biobehavioral Reviews* 35 (7):1562–92.

Dellacherie, D., D. Hasboun, M. Baulac, P. Belin, and S. Samson. 2011. "Impaired recognition of fear in voices and reduced anxiety after unilateral temporal lobe resection." *Neuropsychologia* 49 (4):618–29.

Detre, J. A., H. Y. Rao, D. J. J. Wang, Y. F. Chen, and Z. Wang. 2012. "Applications of arterial spin labeled MRI in the brain." *Journal of Magnetic Resonance Imaging* 35 (5):1026–37.

Dias, R., T. W. Robbins, and A. C. Roberts. 1996. "Dissociation in prefrontal cortex of affective and attentional shifts." *Nature* 380:69–72.

Dikman, Z. V., and J. J. Allen. 2000. "Error monitoring during reward and avoidance learning in high- and low-socialized individuals." *Psychophysiology* 37:43–54.

Dinn, W. M., and C. L. Harris. 2000. "Neurocognitive function in antisocial personality disorder." *Psychiatry Research* 97 (2–3):173–90.

Dmitrieva, T. N., R. D. Oades, B. P. Hauffa, and C. Eggers. 2001. "Dehydroepiandrosterone sulphate and corticotropin levels are high in young male patients with conduct disorder: Comparisons for growth factors, thyroid and gonadal hormones." *Neuropsychobiology* 43:134–40.

Dodge, K. A., and G. S. Pettit. 2003. "A biopsychosocial model of the development of chronic conduct problems in adolescence." *Developmental Psychology* 39 (2):349–71.

Dolan, M. C., and I. M. Anderson. 2003. "The relationship between serotonergic function and the Psychopathy Checklist: Screening Version." *Journal of Pharmacology* 17:216–22.

Dolan, M., J. F. W. Deakin, N. Roberts, and I. M. Anderson. 2002. "Quantitative frontal and temporal structural MRI studies in personality-disordered offenders and control subjects." *Psychiatry Research Neuroimaging* 116:133–49.

Donchin, E., and M. G. H. Coles. 1988. "Is the P300 component a manifestation of context updating?" *Behavioral and Brain Sciences* 11:357–74.

Eagleman, D. 2011. "The brain on trial." *Atlantic Monthly* 308:112–23.

Eastman, N., and C. Campbell. 2006. "Neuroscience and legal determination of criminal responsibility." *Nature Neuroscience* 7:311–18.

Edens, J. F., J. S. Campbell, and J. M. Weir. 2007. "Youth psychopathy and criminal recidivism: A meta-analysis of the psychopathy checklist measures." *Law and Human Behavior* 31 (1):53–75.

Eley, T. C., J. L. Hudson, C. Creswell, M. Tropeano, K. J. Lester, P. Cooper, A. Farmer, C. M. Lewis, H. J. Lyneham, R. M. Rapee, R. Uher, H. M. S. Zavos, and D. A. Collier. 2012. "Therapygenetics: The 5HTTLPR and response to psychological therapy." *Molecular Psychiatry* 17 (3):236–37.

Eslinger, P. J., and A. R. Damasio. 1985. "Severe disturbance of higher cognition after bilateral frontal lobe ablation—patient EVR." *Neurology* 35 (12):1731–41.

Fallgatter, A. J., M. J. Herrmann, J. Roemmler, A.-C. Ehlis, A. Wagener, A. Heidrich, G. Ortega, Y. Zeng, and K.-P. Lesch. 2004. "Allelic variation of serotonin transporter function modulates the brain electrical response for error processing." *Neuropsychopharmacology* 29:1506–11.

Fanselow, M. S. 2000. "Contextual fear, gestalt memories, and the hippocampus." *Behavioral Brain Research* 110:73–81.

Farah, M. J. 2004. "Neuroethics: A guide for the perplexed." *Cerebrum* 6:29–38.

Farrington, D. P. 2000. "Psychosocial predictors of adult antisocial personality and adult convictions." *Behavioral Sciences & the Law* 18:605–22.

————. 2006. "Family background and psychopathy." In *Handbook of Psychopathy*, edited by C. J. Patrick, 229–50. New York: Guilford.

Farrington, D. P., J. W. Coid, L. Harnett, D. Jolliffe, N. Soteriou, R. Turner, and D. J. West. 2006. *The Cambridge Study in Delinquent Development: A Prospective Longitudinal Survey from Age 8 to Age 48*. London: Home Office.

Fecteau, S., D. Knoch, F. Fregni, N. Sultani, P. Boggio, and A. Pascual-Leone. 2007. "Diminishing risk-taking behavior by modulating activity in the prefrontal cortex: A direct current stimulation study." *Journal of Neuroscience* 27 (46):12500–12505.

Fellows, L. K., and M. J. Farah. 2005. "Different underlying impairments in decision-making following ventromedial and dorsolateral frontal lobe damage in humans." *Cerebral Cortex* 15 (1):58–63.

Felmingham, K., A. Kemp, L. Williams, P. Das, G. Hughes, A. Peduto, and R. Bryant. 2007. "Changes in anterior cingulate and amygdala after cognitive behavior therapy of posttraumatic stress disorder." *Psychological Science* 18:127–29.

Fiddick, L., M. V. Spampinato, and J. Grafman. 2005. "Social contracts and precautions activate different neurological systems: An fMRI investigation of deontic reasoning." *NeuroImage* 28 (4):778–86.

Finger, E. C., A. A. Marsh, B. Buzas, N. Kamel, R. Rhodes, M. Vythilingham, D. S. Pine, D. Goldman, and R. J. Blair. 2007. "The impact of tryptophan depletion and 5_HTTLPR genotype on passive avoidance and response reversal instrumental learning tasks." *Neuropsychopharmacology* 32 (1):206–15.

Finger, E. C., A. A. Marsh, D. G. Mitchell, M. E. Reid, C. Sims, S. Budhani, D. S. Kosson, G. Chen, K. E. Towbin, E. Leibenluft, D. Pine, and R. J. Blair. 2008. "Abnormal ventromedial prefrontal cortex function in children with psychopathic traits during reversal learning." *Archives of General Psychiatry* 65:586–94.

Fisher, P. A., M. Stoolmiller, M. R. Gunnar, and B. O. Burraston. 2007. "Effects of a therapeutic intervention for foster preschoolers on diurnal cortisol activity." *Psychoneuroendocrinology* 32 (8–10):892–905.

Flor, H., N. Birbaumer, C. Hermann, S. Ziegler, and C. J. Patrick. 2002. "Aversive Pavlovian conditioning in psychopaths: Peripheral and central correlates." *Psychophysiology* 39:505–18.

Flores, O., H. Perez, L. Valladares, C. Morgan, A. Gatica, H. Burgos, R. Olivares, and A. Hernandez. 2011. "Hidden prenatal malnutrition in the rat: Role of beta(1)-adrenoceptors on synaptic plasticity in the frontal cortex." *Journal of Neurochemistry* 119 (2):314–23.

Focquaert, F., A. L. Glenn, and A. Raine. 2013. "Free will, responsibility, and the punishment of criminals." In *The Future of Punishment*, edited by T. Nadelhoffer, 247–74. Oxford: Oxford University Press.

Fontaine, N. M. G., F. V. Rijsdijk, E. J. P. McCrory, and E. Viding. 2010. "Etiology of different developmental trajectories of callous-unemotional traits." *Journal of the American Academy of Child and Adolescent Psychiatry* 49 (7):656–64.

Forsman, M., P. Lichtenstein, H. Andershed, and H. Larsson. 2008. "Genetic effects explain the stability of psychopathic personality from mid- to late adolescence." *Journal of Abnormal Psychology* 117:606–17.

———. 2010. "A longitudinal twin study of the direction of effects between psycho-pathic personality and antisocial behaviour." *Journal of Child Psychology and Psychiatry* 51:39–47.

Forth, A. E., D. S. Kosson, and R. D. Hare. 2003. *The Psychopathy Checklist: Youth Version.* Toronto: Multi-Health Systems.

Fowler, T., K. Langley, F. Rice, M. B. M. van de Bree, K. Ross, L. S. Wilkinson, M. J. Owen, M. C. O'Donovan, and A. Thapar. 2009. "Psychopathy trait scores in adolescents with childhood ADHD: The contribution of genotypes affecting MAOA, 5HTT and COMT activity." *Psychiatric Genetics* 19:312–19.

Fowler, T., K. Langley, F. Rice, N. Whittinger, K. Ross, S. H. M. van Goozen, M. J. Owen, M. C. O'Donovan, M. B. M. van den Bree, and A. Thapar. 2009. "Psychopathy traits in adolescents with childhood attention-deficit hyperactivity disorder." *British Journal of Psychiatry* 194:62–67.

Fox, E., A. Ridgewell, and C. Ashwin. 2009. "Looking on the bright side: Biased attention and the human serotonin transporter gene." *Proceedings of the Royal Society B* 276:1747–51.

Frick, P. J. 2004. *Inventory of Callous-Unemotional Traits.* New Orleans, LA: University of New Orleans.

Frick, P. J., and R. D. Hare. 2001. *Antisocial Process Screening Device (APSD).* Toronto: Multi-Health Systems.

Frick, P. J., E. R. Kimonis, D. M. Dandreaux, and J. M. Farell. 2003. "The 4 year stability of psychopathic traits in non-referred youth." *Behavioral Sciences & the Law* 21 (6):713–36.

Frick, P. J., B. S. O'Brien, J. M. Wooton, and K. McBurnett. 1994. "Psychopathy and conduct problems in children." *Journal of Abnormal Psychology* 103 (4):700–707.

Fung, M. T., A. Raine, R. Loeber, D. R. Lynam, S. R. Steinhauer, P. H. Venables, and M. Stouthamer-Loeber. 2005. "Reduced electrodermal activity in psychopathy-prone adolescents." *Journal of Abnormal Psychology* 114 (2):187–96.

Furmark, T., M. Tillfors, I. Marteinsdottir, H. Fischer, A. Pissiota, B. Langstrom, and M. Fredrikson. 2002. "Common changes in cerebral blood flow in patients with social phobia treated with citalopram or cognitive-behavioral therapy." *Archives of General Psychiatry* 59 (5):425–33.

Gao, Y., L. A. Baker, A. Raine, H. Wu, and S. Bezdjian. 2009. "Brief report: Interaction between social class and risky decision-making in children with psychopathic tendencies." *Journal of Adolescence* 32 (2):409–14.

Gao, Y., A. L. Glenn, M. Peskin, A. Rudo-Hutt, R. A. Schug, Y. Yang, and A. Raine. 2011. "Neurocriminological approaches." In *Handbook of Criminological Research Methods*, edited by D. Gadd, S. Karstedt, and S. Messner, 63–75. London: Sage.

Gao, Y., and A. Raine. 2009. "P3 event-related potential impairments in antisocial and psychopathic individuals: A meta-analysis." *Biological Psychology* 82:199–210.

———. 2010. "Successful and unsuccessful psychopaths: A neurobiological model." *Behavioral Sciences & the Law* 28:1–17.

Gao, Y., A. Raine, F. Chan, P. H. Venables, and S. A. Mednick. 2010. "Early maternal and paternal bonding, childhood physical abuse and adult psychopathic personality." *Psychological Medicine* 40:1007–16.

Gao, Y., A. Raine, and R. A. Schug. 2011. "P3 event-related potentials and childhood maltreatment in successful and unsuccessful psychopaths." *Brain and Cognition* 77 (2):176–82.

Gao, Y., A. Raine, P. H. Venables, and M. E. Dawson. 2010. "Association of poor childhood fear conditioning and adult crime." *American Journal of Psychiatry* 167:56–60.

Garland, B., and P. W. Glimcher. 2006. "Cognitive neuroscience and the law." *Current Opinion in Neurobiology* 16:130–34.

Garpenstrand, H., P. Annas, J. Ekblom, L. Oreland, and M. Fredrikson. 2001. "Human fear conditioning is related to dopaminergic and serotonergic biological markers." *Behavioral Neuroscience* 115:358–64.

Gatzke-Kopp, L. M., A. Raine, M. S. Buchsbaum, and L. Lacasse. 2001. "Temporal lobe deficits in murderers: EEG findings undetected by PET." *Journal of Neuropsychiatry and Clinical Neuroscience* 13:486–91.

George, M. S., S. H. Lisanby, D. Avery, W. M. McDonald, V. Durkalski, M. Pavlicova, B. Anderson, Z. Nahas, P. Bulow, P. Zarkowski, P. E. Holtzheimer, T. Schwartz, and H. A. Sackeim. 2010. "Daily left prefrontal transcranial magnetic stimulation therapy for major depressive disorder a sham-controlled randomized trial." *Archives of General Psychiatry* 67 (5):507–16.

Gesch, S. M., S. E. Hampson, A. Eves, and M. J. Crowder. 2002. "Influence of supplemental vitamins, minerals and essential fatty acids on the antisocial behaviour of young adult prisoners." *British Journal of Psychiatry* 181:22–28.

Glass, S. J., and J. P. Newman. 2009. "Emotion processing in the criminal psychopath: The role of attention in emotion-facilitated memory." *Journal of Abnormal Psychology* 118:229–34.

Glenn, A. L. 2011. "The other allele: Exploring the long allele of the serotonin transporter gene as a potential risk factor for psychopathy: A review of the parallels in findings." *Neuroscience and Biobehavioral Reviews* 35:612–20.

Glenn, A. L., A. Raine, and W. S. Laufer. 2011. "Is it wrong to criminalize and punish psychopaths?" *Emotion Review* 3:302–4.

Glenn, A. L., A. Raine, and R. A. Schug. 2009. "The neural correlates of moral decision-making in psychopathy." *Molecular Psychiatry* 14:5–6.

Glenn, A. L., A. Raine, R. A. Schug, Y. Gao, and D. A. Granger. 2011. "Increased testosterone-to-cortisol ratio in psychopathy." *Journal of Abnormal Psychology* 120:389–99.

Glenn, A. L., A. Raine, R. A. Schug, L. Young, and M. Hauser. 2009. "Increased DLPFC activity during moral decision-making in psychopathy." *Molecular Psychiatry* 14:909–11.

Glenn, A. L., A. Raine, P. H. Venables, and S. Mednick. 2007. "Early temperamental and psychophysiological precursors of adult psychopathic personality." *Journal of Abnormal Psychology* 116 (3):508–18.

Glenn, A. L., A. Raine, P. S. Yaralian, and Y. Yang. 2010. "Increased volume of the striatum in psychopathic individuals." *Biological Psychiatry* 67:52–58.

Glenn, A. L., and Y. Yang. 2012. "The potential role of the striatum in antisocial behavior and psychopathy." *Biological Psychiatry* 72:817–22.

Glenn, A. L., Y. Yang, A. Raine, and P. Colletti. 2010. "No volumetric differences in the anterior cingulate of psychopathic individuals." *Psychiatry Research Neuroimaging* 183:140–43.

Golub, M. S., C. E. Hogrefe, and S. L. Germann. 2007. "Iron deprivation during fetal development changes the behavior of juvenile rhesus monkeys." *Journal of Nutrition* 137 (4):979–84.

Golub, M. S., C. E. Hogrefe, K. F. Widaman, and J. P. Capitanio. 2009. "Iron deficiency anemia and affective response in rhesus monkey infants." *Developmental Psychobiology* 51 (1):47–59.

Gordon, H. L., A. A. Baird, and A. End. 2004. "Functional differences among those high and low on a trait measure of psychopathy." *Biological Psychiatry* 56:516–21.

Gotlib, I., J. Joormann, K. L. Minor, and J. Hallmayer. 2008. "HPA axis reactivity: A mechanism underlying the associations among 5–HTTLPR, stress, and depression." *Biological Psychiatry* 63:847–51.

Goyer, P. F., P. J. Andreason, W. E. Semple, and A. H. Clayton. 1994. "Positron-emission tomography and personality disorders." *Neuropsychopharmacology* 10:21–28.

Graustella, A. J., and C. MacLeod. 2012. "A critical review of the influence of oxytocin nasal spray on social cognition in humans: Evidence and future directions." *Hormones and Behavior* 61 (3):410–18.

Greene, J., and J. Cohen. 2010. "For the law, neuroscience changes nothing and everything." In *Neuroethics: An Introduction with Readings*, edited by M. J. Farah, 232–58. Cambridge, MA: MIT Press.

Greene, J. D., L. E. Nystrom, A. D. Engell, J. M. Darley, and J. Cohen. 2004. "The neural bases of cognitive conflict and control in moral judgment." *Neuron* 44:389–400.

Greene, J. D., R. B. Sommerville, L. E. Nystrom, J. M. Darley, and J. Cohen. 2001. "An fMRI investigation of emotional engagement in moral judgment." *Science* 293:2105–8.

Gregory, S., D. ffytche, A. Simmons, V. Kumari, M. Howard, S. Hodgins, and N. Blackwood. in press. "The antisocial brain: Psychopathy matters: A structural MRI investigation of antisocial male violent offenders." *Archives of General Psychiatry*.

Guay, J. P., J. Ruscio, R. A. Knight, and R. D. Hare. 2007. "A taxometric analysis of the latent structure of psychopathy: Evidence for dimensionality." *Journal of Abnormal Psychology* 116:701–16.

Gunter, T. D., M. G. Vaughn, and R. A. Philibert. 2010. "Behavioral genetics in antisocial spectrum disorders and psychopathy: A review of the recent literature." *Behavioral Sciences & the Law* 28:148–73.

Haas, S. M., D. A. Waschbusch, W. E. Pelham, S. King, B. F. Andrade, and N. J. Carrey. 2011. "Treatment response in CP/ADHD children with callous/unemotional traits." *Journal of Abnormal Child Psychology* 39 (4):541–52.

Haidt, J. 2001. "The emotional dog and its rational tail: A social intuitionist approach to moral judgment." *Psychological Review* 108:814–34.

Hall, J. R., and S. D. Benning. 2006. "The 'successful' psychopath: Adaptive and subclinical manifestations of psychopathy in the general population." In *Handbook of Psychopathy*, edited by C. J. Patrick, 459–78. New York: Guilford.

Halligan, S. L., J. Herbert, I. M. Goodyer, and L. Murray. 2004. "Exposure to postnatal depression predicts elevated cortisol in adolescent offspring." *Biological Psychiatry* 55 (4):376–81.

Hansen, A. L., B. H. Johnsen, D. Thornton, L. Waage, and J. F. Thayer. 2007. "Facets of psychopathy, heart rate variability and cognitive function." *Journal of Personality Disorders* 21:568–82.

Hare, R. D. 1965. "Psychopathy, fear arousal and anticipated pain." *Psychological Reports* 16:499–502.

———. 1968. "Psychopathy, autonomic functioning, and the orienting response." *Journal of Abnormal Psychology Monograph Supplement* 73 (3):1–24.

———. 1970. *Psychopathy: Theory and Research*. New York: John Wiley.

———. 1978. "Electrodermal and cardiovascular correlates of psychopathy." In *Psychopathic Behavior: Approaches to Research*, edited by R. D. Hare and D. Schalling, 107–44. New York: John Wiley.

———. 1980. "A research scale for the assessment of psychopathy in criminal populations." *Personality and Individual Differences* 1 (2):111–20.

———. 1982. "Psychopathy and physiological activity during anticipation of an aversive stimulus in a distraction paradigm." *Psychophysiology* 19:266–71.

———. 1985. "Comparison of procedures for the assessment of psychopathy." *Journal of Consulting and Clinical Psychology* 53 (1):7–16.

———. 1991. *Manual for the Hare Psychopathy Checklist–Revised*. Toronto: Multi-Health Systems.

———. 1999. *Without Conscience: The Disturbing World of the Psychopaths Among Us*. New York: Guilford.

———. 2003. *Hare Psychopathy Checklist–Revised (PCL-R)*. 2nd ed. Toronto: Multi-Health Systems.

Hare, R. D., J. Frazelle, and D. N. Cox. 1978. "Psychopathy and physiological responses to threat of an aversive stimulus." *Psychophysiology* 15:165–72.

Hare, R. D., and M. J. Quinn. 1971. "Psychopathy and autonomic conditioning." *Journal of Abnormal Psychology* 77:223–35.

Harenski, C. L., and S. Hamann. 2006. "Neural correlates of regulating negative emotions related to moral violations." *NeuroImage* 30:313–24.

Harenski, C. L., K. A. Harenski, M. S. Shane, and K. A. Kiehl. 2010. "Aberrant neural processing of moral violations in criminal psychopaths." *Journal of Abnormal Psychology* 119:863–74.

Hariri, A. R., A. Gorka, L. W. Hyde, M. Kimak, I. Halder, F. Ducci, R. E. Ferrell, D. Goldman, and S. B. Manuck. 2009. "Divergent effects of genetic variation in endocannabinoid signaling on human threat and reward-related brain function." *Biological Psychiatry* 66:9–16.

Hariri, A. R., V. Mattay, A. Tessitore, B. Kolachana, F. Fera, D. Goldman, M. Egan, and D. R. Weinberger. 2002. "Serotonin transporter genetic variation and the response of the human amygdala." *Science* 297:400–403.

Harlow, J. M. 1848. "Passage of an iron bar through the head." *Boston Medical and Surgical Journal* 39:389–93.

Hawes, D. J., and M. R. Dadds. 2005. "The treatment of conduct problems in children with callous-unemotional traits." *Journal of Consulting and Clinical Psychology* 73:737–41.

Heekeren, H. R., I. Wartenburger, H. Schmidt, H. P. Schwintowski, and A. Villringer. 2003. "An fMRI investigation of emotional engagement in moral judgment." *Neuro-Report* 14:1215–19.

Heinz, A., D. F. Braus, M. N. Smolka, J. Wrase, I. Puls, D. Hermann, S. Klein, S. M. Grusser, H. Flor, G. Schumann, K. Mann, and C. Buchel. 2005. "Amygdala-pre-frontal coupling depends on genetic variation of the serotonin transporter." *Nature Neuroscience* 8:20–21.

Herman, A. I., T. S. Conner, R. F. Anton, J. Gelernter, H. R. Kranzler, and J. Covault. in press. "Variation in the gene encoding the serotonin transporter is associated with a measure of sociopathy in alcoholics." *Addiction Biology*.

Hermans, E. J., P. Putman, J. M. Baas, N. M. Gecks, J. L. Kenemans, and J. van Honk. 2007. "Exogenous testosterone attenuates the integrated central stress response in healthy young women." *Psychoneuroendocrinology* 32:1052–61.

Hermans, E. J., P. Putman, J. M. Baas, H. Koppeschaar, and J. van Honk. 2006. "A single administration of testosterone reduces fear-potentiated startle in humans." *Biological Psychiatry* 59:872–74.

Hermans, E. J., P. Putman, and J. van Honk. 2006. "Testosterone administration reduces empathic behavior: A facial mimicry study." *Psychoneuroendocrinology* 31 (7):859–66.

Herpertz, S. C., T. M. Dietrich, and B. Wenning. 2001. "Evidence of abnormal amygdala functioning in borderline personality disorder." *Biological Psychiatry* 50:292–98.

Herpertz, S. C., B. Wenning, B. Mueller, M. Qunaibi, H. Sass, and B. Herpertz-Dahlmann. 2001. "Psychophysiological responses in ADHD boys with and without conduct disorder: Implications for adult antisocial behavior." *Journal of the American Academy of Child and Adolescent Psychiatry* 40:1222–30.

Hessl, D., G. Dawson, K. Frey, H. Panagiotides, H. Self, E. Yamada, and J. Osterling. 1998. "A longitudinal study of children of depressed mothers: Psychobiological findings related to stress." In *Advancing Research on Developmental Plasticity: Integrating the Behavioral Sciences and the Neurosciences of Mental Health*, edited by L. C. Huffman, D. M. Hann, K. K. Lederhendler, and D. Minecke, 256. Bethesda, MD: National Institutes of Mental Health.

Hiatt, K. D., and J. P. Newman. 2007. "Behavioral evidence of prolonged interhemispheric transfer time among psychopathic offenders." *Neuropsychology* 21 (3):313–18.

Hiatt, K. D., W. A. Schmitt, and J. P. Newman. 2004. "Stroop tasks reveal abnormal selective attention among psychopathic offenders." *Neuropsychology* 18 (1):50–59.

Hibbeln, J. R. 2001. "Homicide mortality rates and seafood consumption: A cross-national analysis." *World Review Nutrition and Diet* 88:41–46.

Hicks, B. M., K. E. Markon, C. J. Patrick, R. F. Krueger, and J. P. Newman. 2004. "Identifying psychopathy subtypes on the basis of personality structure." *Psychological Assessment* 16 (3):276–88.

Hicks, B. M., U. Vaidyanathan, and C. J. Patrick. 2010. "Validating female psychopathy subtypes: Differences in personality, antisocial and violent behavior, substance abuse, trauma, and mental health." *Personality Disorders* 1 (1):38–57.

Hirashima, F., A. M. Parow, A. L. Stoll, C. M. Demopulos, K. E. Damico, M. L. Rohan, J. G. Eskesen, C. S. Zuo, B. M. Cohen, and P. F. Renshaw. 2004. "Omega-3 fatty acid treatment and T2 whole brain relaxation times in bipolar disorder." *American Journal of Psychiatry* 161:1922–24.

Hirvonen, M., A. Laakso, K. Nagren, J. O. Rinne, T. Pohjalainene, and J. Hietala. 2004. "C957T polymorphism of the dopamine D2 receptor (DRD2) gene affects striatal DRD2 availability in vivo." *Molecular Psychiatry* 9:1060–61.

Hoenicka, J., G. Ponce, M. A. Jimenez-Arriero, I. Ampuero, R. Rodriguez-Jimenez, G. Rubio, M. Aragues, J. A. Ramos, and T. Palomo. 2007. "Association in alcoholic patients between psychopathic traits and the additive effect of allelic forms of the CNR1 and the FAAH endocannabinoid genes, and the 3' region of the DRD2 gene." *Neurotoxicity Research* 11:51–59.

Holi, M., L. Auvinen-Lintunen, N. Lindberg, P. Tani, and M. Virkkunen. 2006. "Inverse correlation between severity of psychopathic traits and serum cortisol levels in young adult violent male offenders." *Psychopathology* 39:102–4.

Holroyd, C. B., and M. G. H. Coles. 2002. "The neural basis. of human error processing: Reinforcement learning, dopamine, and the error-related negativity." *Psychological Review* 109 (4):679–709.

Houlihan, M., R. Stelmack, and K. Campbell. 1988. "P300 and cognitive ability: Assessing the roles of processing speed, perceptual processing demands and task difficulty." *Intelligence* 26:9–25.

Hugdahl, K. 2001. *Psychophysiology: The Mind-Body Perspective.* Edited by S. M. Kosslyn. Cambridge, MA: Harvard University Press.

Hughes, V. 2010. "Science in court: Head case." *Nature* 464 (7287):340–42.

Huijbregts, S. C. J., S. R. van Berkel, H. Swaab-Barneveld, and S. H. M. van Goozen. 2011. "Neurobiological and behavioral stress reactivity in children prenatally exposed to tobacco." *Psychoneuroendocrinology* 36 (6):913–18.

Hunt, M. K., D. R. Hopko, and R. Bare. 2005. "Construct validity of the Balloon Analog Risk Task (BART)." *Assessment* 12:416–28.

Intrator, J., R. D. Hare, P. Stritzke, K. Brichtswein, D. Dorfman, and T. Harpur. 1997. "A brain imaging (single photon emission computerized tomography) study of semantic and affective processing in psychopaths." *Biological Psychiatry* 42 (96–103).

Iria, C., and F. Barbosa. 2009. "Perception of facial expressions of fear: Comparative research with criminal and non-criminal psychopaths." *Journal of Forensic Psychiatry & Psychology* 20 (1):66–73.

Isen, J., A. Raine, L. A. Baker, M. E. Dawson, S. Bezdjian, and D. I. Lozano. 2010. "Sex-specific association between psychopathic traits and electrodermal reactivity in children." *Journal of Abnormal Psychology* 119:216–25.

Ishikawa, S. S., A. Raine, T. Lencz, S. Bihrle, and L. Lacasse. 2001. "Autonomic stress reactivity and executive functions in successful and unsuccessful criminal psychopaths from the community." *Journal of Abnormal Psychology* 110 (3):423–32.

Johansson, A., P. Santtila, N. Harlaar, B. von der Pahlen, K. Witting, M. Ålgars, K. Alanko, P. Jern, M. Varjonen, and N. K. Sandnabba. 2008. "Genetic effects on male sexual coercion." *Aggressive Behavior* 34 (2):190–202.

Johnson, M. K., C. R. Raye, K. J. Mitchell, S. R. Touryan, E. J. Greene, and S. Nolen-Hoeksema. 2006. "Dissociating the medial frontal and posterior cingulate activity during self-reflection." *Social, Cognitive, and Affective Neuroscience* 1:56–64.

Jones, A. P., K. R. Laurens, C. M. Herba, G. J. Barker, and E. Viding. 2009. "Amygdala hypoactivity to fearful faces in boys with conduct problems and callous-unemotional traits." *American Journal of Psychiatry* 166:95–102.

Justus, A. N., and P. R. Finn. 2007. "Startle modulation in non-incarcerated men and women with psychopathic traits." *Personality and Individual Differences* 43:2057–71.

Jutai, J. W., R. D. Hare, and J. F. Connolly. 1987. "Psychopathy and event-related brain potentials (ERPs) associated with attention to speech stimuli." *Personality and Individual Differences* 8:175–84.

Kagan, J., J. S. Reznick, and N. Snidman. 1988. "Biological bases of childhood shyness." *Science* 240:167–71.

Karpman, B. 1941. "On the need of separating psychopathy into two distinct clinical types: The symptomatic and the idiopathic." *Journal of Criminal Psychopathology* 3:112–37.

Kehoe, P., W. J. Shoemaker, L. Triano, J. Hoffman, and C. Arons. 1996. "Repeated isolation in the neonatal rat produces alterations in behavior and ventral striatal dopamine release in the juvenile after amphetamine challenge." *Behavioral Neuroscience* 110 (6):1435–44.

Kertes, D. A., M. R. Gunnar, N. J. Madsen, and J. D. Long. 2008. "Early deprivation and home basal cortisol levels: A study of internationally adopted children." *Development and Psychopathology* 20 (2):473–91.

Kiehl, K. A. 2006. "A cognitive neuroscience perspective on psychopathy: Evidence for paralimbic system dysfunction." *Psychiatry Research* 142:107–28.

Kiehl, K. A., A. T. Bates, K. R. Laurens, R. D. Hare, and P. F. Liddle. 2006. "Brain potentials implicate temporal lobe abnormalities in criminal psychopaths." *Journal of Abnormal Psychology* 115:443–53.

Kiehl, K. A., R. D. Hare, P. F. Liddle, and J. J. McDonald. 1999. "Reduced P300 responses in criminal psychopaths during a visual oddball task." *Biological Psychiatry* 45:1498–1507.

Kiehl, K. A., A. M. Smith, R. D. Hare, and P. F. Liddle. 2000. "An event-related potential investigation of response inhibition in schizophrenia and psychopathy." *Biological Psychiatry* 48:210–21.

Kiehl, K. A., A. M. Smith, R. D. Hare, A. Mendrek, B. B. Forster, and J. Brink. 2001. "Limbic abnormalities in affective processing by criminal psychopaths as revealed by functional magnetic resonance imaging." *Biological Psychiatry* 50:677–84.

Kiehl, K. A., A. M. Smith, A. Mendrek, B. B. Forster, R. D. Hare, and P. F. Liddle. 2004. "Temporal lobe abnormalities in semantic processing by criminal psychopaths as revealed by functional magnetic resonance imaging." *Psychiatry Research* 130:27–42.

Kimonis, E. R., P. J. Frick, E. Cauffman, A. Goldweber, and J. Skeem. 2012. "Primary and secondary variants of juvenile psychopathy differ in emotional processing." *Development and Psychopathology* 24 (Special Issue 3):1091–1103.

Kimonis, E. R., J. L. Skeem, E. Cauffman, and J. Dmitrieva. 2011. "Are secondary variants of juvenile psychopathy more reactively violent and less psychosocially mature than primary variants?" *Law and Human Behavior* 35 (5):381–91.

Kitajka, K., A. J. Sinclair, R. S. Weisinger, H. S. Weisinger, M. Mathai, A. P. Jayasooriya, J. E. Halver, and L. G. Puskas. 2004. "Effects of dietary omega-3 polyunsaturated fatty acids on brain gene expression." *Proceedings of the National Academy of Sciences USA* 101 (30):10931–36.

Kito, S., T. Hasegawa, and Y. Koga. 2012. "Cerebral blood flow in the ventromedial prefrontal cortex correlates with treatment response to low-frequency right prefrontal repetitive transcranial magnetic stimulation in the treatment of depression." *Psychiatry and Clinical Neurosciences* 66 (2):138–45.

Knoch, D., V. Treyer, M. Regard, R. M. Muri, A. Buck, and B. Weber. 2006. "Lateralized and frequency-dependent effects of prefrontal rTMS on regional cerebral blood flow." *NeuroImage* 31 (2):641–48.

Koenigs, M., A. R. Baskin-Sommers, J. Zeier, and J. P. Newman. 2011. "Investigating the neural correlates of psychopathy: A critical review." *Molecular Psychiatry* 16:792–99.

Koenigs, M., L. Young, R. Adolphs, D. Tranel, F. Cushman, M. Hauser, and A. R. Damasio. 2007. "Damage to the prefrontal cortex increases utilitarian moral judgements." *Nature* 446:908–11.

Kohlboeck, G., C. Glaser, C. Tiesler, H. Demmelmair, M. Standl, M. Romanos, B. Koletzko, I. Lehmann, J. Heinrich, and LISAplus Study Group. 2011. "Effect of fatty acid status in cord blood serum on children's behavioral difficulties at 10 y of age: Results from the LISAplus Study." *American Journal of Clinical Nutrition* 94 (6):1592–99.

Koivisto, H., and J. Haapasalo. 1996. "Childhood maltreatment and adulthood psychopathy in light of file-based assessments among mental state examinees." *Studies on Crime and Crime Prevention* 5:91–104.

Kolko, D. J., L. D. Dorn, O. G. Bukstein, D. Pardini, E. A. Holden, and J. Hart. 2009. "Community vs. clinic-based modular treatment of children with early-onset ODD or CD: A clinical trial with 3–year follow-up." *Journal of Abnormal Child Psychology* 37 (5):591–609.

Kosson, D. S. 1996. "Psychopathy and dual-task performance under focusing conditions." *Journal of Abnormal Psychology* 105:391–400.

———. 1998. "Divided visual attention in psychopathic and nonpsychopathic offenders." *Personality and Individual Differences* 24:373–91.

Kosson, D. S., S. K. Miller, K. A. Byrnes, and C. L. Leveroni. 2007. "Testing neuropsychological hypotheses for cognitive deficits in psychopathic criminals: A study of global-local processing." *Journal of the International Neuropsychological Society* 13 (2):267–76.

Kreuz, L. E., and R. M. Rose. 1972. "Assessment of aggressive behavior and plasma testosterone in a young criminal population." *Psychosomatic Medicine* 34 (4):321–32.

Krischer, M. K., and K. Sevecke. 2008. "Early traumatization and psychopathy in female and male juvenile offenders." *International Journal of Law and Psychiatry* 31:253–62.

Krueger, R. F., K. E. Markon, C. J. Patrick, S. D. Benning, and M. D. Kramer. 2007. "Linking antisocial behavior, substance use, and personality: An integrative quantitative model of the adult externalizing spectrum." *Journal of Abnormal Psychology* 116 (4):645–66.

Kudielka, B. M., and C. Kirschbaum. 2005. "Sex differences in HPA axis responses to stress: A review." *Biological Psychiatry* 69:113–32.

Laakso, A., T. Pohjalainene, J. Bergman, J. Kajander, M. Haaparanta, O. Solin, E. Syvalahti, and J. Hietala. 2005. "The A1 allele of the human D2 dopamine receptor gene is associated with increased activity of striatal L-amino acid decarboxylase in healthy subjects." *Pharmacogenetics and Genomics* 15:387–91.

Laakso, M. P., O. Vaurio, E. Koivisto, L. Savolainen, M. Eronen, and H. J. Aronen. 2001. "Psychopathy and the posterior hippocampus." *Behavioural Brain Research* 118:187–93.

Lalumiere, M. L., and V. L. Quinsey. 1996. "Sexual deviance, antisociality, mating effort, and the use of sexually coercive behaviors." *Personality and Individual Differences* 21:33–48.

Lang, P. J., M. M. Bradley, and B. N. Cuthbert. 1990. "Emotion, attention, and the startle reflex." *Psychological Review* 97 (3):377–95.

Lang, S., B. af Klinteberg, and P. O. Alm. 2002. "Adult psychopathy and violent behavior in males with early neglect and abuse." *Acta Psychiatrica Scandinavica* 106:93–100.

Langevin, R., J. Bain, G. Wortzman, S. Hucker, R. Dickey, and P. Wright. 1988. "Sexual sadism: Brain, blood and behavior." *Annals of the New York Academy of Sciences* 528:163–71.

LaPierre, D., C. M. J. Braun, and S. Hodgins. 1995. "Ventral frontal deficits in psychopathy: Neuropsychological test findings." *Neuropsychologia* 33:139–51.

Larsson, H., H. Andershed, and P. Lichtenstein. 2006. "A genetic factor explains most of the variation in psychopathic personality." *Journal of Abnormal Psychology* 115:221–30.

Larsson, H., C. Tuvblad, F. V. Rijsdijk, H. Andershed, M. Grann, and P. Lichtenstein. 2007. "A common genetic factor explains the association between psychopathic personality and antisocial behavior." *Psychological Medicine* 37:15–26.

LeDoux, J. E. 1998. *The Emotional Brain*. New York: Weidenfeld & Nicolson.

Lee, T. M. C., S. C. Chan, and A. Raine. 2008. "Strong limbic and weak frontal activation to aggressive stimuli in spouse abusers." *Molecular Psychiatry* 13:655–56.

Lee, Z., R. Salekin, and A.-M. Iselin. 2010. "Psychopathic traits in youth: Is there evidence for primary and secondary subtypes?" *Journal of Abnormal Child Psychology* 38 (3):381–93.

Lesch, K.-P., D. Bengel, A. Heils, S. Z. Sabol, B. Greenberg, S. Petri, J. Benjamin, C. R. Muller, D. H. Hamer, and D. L. Murphy. 1996. "Association of anxiety-related traits with a polymorphism in the serotonin transporter gene regulatory region." *Science* 274:1527–31.

Levenson, M. R., K. A. Kiehl, and C. M. Fitzpatrick. 1995. "Assessing psychopathic attributes in a noninstitutionalized population." *Journal of Personality and Social Psychology* 68 (1):151–58.

Levenston, G. K., C. J. Patrick, M. M. Bradley, and P. J. Lang. 2000. "The psychopath as an observer: Emotion and attention in picture processing." *Journal of Abnormal Psychology* 109:373–86.

Lezak, M. D., D. B. Howieson, D. W. Loring, H. J. Hannay, and J. S. Fischer. 2004. *Neuropsychological Assessment*. 4th ed. New York: Oxford University Press.

Lilienfeld, S. O., and B. P. Andrews. 1996. "Development and preliminary validation of a self-report measure of psychopathic personality traits in noncriminal populations." *Journal of Personality Assessment* 66:488–524.

Lilienfeld, S. O., and M. R. Widows. 2005. *Psychopathic Personality Inventory–Revised (PPI-R) professional manual*. Odessa, FL: Psychological Assessment Resources.

Lim, M. M., and L. J. Young. 2006. "Neuropeptidergic regulation of affiliative behavior and social bonding in animals." *Hormones and Behavior* 50 (4):506–17.

Lindberg, N., P. Tani, M. Virkkunen, T. Porkka-Heiskanen, B. Appelberg, H. Naukkarinen, and T. Salmi. 2005. "Quantitative electroencephalographic measures in homicidal men with antisocial personality disorder." *Psychiatry Research* 136 (1):7–15.

Liu, J. H. 2011. "Early health risk factors for violence: Conceptualization, evidence, and implications." *Aggression and Violent Behavior* 16 (1):63–73.

Liu, J. H., L. McCauley, C. Compher, C. H. Yan, X. M. Shen, H. Needleman, and J. A. Pinto-Martin. 2011. "Regular breakfast and blood lead levels among preschool children." *Environmental Health* 10:28–36.

Liu, J. H., A. Raine, P. H. Venables, and S. Mednick. 2004. "Malnutrition at age 3 years and externalizing behavior problems at ages 8, 11 and 17 years." *American Journal of Psychiatry* 161:2005–13.

Llanes, S. J., and D. S. Kosson. 2006. "Divided visual attention and left hemisphere activation among psychopathic and nonpsychopathic offenders." *Journal of Psychopathology and Behavioral Assessment* 28 (1):9–18.

Loney, B. R., M. A. Butler, E. N. Lima, C. A. Counts, and L. A. Eckel. 2006. "The relation between salivary cortisol, callous-unemotional traits, and conduct problems in an adolescent non-referred sample." *Journal of Child Psychology and Psychiatry* 47 (1):30–36.

Loney, B. R., J. Taylor, M. A. Butler, and W. G. Iacono. 2007. "Adolescent psychopathy features: 6-year temporal stability and the prediction of externalizing symptoms during the transition to adulthood." *Aggressive Behavior* 33:242–52.

Lonsdorf, T. B., A. I. Weike, P. Nikamo, M. Schalling, A. O. Hamm, and A. Ohman. 2009. "Genetic gating of human fear learning and extinction: Possible implications for gene-environment interaction in anxiety disorder." *Psychological Science* 20:198–206.

Lorber, M. F. 2004. "Psychophysiology of aggression, psychopathy, and conduct problems: A meta-analysis." *Psychological Bulletin* 130 (4):531–52.

Lu, R. B., J. F. Lee, H. C. Ko, and W. W. Lin. 2001. "Dopamine D2 receptor gene (DRD2) is associated with alcoholism with conduct disorder." *Alcoholism: Clinical Experimental Research* 25:177–84.

Lykken, D. 1957. "A study of anxiety in the sociopathic personality." *Journal of Abnormal and Social Psychology* 55:6–10.

Lynam, D. R. 1997. "Pursuing the psychopath: Capturing the fledgling psychopath in a nomological net." *Journal of Abnormal Psychology* 106 (3):425–38.

Lynam, D. R., A. Caspi, T. E. Moffitt, R. Loeber, and M. Stouthamer-Loeber. 2007. "Longitudinal evidence that psychopathy scores in early adolescence predict adult psychopathy." *Journal of Abnormal Psychology* 116:155–65.

Lynam, D. R., and K. J. Derefinko. 2006. "Psychopathy and personality." In *Handbook of Psychopathy*, edited by C. J. Patrick, 133–55. New York: Guilford.

Lynam, D. R., E. T. Gaughan, J. D. Miller, D. J. Miller, S. Mullins-Sweatt, and T. A. Widiger. 2011. "Assessing the basic traits associated with psychopathy: Development and validation of the elemental psychopathy assessment." *Psychological Assessment* 23 (1):108–24.

Lynam, D. R., S. Whiteside, and S. Jones. 1999. "Self-reported psychopathy: A validation study." *Journal of Personality Assessment* 73 (1):110–32.

Mahmut, M. K., J. Homewood, and R. J. Stevenson. 2008. "The characteristics of non-criminals with high psychopathy traits: Are they similar to criminal psychopaths?" *Journal of Research in Personality* 42 (3):679–92.

Mahmut, M. K., C. Menictas, R. J. Stevenson, and J. Homewood. 2011. "Validating the factor structure of the Self-Report Psychopathy Scale in a community sample." *Psychological Assessment* 23 (3):670–78.

Maibom, H. L. 2008. "The mad, the bad, and the psychopath." *Neuroethics* 1:167–84.

Maras, A., M. Laucht, D. Gerdes, C. Wilhelm, S. Lewicka, D. Haack, L. Malisova, and M. H. Schmidt. 2003. "Association of testosterone and dihydrotestosterone with externalizing behavior in adolescent boys and girls." *Psychoneuroendocrinology* 28 (7):932–40.

Maratos, E. J., R. J. Dolan, J. S. Morris, R. N. A. Henson, and M. D. Rugg. 2001. "Neural activity associated with episodic memory for emotional context." *Neuropsychologia* 39:910–20.

Marsh, A. A., E. C. Finger, D. G. V. Mitchell, M. E. Reid, C. Sims, D. S. Kosson, K. E. Towbin, E. Leibenluft, D. Pine, and R. J. Blair. 2008. "Reduced amygdala response to fearful expressions in children and adolescents with callous-unemotional traits and disruptive behavior disorders." *American Journal of Psychiatry* 165:712–20.

Marshall, L. A., and D. J. Cooke. 1999. "The childhood experiences of psychopaths: A retrospective study of familial and societal factors." *Journal of Personality Disorders* 13:211–25.

Martin, G. 2003. "The effectiveness of community-based sanctions in reducing recidivism." *Corrections Today* 65 (1):26–29.

Mathieu, C., R. D. Hare, D. N. Jones, P. Babiak, and C. S. Neumann. 2013. "Factor structure of the B-Scan 360: A measure of corporate psychopathy." *Psychological Assessment* 25:288–93.

Maughan, B., A. Taylor, A. Caspi, and T. E. Moffitt. 2004. "Prenatal smoking and early childhood conduct problems." *Archives of General Psychiatry* 61:836–43.

Mayberg, H. S., M. Liotti, S. K. Brannan, S. McGinnis, R. K. Mahurin, and P. A. Jerabek. 1999. "Reciprocal limbic-cortical function and negative mood: Converging PET findings in depression and normal sadness." *American Journal of Psychiatry* 156:675–82.

Mazur, A., and A. Booth. 1998. "Testosterone and dominance in men." *Behavioral and Brain Sciences* 21:353–97.

McCabe, D. P., and A. D. Castel. 2008. "Seeing is believing: The effect of brain images on judgments of scientific reasoning." *Cognition* 107 (1):343–52.

McClure, E. B., A. Adler, C. S. Monk, J. Cameron, S. Smith, E. E. Nelson, E. Leibenluft, M. Ernst, and D. Pine. 2007. "fMRI predictors of treatment outcome in pediatric anxiety disorders." *Psychopharmacology* 191:97–105.

McDonald, R., M. C. Dodson, D. Rosenfield, and E. N. Jouriles. 2011. "Effects of a parenting intervention on features of psychopathy in children." *Journal of Abnormal Child Psychology* 39 (7):1013–23.

McNamara, R. K., J. Able, R. Jandacek, T. Rider, P. Tso, J. C. Eliassen, D. Alfieri, W. Weber, K. Jarvis, M. P. DelBello, S. M. Strakowski, and C. M. Adler. 2010. "Docosahexaenoic acid supplementation increases prefrontal cortex activation during sustained attention in healthy boys: A placebo-controlled, dose-ranging, functional magnetic resonance imaging study." *American Journal of Clinical Nutrition* 91:1060–67.

Mendez, M. F. 2010. "The unique predisposition to criminal violations in frontotemporal dementia." *Journal of the American Academy of Psychiatry and the Law* 38 (3):318–23.

Mendez, M. F., E. Anderson, and J. S. Shapira. 2005. "An investigation of moral judgment in frontotemporal dementia." *Cognitive and Behavioral Neurology* 18:193–97.

Meyer-Lindenberg, A., J. W. Buckholtz, B. Kolachana, A. R. Hariri, L. Pezawas, G. Blasi, A. Wabnitz, R. Honea, B. Verchinski, J. H. Callicott, M. Egan, V. Mattay, and D. R. Weinberger. 2006. "Neural mechanisms of genetic risk for impulsivity and violence in humans." *Proceedings of the National Academy of Sciences USA* 103:6269–74.

Mitchell, D. G. V., E. Colledge, A. Leonard, and R. J. R. Blair. 2002. "Risky decisions and response reversal: Is there evidence of orbitofrontal cortex dysfunction in psychopathic individuals?" *Neuropsychologia* 40 (12):2013–22.

Mobbs, D., H. C. Lau, O. D. Jones, and C. D. Frith. 2007. "Law, responsibility, and the brain." *Public Library of Science: Biology* 5 (4):e103.

Moffitt, T. E. 2005. "The new look of behavioral genetics in developmental psychopathology: Gene-environment interplay in antisocial behaviors." *Psychological Bulletin* 131:533–54.

Moffitt, T. E., S. Ross, and A. Raine. 2011. "Crime and biology." In *Crime and Public Policy*, edited by J. Q. Wilson and J. Petersilia, 53–87. Oxford: Oxford University Press.

Mol, B., P. Van den Bos, Y. Derks, and J. Egger. 2009. "Executive functioning and the two-factor model of psychopathy: No differential relation?" *International Journal of Neuroscience* 119 (1):124–40.

Moll, J., P. J. Eslinger, and R. de Oliveira-Souza. 2001. "Frontopolar and anterior temporal cortex activation in a moral judgment task." *Arquivos de Neuro-Psiquiatria* 59 (3B):657–64.

Moll, J., R. de Oliveira-Souza, and P. J. Eslinger. 2003. "Morals and the human brain: A working model." *NeuroReport* 14:299–305.

Moll, J., R. de Oliveira-Souza, P. J. Eslinger, I. E. Bramati, J. Mourao-Miranda, P. A. Andreiuolo, and L. Pessoa. 2002. "The neural correlates of moral sensitivity: A functional magnetic resonance imaging investigation of basic and moral emotions." *Journal of Neuroscience* 22 (7):2730–36.

Moll, J., R. de Oliveira-Souza, F. T. Moll, F. A. Ignacio, I. E. Bramati, E. M. Caparelli-Daquer, and P. J. Eslinger. 2005. "The moral affiliations of disgust: A functional MRI study." *Cognitive Behavioral Neurology* 18:68–78.

Molto, J., R. Poy, P. Segarra, M. C. Pastor, and S. Montanes. 2007. "Response perseveration in psychopaths: Interpersonal/affective or social deviance traits?" *Journal of Abnormal Psychology* 116 (3):632–37.

Morgan, A. B., and S. O. Lilienfeld. 2000. "A meta-analytic review of the relation between antisocial behavior and neuropsychological measures of executive function." *Clinical Psychology Review* 20:113–36.

Morse, S. J. 2008. "Psychopathy and criminal responsibility." *Neuroethics* 1:205–12.

Muhammad, A., S. Hossain, S. M. Pellis, and B. Kolb. 2011. "Tactile stimulation during development attenuates amphetamine sensitization and structurally reorganizes prefrontal cortex and striatum in a sex-dependent manner." *Behavioral Neuroscience* 125 (2):161–74.

Müller, J. L., S. Gänßbauer, M. Sommer, K. Döhnel, T. Weber, T. Schmidt-Wilcke, and G. Hajak. 2008. "Gray matter changes in right superior temporal gyrus in criminal psychopaths: Evidence from voxel-based morphometry." *Psychiatry Research: Neuroimaging* 163:213–22.

Müller, J. L., M. Sommer, V. Wagner, K. Lange, H. Taschler, C. H. Roder, G. Schuierer, H. E. Klein, and G. Hajak. 2003. "Abnormalities in emotion processing within cortical and subcortical regions in criminal psychopaths: Evidence from a functional magnetic resonance imaging study using pictures with emotional content." *Biological Psychiatry* 54:152–62.

Muneoka, K., T. Ogawa, K. Kamei, S. Muraoka, R. Tomiyoshi, Y. Mimura, H. Kato, M. R. Suzuki, and M. Takigawa. 1997. "Prenatal nicotine exposure affects the development of the central serotonergic system as well as the dopaminergic system in rat offspring: Involvement of route of drug administrations." *Developmental Brain Research* 102 (1):117–26.

Muñoz, L. C., V. Pakalniskiene, and P. J. Frick. 2011. "Parental monitoring and youth behavior problems: Moderation by callous-unemotional traits over time." *European Child and Adolescent Psychiatry* 20:261–69.

Munro, G. E. S., J. Dywan, G. T. Harris, S. McKee, A. Unsal, and S. J. Segalowitz. 2007a. "ERN varies with degree of psychopathy in an emotion discrimination task." *Biological Psychology* 76:31–42.

———. 2007b. "Response inhibition in psychopathy: The frontal N2 and P3." *Neuroscience Letters* 418:149–53.

National Institute on Drug Abuse. 2011. "Prenatal exposure to drugs of abuse." http://www.drugabuse.gov/sites/default/files/prenatal.pdf.

Needleman, H. L., J. A. Riess, M. J. Tobin, G. E. Biesecker, and J. B. Greenhouse. 1996. "Bone lead levels and delinquent behavior." *Journal of the American Medical Association* 275 (5):363–69.

Neugebauer, R., H. W. Hoek, and E. Susser. 1999. "Prenatal exposure to wartime famine and development of antisocial personality disorder in early adulthood." *Journal of the American Medical Association* 282 (5):455–62.

Newman, J. P. 1998. "Psychopathic behavior: An information processing perspective." In *Psychopathy: Theory, Research and Implications for Society*, edited by D. J. Cooke, A. E. Forth, and R. D. Hare, 81–104. Dordrecht, Netherlands: Kluwer.

Newman, J. P., J. J. Curtin, J. D. Bertsch, and A. R. Baskin-Sommers. 2010. "Attention moderates the fearlessness of psychopathic offenders." *Biological Psychiatry* 67:66–70.

Newman, J. P., and D. S. Kosson. 1986. "Passive avoidance learning in psychopathic and nonpsychopathic offenders." *Journal of Abnormal Psychology* 95:252–56.

Newman, J. P., C. M. Patterson, and D. S. Kosson. 1987. "Response perseveration in psychopaths." *Journal of Abnormal Psychology* 96 (2):145–48.

Newman, J. P., and W. A. Schmitt. 1998. "Passive avoidance in psychopathic offenders: A replication and extension." *Journal of Abnormal Psychology* 107:563–75.

Ochsner, K. N., J. S. Beer, E. R. Robertson, J. C. Cooper, J. D. E. Gabrieli, J. F. Kihlstrom, and M. D'Esposito. 2005. "The neural correlates of direct and reflected self-knowledge." *NeuroImage* 28 (4):797–814.

Ochsner, K. N., S. A. Bunge, J. J. Gross, and J. D. E. Gabrieli. 2002. "Rethinking feel-ings: An fMRI study of the cognitive regulation of emotion." *Journal of Cognitive Neuroscience* 14 (8):1215–29.

O'Doherty, J. 2004. "Reward representations and reward-related learning in the human brain: Insights from neuroimaging." *Current Opinion in Neurobiology* 14:769–76.

Ogilvie, J. M., A. L. Stewart, R. C. K. Chan, and D. H. K. Shum. 2011. "Neuropsycho-logical measures of executive function and antisocial behavior: A meta-analysis." *Criminology* 49 (4):1063–1107.

Ogloff, J. R., and S. Wong. 1990. "Electrodermal and cardiovascular evidence of a cop-ing response in psychopaths." *Criminal Justice and Behavior* 17:231–45.

Olds, D. L. 2008. "Preventing child maltreatment and crime with prenatal and infancy support of parents: The nurse-family partnership." *Journal of Scandinavian Studies in Criminology and Crime Prevention* 9:2–24.

O'Leary, M. M., B. R. Loney, and L. A. Eckel. 2007. "Gender differences in the associa-tion between psychopathic personality traits and cortisol response to induced stress." *Psychoneuroendocrinology* 32 (2):183–91.

O'Leary, M. M., J. Taylor, and L. A. Eckel. 2010. "Psychopathic personality traits and cortisol response to stress: The role of sex, type of stressor, and menstrual phase." *Hormones and Behavior* 58:250–56.

Olivares, R., C. Morgan, H. Perez, A. Hernandez, F. Aboitiz, R. Soto-Moyano, J. Gil, A. Ortiz, O. Flores, M. Gimeno, and J. Laborda. 2012. "Anatomy of corpus callosum in prenatally malnourished rats." *Biological Research* 45 (1):87–92.

Olsen, S. F., and N. J. Secher. 2002. "Low consumption of seafood in early pregnancy as a risk factor for preterm delivery: Prospective cohort study." *British Medical Journal* 324 (7335):447–50.

O'Neal, C. R., L. M. Brotman, K. Y. Huang, K. K. Gouley, D. Kamboukos, E. J. Calzada, and D. Pine. 2010. "Understanding relations among early family environment, cor-tisol response, and child aggression via a prevention experiment." *Child Develop-ment* 81:290–305.

Osinsky, R., M. Reuter, Y. Kupper, A. Schmitz, E. Kozyra, N. Alexander, and J. Hennig. 2008. "Variation in the serotonin transporter gene modulates selective attention to threat." *Emotion* 8:584–88.

Pajer, K., R. Tabbah, W. Gardner, R. T. Rubin, R. K. Czambel, and Y. Wang. 2006. "Adrenal androgen and gonadal hormone levels in adolescent girls with conduct disorder." *Psychoneuroendocrinology* 31 (10):1245–56.

Palca, J. 1992. "NIH wrestles with furor over conference." *Science* 257:739.

Paquette, V., J. Levesque, B. Mensour, J. M. Leroux, G. Beaudoin, P. Bourgouin, and M. Beauregard. 2003. "'Change the mind and you change the brain': Effects of cognitive-behavioral therapy on the neural correlates of spider phobia." *NeuroImage* 18:401–9.

Pardini, D. A., and A. L. Byrd. 2012. "Perceptions of aggressive conflicts and others' distress in children with callous-unemotional traits: 'I'll show you who's boss, even if you suffer and I get in trouble.'" *Journal of Child Psychology and Psychiatry* 53 (3):283–91.

Parker, C. R. J. 1999. "Dehydroepiandrosterone and dehydroepiandrosterone sulfate production in the human adrenal during development and aging." *Steroids* 64:640–47.

Pastor, M. C., J. Molto, J. Vila, and P. J. Lang. 2003. "Startle reflex modulation, affective ratings and autonomic reactivity in incarcerated Spanish psychopaths." *Psychophysiology* 40:934–38.

Patrick, C. J. 1994. "Emotion and psychopathy: Startling new insights." *Psychophysiology* 31:319–30.

———. 2008. "Psychophysiological correlates of aggression and violence: An integrative review." *Philosophical Transactions of the Royal Society B—Biological Sciences* 363 (1503):2543–55.

Patrick, C. J., and E. M. Bernat. 2009. "Neurobiology of psychopathy: A two-process theory." In *Handbook of Neuroscience for the Behavioral Sciences*, edited by G. G. Berntson and J. T. Cacioppo, 1110–31. New York: John Wiley.

Patrick, C. J., M. M. Bradley, and P. J. Lang. 1993. "Emotion in the criminal psychopath: Startle reflex modulation." *Journal of Abnormal Psychology* 102:82–92.

Patrick, C. J., B. N. Cuthbert, and P. J. Lang. 1994. "Emotion in the criminal psychopath: Fear image processing." *Journal of Abnormal Psychology* 103:523–34.

Patrick, C. J., D. C. Fowles, and R. F. Krueger. 2009. "Triarchic conceptualization of psychopathy: Developmental origins of disinhibition, boldness, and meanness." *Development and Psychopathology* 21 (Special Issue 3):913–38.

Patrick, C. J., N. C. Venables, and J. Skeem. 2012. "Psychopathy and brain function: Empirical findings and legal implications." In *Psychopathy and Law: A Practitioner's Guide*, edited by H. Häkkänen-Nyholm and J.-O. Nyholm, 39–78. New York: John Wiley.

Patrick, C. J., K. A. Zempolich, and G. K. Levenston. 1997. "Emotionality and violent behavior in psychopaths: A biosocial analysis." In *Biosocial Basis of Violence*, edited by A. Raine, P. A. Brennan, D. P. Farrington, and S. A. Mednick, 145–61. New York: Plenum.

Patterson, C. M., and J. P. Newman. 1993. "Reflectivity and learning from aversive events: Toward a psychological mechanism for the syndromes of disinhibition." *Psychological Review* 100 (4):716–36.

Paulhus, D. L., C. S. Neumann, and R. D. Hare. in press. *Manual for the Self-Report Psychopathy Scale 4th edition*. Toronto: Multi-Health Systems.

Pearson, T. A., and T. A. Manolio. 2008. "How to interpret a genome-wide association study." *Journal of the American Medical Association* 299:1335–44.

Peng, H. J., H. R. Zheng, L. J. Li, J. B. Liu, Y. Zhang, B. C. Shan, L. Zhang, Y. Yin, J. Liu, W. H. Li, J. S. Zhou, Z. X. Li, H. C. Yang, and Z. J. Zhang. 2012. "High-frequency rTMS treatment increases white matter FA in the left middle frontal gyrus in young patients with treatment-resistant depression." *Journal of Affective Disorders* 136 (3):249–57.

Pezawas, L., A. Meyer-Lindenberg, E. M. Drabant, B. Verchinski, K. E. Munoz, B. Kolachana, M. Egan, V. Mattay, A. R. Hariri, and D. R. Weinberger. 2005. "5-HTTLPR polymorphism impacts human cingulate-amygdala interactions: A genetic susceptibility mechanism for depression." *Nature Neuroscience* 8:828–34.

Phillips, M. L., W. C. Drevets, S. L. Rauch, and R. Lane. 2003. "Neurobiology of emotion perception I: The neural basis of normal emotion perception." *Biological Psychiatry* 54:504–14.

Pike, A., and R. Plomin. 1997. "A behavioral genetic perspective on close relationships." *International Journal of Behavioral Development* 21:647–68.

Plomin, R., M. A. Haworth, and O. S. P. Davis. 2009. "Common disorders are quantitative traits." *Nature Reviews: Genetics* 10:872–78.

Poffenberger, A. T., Jr. 1912. "Reaction time to retinal stimulation with special reference to the time lost in conduction through nerve centers." *Archives of Psychology* 23:1–73.

Pokora, M. J., E. K. Richfield, and D. A. CorySlechta. 1996. "Preferential vulnerability of nucleus accumbens dopamine binding sites to low-level lead exposure: Time course of effects and interactions with chronic dopamine agonist treatments." *Journal of Neurochemistry* 67 (4):1540–50.

Ponce, G., J. Hoenicka, M. A. Jimenez-Arriero, R. Rodriguez-Jimenez, M. Aragues, N. Martin-Sune, E. Huertas, and T. Palomo. 2008. "DRD2 and ANKK1 genotype in alcohol-dependent patients with psychopathic traits: Association and interaction study." *British Journal of Psychiatry* 193:121–25.

Ponce, G., J. Hoenicka, G. Rubio, I. Ampuero, M. A. Jimenez-Arriero, and R. Rodriguez-Jimenez. 2003. "Association between cannabinoid receptor gene (CNR1) and childhood attention deficit/hyperactivity disorder in Spanish male alcoholic patients." *Molecular Psychiatry* 8:466–67.

Poythress, N. G., and J. Skeem. 2006. "Disaggregating psychopathy: Where and how to look for subtypes." In *Handbook of Psychopathy*, edited by C. J. Patrick, 172–92. New York: Guilford.

Psychological Assessment Resources. 2003. *Computerised Wisconsin Card Sorting Test Version 4 (WCST)*. Lutz, FL: Psychological Assessment Resources.

Qiu, A., A. Rifkin-Graboi, J. Zhong, D. Y.-L. Phua, Y. K. Lai, and M. J. Meaney. 2012. "Birth weight and gestation influence striatal morphology and motor response in normal six-year-old boys." *NeuroImage* 59 (2):1065–70.

Racer, K. H., T. T. Gilbert, P. Luu, J. Felver-Gant, Y. Abdullaev, and T. J. Dishion. 2011. "Attention network performance and psychopathic symptoms in early adolescence: An ERP study." *Journal of Abnormal Child Psychology* 39 (7):1001–12.

Rafter, N. H. 2008. *The Criminal Brain: Understanding Biological Theories of Crime.* New York: New York University Press.

Raine, A. 1993. *The Psychopathology of Crime: Criminal Behavior as a Clinical Disorder.* San Diego, CA: Academic Press.

———. 2002. "Biosocial studies of antisocial and violent behavior in children and adults: A review." *Journal of Abnormal Child Psychology* 30:311–26.

———. 2008. "From genes to brain to antisocial behavior." *Current Directions in Psychological Science* 17:323–28.

Raine, A., P. A. Brennan, and S. Mednick. 1994. "Birth complications combined with early maternal rejection at age 1 year predispose to violent crime at age 18 years." *Archives of General Psychiatry* 51:984–88.

Raine, A., M. S. Buchsbaum, and L. Lacasse. 1997. "Brain abnormalities in murderers indicated by positron emission tomography." *Biological Psychiatry* 42:495–508.

Raine, A., M. S. Buchsbaum, J. Stanley, S. Lottenberg, L. Abel, and J. Stoddard. 1994. "Selective reductions in prefrontal glucose metabolism in murderers." *Biological Psychiatry* 36 (6):365–73.

Raine, A., S. S. Ishikawa, E. Arce, T. Lencz, K. H. Knuth, S. Bihrle, L. Lacasse, and P. Colletti. 2004. "Hippocampal structural asymmetry in unsuccessful psychopaths." *Biological Psychiatry* 55:185–91.

Raine, A., L. Lee, Y. Yang, and P. Colletti. 2010. "Neurodevelopmental marker for limbic maldevelopment in antisocial personality disorder and psychopathy." *British Journal of Psychiatry* 197:186–92.

Raine, A., T. Lencz, K. Taylor, J. B. Hellige, S. Bihrle, L. Lacasse, M. Lee, S. S. Ishikawa, and P. Colletti. 2003. "Corpus callosum abnormalities in psychopathic antisocial individuals." *Archives of General Psychiatry* 60:1134–42.

Raine, A., J. R. Meloy, S. Bihrle, J. Stoddard, L. Lacasse, and M. S. Buchsbaum. 1998. "Reduced prefrontal and increased subcortical brain functioning assessed using positron emission tomography in predatory and affective murderers." *Behavioral Sciences & the Law* 16:319–32.

Raine, A., and P. H. Venables. 1988a. "Enhanced P3 evoked potentials and longer P3 recovery times in psychopaths." *Psychophysiology* 25:30–38.

———. 1988b. "Skin conductance responsivity in psychopaths to orienting, defensive, and consonant-vowel stimuli." *Journal of Psychophysiology* 2:221–25.

Raine, A., P. H. Venables, and M. Williams. 1996. "Better autonomic conditioning and faster electrodermal half-recovery time at age 15 years as possible protective factors against crime at 29 years." *Developmental Psychology* 32 (4):624–30.

Raine, A., and Y. Yang. 2006. "Neural foundations to moral reasoning and antisocial behavior." *Social, Cognitive, and Affective Neuroscience* 1:203–13.

Ramlau-Hansen, C. H., L. B. Hakonsen, M. Christensen, J. P. Bonde, J. Olsen, and A. M. Thulstrup. 2011. "Maternal shift work during pregnancy and biomarkers of reproductive function among the male offspring—A pilot follow-up study." *Scandinavian Journal of Work, Environment & Health* 37 (6):533–38.

Reist, C., C. Mazzanti, R. Vu, D. Tran, and D. Goldman. 2001. "Serotonin transporter promoter polymorphism is associated with attenuated prolactin response to fenfluramine." *American Journal of Medical Genetics Part B (Neuropsychiatric Genetics)* 105:363–68.

Rhee, S. H., and I. D. Waldman. 2002. "Genetic and environmental influences on antisocial behavior: A meta-analysis of twin and adoption studies." *Psychological Bulletin* 128:490–529.

Richell, R. A., D. G. V. Mitchell, K. S. Peschardt, J. S. Winston, A. Leonard, R. J. Dolan, and R. J. R. Blair. 2005. "Trust and distrust: The perception of trustworthiness of faces in psychopathic and non-psychopathic offenders." *Personality and Individual Differences* 38 (8):1735–44.

Ridderinkhof, K. R., M. Ullsperger, E. A. Crone, and S. Nieuwenhuis. 2004. "The role of the medial frontal cortex in cognitive control." *Science* 306:443–47.

Rijsdijsk, F. V., E. Viding, S. A. De Brito, M. Forgiarini, A. Mechelli, A. P. Jones, and E. McCrory. 2010. "Heritable variations in gray matter concentration as a potential endophenotype for psychopathic traits." *Archives of General Psychiatry* 67:406–13.

Rilling, J. K., A. L. Glenn, M. R. Jairam, G. Pagnoni, D. R. Goldsmith, H. A. Elfenbein, and S. O. Lilienfeld. 2007. "Neural correlates of social cooperation and non-cooperation as a function of psychopathy." *Biological Psychiatry* 61:1260–71.

Rizwan, S., J. T. Manning, and B. J. Brabin. 2007. "Maternal smoking during pregnancy and possible effects of in utero testosterone." *Early Human Development* 83:97–90.

Robertson, D., J. Snarey, O. Ousley, K. Harenski, F. D. Bowman, R. Gilkey, and C. Kilts. 2007. "The neural processing of moral sensitivity to issues of justice and care." *Neuropsychologia* 45:755–66.

Rogers, R. D. 2006. "The functional architecture of the frontal lobes." In *Handbook of Psychopathy*, edited by C. J. Patrick, 313–33. New York: Guilford.

Rogers, R., R. L. Jackson, K. W. Sewell, and J. Johansen. 2004. "Predictors of treatment outcome in dually diagnosed antisocial youth: An initial study of forensic inpatients." *Behavioral Sciences & the Law* 22:215–22.

Roiser, J. P., R. D. Rogers, L. J. Cook, and B. J. Sahakian. 2006. "The effect of polymorphism at the serotonin transporter gene on decision-making, memory and executive function in ecstasy users and controls." *Psychopharmacology* 188:213–27.

Rolls, E. T. 2000. "The orbitofrontal cortex and reward." *Cerebral Cortex* 10:284–94.

Rolls, E. T., J. Hornak, D. Wade, and J. McGrath. 1994. "Emotion-related learning in patients with social and emotional changes associated with frontal lobe damage." *Journal of Neurology, Neurosurgery and Psychiatry* 57:1518–24.

Rosen, G. M., A. S. Deinard, S. Schwartz, C. Smith, B. Stephenson, and B. Grabenstein. 1985. "Iron deficiency among incarcerated juvenile delinquents." *Journal of Adolescent Healthcare* 6 (6):419–23.

Rosen, J. B., and J. Schulkin. 1998. "From normal fear to pathological anxiety." *Psychological Review* 105:325–50.

Rosenblitt, J. C., H. Soler, S. E. Johnson, and D. M. Quadagno. 2002. "Sensation seeking and hormones in men and women: Exploring the link." *Hormones and Behavior* 40 (3):396–402.

Roussy, S., and J. Toupin. 2000. "Behavioral inhibition deficits in juvenile psychopaths." *Aggressive Behavior* 26 (6):413–24.

Royal Society. 2011. *Brain Waves Module 4: Neuroscience and the Law*. London: Royal Society.

Sadeh, N., S. Javdani, J. J. Jackson, E. K. Reynolds, M. N. Potenza, J. Gelernter, C. W. Lejuez, and E. Verona. 2010. "Serotonin transporter gene associations with psychopathic traits in youth vary as a function of socioeconomic resources." *Journal of Abnormal Psychology* 119:604–9.

Sadeh, N., and E. Verona. 2008. "Psychopathic personality traits associated with abnormal selective attention and impaired cognitive control." *Neuropsychology* 22 (5):669–80.

Salaria, S., G. Chana, F. Caldara, E. Feltrin, M. Altieri, F. Faggioni, E. Domenici, E. Merlo-Pich, and I. P. Everall. 2006. "Microarray analysis of cultured human brain aggregates following cortisol exposure: Implications for cellular functions relevant to mood disorders." *Neurobiology of Disease* 23 (3):630–36.

Salekin, R. T. 2002. "Psychopathy and therapeutic pessimism: Clinical lore or clinical reality?" *Clinical Psychology Review* 22:79–112.

Salekin, R. T., and D. R. Lynam. 2010. *Handbook of Child and Adolescent Psychopathy*. New York: Guilford.

Salekin, R. T., J. G. Tippey, and A. D. Allen. 2012. "Treatment of conduct problem youth with interpersonal callous traits using mental models: Measurement of risk and change." *Behavioral Sciences & the Law* 30 (4):470–86.

Salekin, R. T., C. Worley, and R. D. Grimes. 2010. "Treatment of psychopathy: A review and brief introduction to the mental model approach for psychopathy." *Behavioral Sciences & the Law* 28 (2):235–66.

Schneider, F., U. Habel, C. Kessler, S. Posse, W. Grodd, and H. W. Muller-Gartner. 2000. "Functional imaging of conditioned aversive emotional responses in antisocial personality disorder." *Neuropsychobiology* 42:192–201.

Schoenbaum, G., A. A. Chiba, and M. Gallagher. 1999. "Neural encoding in orbitofrontal cortex and basolateral amygdala during olfactory discrimination learning." *Journal of Neuroscience* 19 (5):1876–84.

Schug, R. A., Y. Gao, A. L. Glenn, M. Peskin, Y. Yang, and A. Raine. 2010. "The developmental evidence base: Neurobiological research and forensic applications." In *Textbook of Forensic Psychology*, edited by G. Towl and D. Crighton, 73–87. Hoboken, NJ: Wiley-Blackwell.

Schulkin, J. 2003. "Allostasis: A neural behavioral perspective." *Hormones and Behavior* 43:21–27.

Schulkin, J., P. W. Gold, and B. S. McEwen. 1998. "Induction of corticotropin-releasing hormone gene expression by glucocorticoids: Implication for understanding the states of fear and anxiety and allostatic load." *Psychoneuroendocrinology* 23:219–43.

Schutter, D. J. L. G., and J. van Honk. 2004. "Decoupling of midfrontal delta-beta oscillations after testosterone administration." *International Journal of Psychophysiology* 53 (1):71–73.

———. 2005. "Salivary cortisol levels and the coupling of midfrontal delta-beta oscillations." *International Journal of Psychophysiology* 55 (1):127–29.

Scott, S. K., A. W. Young, A. J. Calder, D. J. Hellawell, J. P. Aggleton, and M. Johnson. 1997. "Impaired auditory recognition of fear and anger following bilateral amygdala lesions." *Nature* 385 (6613):254–57.

Sellbom, M., and E. Verona. 2007. "Neuropsychological correlates of psychopathic traits in a non-incarcerated sample." *Journal of Research in Personality* 41 (2):276–94.

Serafim, A. D., D. M. de Barros, A. Valim, and C. Gorenstein. 2009. "Cardiac response and anxiety levels in psychopathic murderers." *Revista Brasileira De Psiquiatria* 31 (3):214–18.

Shamay-Tsoory, S. G., R. Tomer, B. D. Berger, D. Goldsher, and J. Aharon-Peretz. 2005. "Impaired 'affective theory of mind' is associated with right ventromedial prefrontal damage." *Cognitive Behavioral Neurology* 18 (1):55–67.

Shea, A., C. Walsh, H. MacMillan, and M. Steiner. 2005. "Child maltreatment and HPA axis dysregulation: Relationship to major depressive disorder and post traumatic stress disorder in females." *Psychoneuroendocrinology* 30 (2):162–78.

Shirtcliff, E. A., M. M. Vitacco, A. R. Graf, A. J. Gostisha, J. L. Merz, and C. Zahn-Waxler. 2009. "Neurobiology of empathy and callousness: Implications for the development of antisocial behavior." *Behavioral Sciences & the Law* 27:131–71.

Sipe, J. C., K. Chiang, A. L. Gerber, E. Beutler, and B. F. Cravatt. 2002. "A missense mutation in human fatty acid amide hydrolase associated with problem drug use." *Proceedings of the National Academy of Sciences USA* 99:8394–99.

Skeem, J., P. Johansson, H. Andershed, M. Kerr, and J. E. Louden. 2007. "Two subtypes of psychopathic violent offenders that parallel primary and secondary variants." *Journal of Abnormal Psychology* 116 (2):395–409.

Skeem, J. L., N. Poythress, J. F. Edens, S. O. Lilienfeld, and E. M. Cale. 2003. "Psychopathic personality or personalities? Exploring potential variants of psychopathy and their implications for risk assessment." *Aggression and Violent Behavior* 8 (5):513–46.

Skranes, J., T. R. Vangberg, S. Kulseng, M. S. Indredavik, K. A. I. Evensen, M. Martinussen, A. M. Dale, O. Haraldseth, and A. M. Brubakk. 2007. "Clinical findings and white matter abnormalities seen on diffusion tensor imaging in adolescents with very low birth weight." *Brain* 130:654–66.

Smith, E. E., and J. Jonides. 1999. "Storage and executive processes in the frontal lobes." *Science* 283:1657–61.

Smith, S. S., J. P. Newman, A. Evans, R. Pickens, J. Wydeven, G. R. Uhl, and D. B. Newlin. 1993. "Comorbid psychopathy is not associated with increased D2 dopamine receptor TaqI A or B gene marker frequencies in incarcerated substance abusers." *Biological Psychiatry* 33:845–48.

Soderstrom, H., L. Hultin, M. Tullberg, C. Wikkelso, S. Ekholm, and A. Forsman. 2002. "Reduced frontotemporal perfusion in psychopathic personality." *Psychiatry Research: Neuroimaging* 114:81–94.

Sowell, E. R., L. H. Lu, E. D. O'Hare, S. T. McCourt, S. N. Mattson, M. J. O'Connor, and S. Y. Bookheimer. 2007. "Functional magnetic resonance imaging of verbal learning in children with heavy prenatal alcohol exposure." *NeuroReport* 18 (7):635–39.

Spain, S. E., K. S. Douglas, N. G. Poythress, and M. K. Epstein. 2004. "The relationship between psychopathy, violence, and treatment outcome: A comparison of three youth psychopathy measures." *Behavioral Sciences & the Law* 22:85–102.

Stalenheim, E. G., E. Eriksson, L. von Knorring, and L. Wide. 1998. "Testosterone as a biological marker in psychopathy and alcoholism." *Psychiatry Research* 77:79–88.

Suchy, Y., and D. S. Kosson. 2005. "State-dependent executive deficits among psychopathic offenders." *Journal of the International Neuropsychological Society* 11 (3):311–21.

———. 2006. "Forming, switching, and maintaining mental sets among psychopathic offenders during verbal and nonverbal tasks: Another look at the left-hemisphere activation hypothesis." *Journal of the International Neuropsychological Society* 12 (4):538–48.

Sutton, S. K., J. E. Vitale, and J. P. Newman. 2002. "Emotion among women with psychopathy during picture perception." *Journal of Abnormal Psychology* 111 (4):610–19.

Sylvers, P. D., P. A. Brennan, and S. O. Lilienfeld. 2011. "Psychopathic traits and preattentive threat processing in children: A novel test of the fearlessness hypothesis." *Psychological Science* 22 (10):1280–87.

Takahashi, H., N. Yahata, M. Koeda, T. Matsuda, K. Asai, and Y. Okubo. 2004. "Brain activation associated with evaluative processes of guilt and embarrassment: An fMRI study." *NeuroImage* 23 (3):967–74.

Tassy, S., O. Oullier, Y. Duclos, O. Coulon, J. Mancini, C. Deruelle, S. Attarian, O. Felician, and B. Wicker. 2012. "Disrupting the right prefrontal cortex alters moral judgement." *Social Cognitive and Affective Neuroscience* 7 (3):282–88.

Tatar, J. R., E. Cauffman, E. R. Kimonis, and J. L. Skeem. 2012. "Victimization history and posttraumatic stress: An analysis of psychopathy variants in male juvenile offenders." *Journal of Child & Adolescent Trauma* 5 (2):102–13.

Taylor, J., B. R. Loney, L. Bobadilla, W. G. Iacono, and M. McGue. 2003. "Genetic and environmental influences on psychopathy trait dimensions in a community sample of male twins." *Journal of Abnormal Child Psychology* 31:633–45.

Terburg, D., B. Morgan, and J. Van Honk. 2009. "The testosterone-cortisol ratio: A hormonal marker for proneness to social aggression." *International Journal of Law and Psychiatry* 32:216–23.

Thapar, A., K. Langley, K. A. Fowler, F. Rice, D. Turic, N. Whittinger, J. Aggleton, M. Van den Bree, M. Owen, and M. O'Donovan. 2005. "Catechol O-methyltransferase gene variant and birth weight predict early-onset antisocial behavior in children with attention-deficit/hyperactivity disorder." *Archives of General Psychiatry* 62:1275–78.

Tiihonen, J., R. Rossi, M. P. Laakso, S. Hodgins, C. Testa, J. Perez, E. Repo-Tiihonen, O. Vaurio, H. Soininen, H. J. Aronen, M. Kononen, P. Thompson, and G. B. Frisoni. 2008. "Brain anatomy of persistent violent offenders: More rather than less." *Psychiatry Research: Neuroimaging* 163:201–12.

Tranel, D., G. Gullickson, M. Koch, and R. Adolphs. 2006. "Altered experience of emotion following bilateral amygdala damage." *Cognitive Neuropsychiatry* 11:219–32.

Tremblay, R. E. 2008. "Understanding development and prevention of chronic physical aggression: Towards experimental epigenetics studies." *Philosophical Transactions of the Royal Society B—Biological Sciences* 363:2613–22.

Tunbridge, E. M., P. J. Harrison, and D. R. Weinberger. 2006. "Catechol-o-methyl-transferase, cognition, and psychosis: Val158Met and beyond." *Biological Psychiatry* 60:141–51.

Tyrka, A. R., L. Wier, L. H. Price, N. Ross, G. M. Anderson, C. W. Wilkinson, and L. L. Carpenter. 2008. "Childhood parental loss and adult hypothalamic-pituitary-adrenal function." *Biological Psychiatry* 63 (12):1147–54.

Udry, J. R., and L. M. Talbert. 1988. "Sex hormone effects on personality at puberty." *Journal of Personality and Social Psychology* 54:291–95.

Ueno, S., M. Nakamura, M. Mikami, K. Kondoh, H. Ishiguro, and T. Arinami. 1999. "Identification of a novel polymorphism of the human dopamine transporter (DAT1) gene and the significant association with alcoholism." *Molecular Psychiatry* 4:552–57.

Vachon, D. D., D. R. Lynam, R. Loeber, and M. Stouthamer-Loeber. 2012. "Generalizing the nomological network of psychopathy across populations differing on race and conviction status." *Journal of Abnormal Psychology* 121 (1):263–69.

Vaidyanathan, U., J. R. Hall, C. J. Patrick, and E. M. Bernat. 2011. "Clarifying the role of defensive reactivity deficits in psychopathy and antisocial personality using startle reflex methodology." *Journal of Abnormal Psychology* 120 (1):253–58.

Vaidyanathan, U., C. J. Patrick, and E. M. Bernat. 2009. "Startle reflex potentiation during aversive picture viewing as an indicator of trait fear." *Psychophysiology* 46 (1):75–85.

van den Hoofdakker, B. J., M. H. Nauta, D. A. J. Dijck-Brouwer, L. van der Veen-Mulders, S. Sytema, P. M. G. Emmelkamp, R. B. Minderaa, and P. J. Hoekstra. 2012. "Dopamine transporter gene moderates response to behavioral parent training in children with ADHD: A pilot study." *Developmental Psychology* 48 (2):567–74.

van Goozen, S. H. M., W. Matthys, P. T. Cohen-Kettenis, J. H. H. Thijssen, and H. van Engeland. 1998. "Adrenal androgens and aggression in conduct disorder prepubertal boys and normal controls." *Biological Psychiatry* 43:156–58.

van Honk, J., J. S. Peper, and D. J. L. G. Schutter. 2005. "Testosterone reduces unconscious fear but not consciously experienced anxiety: Implications for the disorders of fear and anxiety." *Biological Psychiatry* 58:218–25.

van Honk, J., and D. J. L. G. Schutter. 2006. "Unmasking feigned sanity: A neurobiological model of emotion processing in primary psychopathy." *Cognitive Neuropsychiatry* 11 (3):285–306.

———. 2007. "Testosterone reduces conscious detection of signals serving social correction: Implications for antisocial behavior." *Psychological Science* 18:663–67.

van Honk, J., D. J. L. G. Schutter, E. J. Hermans, and P. Putman. 2003. "Low cortisol levels and the balance between punishment sensitivity and reward dependency." *NeuroReport* 14 (15):1993–96.

van Honk, J., D. J. L. G. Schutter, E. J. Hermans, P. Putman, A. Tuiten, and H. Koppe-schaar. 2004. "Testosterone shifts the balance between sensitivity for punishment and reward in healthy young women." *Psychoneuroendocrinology* 29:937–43.

van Peer, J. M., K. Roelofs, and P. Spinhoven. 2008. "Cortisol administration enhances the coupling of midfrontal delta and beta oscillations." *International Journal of Psychophysiology* 67:144–50.

van Wingen, G., C. Mattern, R. J. Verkes, J. K. Buitelaar, and G. Fernandez. 2010. "Testosterone reduces amygdala-orbitofrontal cortex coupling." *Psychoneuroendocrinology* 35:105–13.

Vandevelde, S., V. Soyez, T. Vander Beken, S. De Smet, A. Boers, and E. Broekaert. 2011. "Mentally ill offenders in prison: The Belgian case." *International Journal of Law and Psychiatry* 34 (1):71–78.

Vanman, E. J., V. Y. Mejia, M. E. Dawson, A. M. Schell, and A. Raine. 2003. "Modification of the startle reflex in a community sample: Do one or two dimensions of psychopathy underlie emotional processing?" *Personality and Individual Differences* 35 (8):2007–21.

Varlamov, A., N. Khalifa, P. F. Liddle, C. Duggan, and R. Howard. 2010. "Cortical correlates of impaired self-regulation in personality disordered patients with traits of psychopathy." *Journal of Personality Disorders* 25:74–87.

Varvarigou, A. A., S. G. Liatsis, P. Vassilakos, G. Decavalas, and N. G. Beratis. 2009. "Effect of maternal smoking on cord blood estriol, placental lactogen, chorionic gonadotropin, FSH, LH, and cortisol." *Journal of Perinatal Medicine* 37 (4):364–69.

Vernon, P. A., V. C. Villani, L. C. Vickers, and J. A. Harris. 2008. "A behavioral genetic investigation of the Dark Triad and the Big 5." *Personality and Individual Differences* 44:445–52.

Verona, E., C. J. Patrick, J. J. Curtin, M. M. Bradley, and P. J. Lang. 2004. "Psychopathy and physiological response to emotionally evocative sounds." *Journal of Abnormal Psychology* 113:99–108.

Viding, E., R. J. Blair, T. E. Moffitt, and R. Plomin. 2005. "Evidence for substantial genetic risk for psychopathy in 7-year-olds." *Journal of Child Psychology and Psychiatry* 46:592–97.

Viding, E., K. B. Hanscombe, C. J. C. Curtis, O. S. P. Davis, E. L. Meaburn, and R. Plomin. 2010. "In search of genes associated with risk for psychopathic tendencies in children: A two-stage genome-wide association study of pooled DNA." *Journal of Child Psychology and Psychiatry* 51:780–88.

Viet, R., H. Flor, M. Erb, C. Hermann, M. Lotze, W. Grodd, and N. Birbaumer. 2002. "Brain circuits involved in emotional learning in antisocial behavior and social phobia in humans." *Neuroscience Letters* 328:233–36.

Vollm, B., P. Richardson, S. McKie, R. Elliot, J. Deakin, and I. M. Anderson. 2006. "Serotonergic modulation of neuronal responses to behavioural inhibition and reinforcing stimuli: An fMRI study in healthy volunteers." *European Journal of Neuroscience* 23 (2):552–60.

von Borries, A. K. L., I. A. Brazil, B. H. Bulten, J. K. Buitelaar, R. J. Verkes, and E. R. A. Bruijn. 2010. "Neural correlates of error-related learning deficits in individuals with psychopathy." *Psychological Medicine* 40:1559–68.

Waschbusch, D. A., N. J. Carrey, M. T. Willoughby, S. King, and B. F. Andrade. 2007. "Effects of methylphenidate and behavior modification on the social and academic behavior of children with disruptive behavior disorders: The moderating role of callous/unemotional traits." *Journal of Clinical Child and Adolescent Psychology* 36 (4):629–44.

Way, B. M., and S. E. Taylor. 2010. "The serotonin transporter promoter polymorphism is associated with cortisol response to psychosocial stress." *Biological Psychiatry* 67:487–92.

Weaver, I. C. G., M. J. Meaney, and M. Szyf. 2006. "Maternal care effects on the hippocampal transcriptome and anxiety-mediated behaviors in the offspring that are reversible in adulthood." *Proceedings of the National Academy of Sciences USA* 103:3480–85.

Weiler, B., and C. S. Widom. 1996. "Psychopathy and violent behavior in abused and neglected young adults." *Criminal Behavior and Mental Health* 6:253–71.

Widom, C. S. 1977. "A methodology for studying noninstitutionalized psychopaths." *Journal of Consulting and Clinical Psychology* 45:674–83.

Widom, C. S., and J. P. Newman. 1985. "Characteristics of non-institutionalized psychopaths." In *Aggression and Dangerousness*, edited by D. P. Farrington and J. Gunn, 57–80. New York: John Wiley.

Williams, K. M., and D. L. Paulhus. 2004. "Factor structure of the Self-Report Psychopathy scale (SRP-II) in non-forensic samples." *Personality and Individual Differences* 37:765–78.

Wright, J. P., K. N. Dietrich, M. D. Ris, R. W. Hornung, S. D. Wessel, B. P. Lanphear, M. Ho, and M. N. Rae. 2008. "Association of prenatal and childhood blood lead concentrations with criminal arrests in early adulthood." *PLOS Medicine* 5 (5):732–40.

Yang, Y. L., A. L. Glenn, and A. Raine. 2008. "Brain abnormalities in antisocial individuals: Implications for the law." *Behavioral Sciences & the Law* 26 (1):65–83.

Yang, Y., and A. Raine. 2009. "Prefrontal structural and functional brain imaging findings in antisocial, violent, and psychopathic individuals: A meta-analysis." *Psychiatry Research* 174:81–88.

Yang, Y., A. Raine, P. Colletti, A. W. Toga, and K. L. Narr. 2009. "Abnormal temporal and prefrontal cortical gray matter thinning in psychopaths." *Molecular Psychiatry* 14:561–62.

———. 2010. "Morphological alterations in the prefrontal cortex and the amygdala in unsuccessful psychopaths." *Journal of Abnormal Psychology* 119 (3):546–54.

———. 2011. "Abnormal structural correlates of response perseveration in individuals with psychopathy." *Journal of Neuropsychiatry and Clinical Neuroscience* 23:107–10.

Yang, Y., A. Raine, T. Lencz, S. Bihrle, L. Lacasse, and P. Colletti. 2005. "Volume reduction in prefrontal gray matter in unsuccessful criminal psychopaths." *Biological Psychiatry* 15 (57):1103–8.

Yang, Y., A. Raine, K. L. Narr, P. Colletti, and A. W. Toga. 2009. "Localization of deformations within the amygdala in individuals with psychopathy." *Archives of General Psychiatry* 66:986–94.

Yehuda, S., S. Rabinovitz, and D. I. Mostofsky. 2005. "Essential fatty acids and the brain: From infancy to aging." *Neurobiology of Aging* 26:98–102.

Zaalberg, A., H. Nijman, E. Bulten, L. Stroosma, and C. van der Staak. 2010. "Effects of nutritional supplements on aggression, rule-breaking, and psychopathology among young adult prisoners." *Aggressive Behavior* 36 (2):117–26.

Zhou, D. M., C. Lebel, C. Lepage, C. Rasmussen, A. Evans, K. Wyper, J. Pei, G. Andrew, A. Massey, D. Massey, and C. Beaulieu. 2011. "Developmental cortical thinning in fetal alcohol spectrum disorders." *NeuroImage* 58 (1):16–25.

Andrea L. Glenn, PhD, is Assistant Professor in the Center for the Prevention of Youth Behavior Problems and the Department of Psychology at the University of Alabama. Her research focuses on understanding the biological correlates of psychopathy and using biological information in the development of interventions for youth with conduct problems. She is a past recipient of a Ruth L. Kirschstein National Research Service Award (NRSA) from the National Institutes of Health and an AXA Research Fund Postdoctoral Fellowship.

Adrian Raine, PhD, is University Professor and the Richard Perry Professor of Criminology, Psychiatry, and Psychology at the University of Pennsylvania. He has published five books and 297 journal articles and book chapters and has given 268 invited presentations in 25 countries.

65228894R00158

Made in the USA
San Bernardino, CA
29 December 2017